Y0-BEC-190

Neurosis and Narrative

The Decadent Short Fiction of Proust, Lorrain, and Rachilde

Renée A. Kingcaid

Southern
Illinois
University
Press

*Carbondale
and
Edwardsville*

95 94 93 92   4 3 2 1

Library of Congress Cataloging-in-Publication Data

Kingcaid, Renée A., 1952–
Neurosis and narrative: the decadent short fiction of Proust, Lorrain,
and Rachilde/Renée A. Kingcaid.
p. cm.
Includes bibliographical references and index.
1. French fiction—20th century—History and criticism. 2. French
fiction—19th century—History and criticism.   3. Decadence
(Literary movement)—France. 4. Proust, Marcel, 1871–1922—
Knowledge—Psychology. 5. Lorrain, Jean, 1855–1906—Knowledge—
Psychology. 6. Rachilde, 1860–1953—Knowledge—Psychology.
7. Psychoanalysis and literature. 8. Semiotics and literature.
9. Neuroses in literature. 10. Narration (Rhetoric) I. Title.
PQ673.K58 1992
843'.9109353—dc20   91-22156
ISBN 0-8093-1753-2   CIP

To Michael

Contents

Preface   ix

1. Neurosis and Narrative: 1
   Principles and Strategies

2. Common Ground: 18
   Freud and the Decadence

3. Plotting the Fetish: 35
   Proust's *Pleasures
   and Regrets*

4. The Return of the Repressed: 75
   Lorrain's *Masked Figures
   and Phantoms*

5. The Epithalamic Horror: 111
   Displacement in Rachilde

6. Neurosis and Nostalgia: 145
   "Decadent" Desire?

Notes   155

Bibliography   183

Index   201

Preface

To make this study as widely accessible as possible, I have provided translations of all of my original French sources, both primary and secondary. Of the primary works—Proust's *Pleasures and Regrets,* Jean Lorrain's *Masked Figures and Phantoms,* and Rachilde's *Stories* and *Demon of the Absurd*—only the Proust, to my knowledge, is available in English translation. That translation, done by Louise Varese and published by Ecco Press in 1949, offers only selected parts of the original *Les plaisirs et les jours:* the four major short stories of the work—the four I will be looking at here— the preface by Anatole France, two minor short stories, the society portraits known as the "Fragments of Italian Comedy," and the prose poems "Regrets, Reveries, Changing Skies." The translation does not include Proust's own preface to the work, that is, the extended dedication to Willie Heath in which Proust develops the theme of illness as poetic inspiration, the theme that opens the work on a distinct note of Decadence.

I have used Varese's translation for my citations from the major short stories of *Pleasures and Regrets:* "The Death of Baldassare Silvande," "The Melancholy Summer of Madame de Breyves," "A Young Girl's Confession," and "The End of Jealousy." Page references to these stories in the text refer directly, therefore, to Varese's text. The translations from Proust's own preface, however, are my own, as are all of the translations from Lorrain and Rachilde; my page references to these works are therefore to the French editions cited in the bibliography. In each instance of my own translation of a primary source, I have additionally supplied the French original in the notes. Readers of French will undoubtedly wish to evaluate both my translations and my literary analyses on the basis of the original texts from which I worked. In all translations, I have attempted to retain both the literal meaning and the suggestive nuance of the original passages. This exercise in translation has been no less instructive to me than was the initial work of analysis: there is nothing like rendering lurid prose into one's native language to make one fully aware of just how lurid it is!

Similarly, I have done my own translations of all citations from my secondary sources in French. However, in the dual interests of space and textual flow, I have not appended the original French; readers wishing to consult these sources will find them listed in the bibliography. In the few cases in which I have substituted my own translation for a previously published one, I have made this substitution clear in the text.

As this book makes its way to press, I would like to publicly acknowledge the support that my home institution, Saint Mary's College at Notre Dame, Indiana, has given to this project since its inception. In the long course of my research and writing, from 1985 to 1989, the college has twice awarded me faculty research grants, supporting such critical needs as interlibrary loan, library work space, manuscript production costs, and day care. The Cushwa-Leighton Library at Saint Mary's College has also been most generous in its acquisitions relating to my work; I owe a particular debt of gratitude to Lola Mae Philippsen, Director of Interlibrary Loan and Acquisitions, for her unfailing courtesy and efficiency.

A grant to the Department of Modern Languages at Saint Mary's College by the Charles P. Culpeper Foundation provided valuable travel funds that enabled me to consult original editions of Rachilde's novels at the Bibliothèque Nationale in Paris during the summer of 1989. Without this support, I would have remained without the benefit of Rachilde's preface to her novel *Madame Adonis,* an important reflection on the state of the female novelist that is not often reprinted in modern editions of the novel.

Working with Southern Illinois University Press has proven a pleasure. Curtis Clark, acquisitions editor, is a sure hand to guide a new author, and eagle-eyed copy editors Carol Burns and Dan Gunter turned my computer pixels into print.

Throughout this project, I have benefited from the encouragement and support of numerous friends and colleagues. In particular, I wish to thank Nicholas J. Meyerhofer, formerly of Saint Mary's and now chair of the Department of Modern Languages at Northern Arizona University, and Gerald Gingras, Associate Professor of

Spanish at Saint Mary's, for their painstaking readings of the manuscript in its early stages. Their questions and insights forced me to clarify my discussions of theory and to smooth out many a sentence structure. I am also deeply grateful to my friend and colleague Mana Derakhshani for so patiently checking my English translations.

Finally, as always, the lion's share of my gratitude belongs to my husband, Michael Langthorne. This is not the book we had originally thought I would write, but his confidence in me and in the value of my ideas outlasted my difficulties and doubts during these past several years to make the difference between *Neurosis and Narrative* and just plain neurosis. This book then, at long last, belongs to him.

*Neurosis
and
Narrative*

Neurosis and Narrative

Principles and Strategies

Reading Dora: The Place of the Trope

The original plan was to write about Dora. Dora, the wily heroine of Freud's *Fragment of an Analysis of a Case of Hysteria.* Dora who would not tell where she had learned about sex. Dora whose hands played suggestively with objects around her while she insisted they had no meaning. Dora who kept Freud guessing and left him musing. Dora who walked away.

The Dora case and the splendid array of critical studies it has inspired have done more than anything else to temper my critical appreciation of Freud. Before Dora, Freud was the *magister,* endlessly resourceful, eminently quotable, usually reliable. After Dora, it became clear that Freud was a shifty old craftsman, never quite to be taken again at face value. Dora's refusal to be cured, her willful failure to agree with Freud's interpretations, gave me to understand finally the connection between psychoanalysis and rhetoric I had been groping for in my earlier fascination with Freud's first collection of case studies, the *Studies on Hysteria.* Reading and rereading the Dora case, I understood how, in the rhetoric of the psyche, neurosis functions as a trope, as a deviation from an unstated but assumed norm, as a figure of speech that both cries out for and resists interpretation. Watching Dora wiggle and squirm under Freud's questioning and ultimately reserve her opinions for herself, I understood why repression splits the signifier from the signified.

Meaning does not exist because of language. Meaning is more often created in spite of it.

This is not a book about Dora, though the insights gained from her case are central to it. Thus it may be helpful to briefly review her story. Dora (in real life Ida Bauer) was brought to Freud by her father when she was eighteen years old. She had been exhibiting hysterical symptoms; a suicide note in her handwriting seriously alarmed her father (who had been previously treated by Freud for syphilis) and precipitated her entry into treatment. After some months in a treatment based chiefly on the analysis of two of her dreams, Dora announced her intention not to return to Freud. She did return, however, one year later, complaining of a facial tic that had set in shortly after she had read in the paper of Freud's appointment to the rank of professor. On that occasion, it was also clear to Freud that she had no intention of resuming analysis.

Perhaps the most compelling aspect of the Dora case, which Freud published in 1905 as *Fragment of an Analysis of a Case of Hysteria,* is the manner in which the case presents both patient and doctor as protagonists in a subtle and dramatic war of words. Who is to be convinced of what? Should Dora accept Freud's judgment that Herr K., her father's close friend and husband of her father's mistress, is an acceptable love object for her? Or should Freud believe Dora when she professes to know she is being used as an object of barter: traded off by her father to Herr K. so that her father can have Frau K.?

It is equally interesting that critical analyses of the Dora case, medical or literary in nature, most often center on Freud's failures in the case. In this approach, they take their lead from Freud himself, who confesses in the study that he had not been able to cure Dora in part because he had failed to recognize the operation of transference between them; that is, Dora too strongly identified him with the dominant males in her life—her father and Herr K.—to allow the theoretically neutral exchange of analysis to take effect. The question of who wins in the case and the nature of that victory also vary with the difference in viewpoint between the clinical or the literary. From the medical viewpoint adopted, for example, by Jules Glenn, M.D., in "Freud's Adolescent Patients," Freud was bound to disappoint Dora by his failure to understand her as an adolescent. The analysis was unnecessarily complicated, Glenn suggests, by Freud's unfamiliarity with the ambiguous and rebellious patterns of behavior that adolescent psychology has since added to the store of psychoanalytic knowledge.

Similarly, Robert J. Langs, M.D., points out in "The Misalliance Dimension in the Case of Dora" that Freud's overinvolvement with Dora's family interfered with his clinical objectivity, his ability to create the emotionally neutral relationship necessary for the therapeutic "alliance" between himself and his patient. Freud, Langs suggests, was too willing to believe the adults' side of things to be able to do justice to Dora. Instead, Freud professed to see nothing wrong in the planned exchange of Dora for Frau K. The failure of psychoanalytic technique, demanding strict neutrality on the part of the analyst, accounted for the failure of the analysis, as Langs concludes: "to the very end, [Freud's] deviation in 'technique' contributed to Dora's 'transference' fantasies, and to the premature interruption of her analysis. Freud's overriding interest in having Dora confirm his theories of infantile sexuality is also reaffirmed here as a source of misalliance and flight" (69).

Even as they judge Freud in light of subsequent psychological insight, medical reviews of the Dora case tend not to blame Freud for the understandable inadequacies of his practice at its birth; if anything, they seem pleased to note that Dora, having spurned Freud's help, grew up to be an unhappy and dissatisfied, crotchety matron. The literary critiques, however, have no such scruples toward the "Master." If these literary studies, particularly those from a feminist point of view, have a common axe to grind, it is that in this case study Freud significantly overstepped his place as (male) narrator with respect to Dora, his (female) narrated. In "Nadja, Dora, Lol V. Stein: Women, Madness and Narrative," Susan Rubin Suleiman summarizes this strain of criticism. She first cites from Stephen Marcus's seminal article "Freud and Dora: Story, History, Case History" the observation that Dora ended her treatment because she "'refused to be a character in the story that Freud was composing for her'" (129); Suleiman then focuses on the complexities of narration that both engender and undermine psychoanalysis.

> One great virtue of the Dora case—which may explain its apparently endless capacity to generate commentaries and "rewritings"—is that it dramatizes, as perhaps no

other of Freud's writings does, the ways in which the desire of the narrating and of the interpreting subject is caught up, entangled with, contaminated by its object. Freud's multiple entanglements with Dora—on the levels of discourse, of desire and of sexuality—can be read as an allegory of psychoanalysis, which is at the same time, paradoxically, its greatest success: the failure to achieve complete "mastery of the material.". . . Interpreters beware: desire is contagious. (132–33)

The perspective of failure to "master the material" demands in part that my study confine itself to speaking of Dora obliquely, in relation to the more general questions of narration and desire "her" case study evokes. This would seem a prudent choice. After all, as Suzanne Gearhart has observed in her trenchant study of Jacques Lacan's analysis of Freud's analysis of Dora, an "endless process of identification" between Dora and the various adults in her story— each of her parents, each of the K.'s, and Freud himself—effectively precludes resolution of her case (126).[1]

Thus, rather than attempt to add another circle to the critical go-round between Freud and Dora, subject and object, narrator and narrated, I prefer to reverse the insights into language, rhetoric, and psychoanalysis opened up by Dora's impressive critical history. In other words, if neurosis can be read as a trope, as a deviation in the rhetoric of the psyche, under what conditions can troping or the use of figurative language be read as neurosis?

The Test Case: A Semiotics of Decadence

We do not have to look far in French literature for a test case of figurative language that begs to be read as neurotic. Characterized by language as overwrought and worried as its haggard protagonists, Decadent fiction invites us to read neurosis as a meaning maker, not just as a theme but as part and parcel of the process of signification.

If any single word can sum up the late nineteenth century in France, its generalized sense of exhaustion and degeneration that begins with the individual and extends to the entire range of political, aesthetic, and social structures, that word is certainly

4

neurosis. In "Degeneration and the Medical Model of Cultural Crisis in the French Belle Epoque," Robert A. Nye describes the influence of medical discourse on the national sense of decline that permeated offical and literary discourse in France in the two decades before the turn of the twentieth century:

> The medical and "hygienic" sources of degeneracy were, if anything, more important elements in public discourse than the "moral" notion of degeneracy popularized in literature and criticism. . . . a strictly medical notion of degeneracy could convincingly demonstrate the relationship that was assumed to exist between degenerate individuals and the various social pathologies from which the [French] nation suffered: depopulation, crime, mental illness, prostitution, suicide, and various organic diseases. (20)

As one such borrowing from medical parlance, *neurosis* proved immensely useful to the writers of the fin de siècle. A. E. Carter points out in *The Idea of Decadence* that obsessive reference to impaired heredity and nervous debility created nothing less than a revolution in literary psychology, roughly comprehensible as a shift from *idéal* to *ennui*. "The emotional hypertrophy of Romanticism," Carter explains, "and the theoretical perversities of Gautier and Baudelaire, are no longer presented [in Decadent literature] as the fruits of aspirations towards the infinite or thwarted idealism. They are symptoms of neurosis" (66).

If we define *neurosis,* for the moment, as an acute hypersensitivity of the nervous system resulting from extenuation of the race, neurosis and its symptoms are the common ground between Huysmans's Des Esseintes and Mallarmé's Igitur, Jean Lorrain's Monsieur de Phocas and Maeterlinck's Pelléas, Zola's Nana and the Goncourts' Renée Mauperin. What was contemporary literature after all, queried Henri Beauclair and Gabriel Vicaire in their 1885 parody, *Les déliquescences, poèmes décadents d'Adoré Floupette,* if not an "attack of nerves on paper" ("une attaque de nerfs sur du papier"; qtd. in Richard 310)? And what are the Decadents themselves if not the "bad boys" of nineteenth-century French literature, products of diseased psyches producing a literature devoted to disease? In "The

Neurosis and Narrative

Literary Concept of Decadence," Alice R. Kaminsky writes, "Decadents, unlike romantics, classicists, or realists, or even naturalists, have a bad reputation. Exactly what the badness consists of we are not sure, but clearly some kind of perverted notion or action is expected of the decadent" (371).

It is not my intention to settle here once and for all the pesky debate that opposes Decadence and Symbolism, *décadence* and *décadentisme,* or, as in John R. Reed's contribution, "Decadent fiction" and "fictions of decadence." I am assuming, rather, a general familiarity with the recurrent themes and ambiance of fin de siècle literature, those connotations of ill repute and sickened psyche that send well-known shivers into the soul: ambiguous sexualities that find sensual delight in pain and refusal, beauty that is most beautiful when excessive and excessively grotesque, and perverse consolation discovered in the contemplation of the horrible. Under the impetus of neurosis, French literature of the fin de siècle, the literature that I am calling "Decadent," invests ultimate value in the rare, the diseased, the overdone and the decaying, in that which is running down or running out, in that which is coming to an end.

Lest I appear to be dealing only in connotation, let me try to propose a more coherent statement of what I consider Decadent fiction. By *Decadent* I mean a specific type of literature, clustered around the turn of the twentieth century in France and rooted in the following assumptions: (1) art is innately superior to life; (2) neurosis is a fertile source of inspiration for art; and (3) art inspired by neurosis is the highest form of art to which one might aspire. By this definition Des Esseintes remains the prototype of the (redundantly) Decadent neurotic; Huysmans's *Against the Grain* (*A rebours,* 1884), which relates and exacerbates this neurosis, remains the Bible of the "movement." But it is a definition that allows me to discuss in one breath authors as ostensibly disparate as Proust and Jean Lorrain and to return to Rachilde's "pulp" fiction as a work of high art.

It has been typical in critical writing to discuss the French Decadence—with its etymological meaning of "falling away"—in terms of what the Decadence was "decadent" or "falling away" from. But this approach runs up short against another problem of definition: where do we situate the Golden Age with respect to which "decadence" is a diminution or degrading? For Hippolyte Taine, as

6

we shall see, the Golden Age was the Italian Renaissance, but this is not, as we shall also see, by any means an objective criterion.

In "Decadence politique et littéraire à la fin du XIXe siècle," Jean El Gammal gives some idea of the complexities raised by the tandem definition of the Decadence and its previous Golden Age. Tracing the references to decadence and its antecedents in a wide range of political and literary groups in fin de siècle France, he discovers that, for the political Right, the very existence of the Republic was evidence of political decline. The extreme Right (legitimists, Orleanists, and Bonapartists) exaggerated this standard of decline into a choice of lost Edens: the thirteenth century and the Catholic throne for the legitimists; the July Monarchy for the Orleanists; the Empire, naturally enough, for the Bonapartists (23–25). For the Left, on the other hand, the Republic was "decadent" to the extent that it still recognized the Church, to the extent, that is, to which it fell short of the ideal of laicization. The literary decadence is no less difficult to define. El Gammal concedes that the "common denominator" of almost all literature in late nineteenth-century France is decadence, adding, however, that if the theme is present from the beginning of the century, it is particularly so from the time of the Second Empire (29). Only Huysmans, in El Gammal's opinion, demonstates a historical sense of decadence, a sense that brings us back to the political nostalgia of the far Right: "Progressively evolving toward an exalted Catholicism, which recalls that of certain rightists, but with more energy in its expression, [Huysmans] arrived at a distinct partiality for the Middle Ages" (29).

France's defeat by Prussia in the War of 1870 is certainly a convenient watershed for an evolutionary concept of Decadent fin de siècle France. Yet the analogy that followed the defeat—the comparison between a demoralized France and Imperial Rome on the brink of dissolution—has little more to sustain it than its imaginative appeal.[2] Overwhelmingly complicated and historically inexact, the historical model of Decadence does not "define" fin de siècle France any more than does the equally popular organic model—the belief that civilizations, like people, are destined to be born, live, and die in inevitable cycles that flourish and fade. Both still leave us with the question: what is the Decadence decadent from?

A semiotic approach to the Decadence poses the question in a different, and I think more accessible, way. In conjunction with the psychoanalysis suggested by the emphasis of this literature on neurosis, semiotics would realign the action of the signifier with the (un)repression of neurotic desire in fiction to present the literature of the fin de siècle not only as an "attack of nerves on paper" but as an "attack of the signifier" as well. Decadence could be seen as Decadence, therefore, not by looking at what it followed but by considering what it preceded. The fiction of the Decadence anticipated Freud by elaborating a cult of willfully abstruse signification around a central theme of neurosis. Conceived in semiotic terms, Decadence would designate the implicit recognition occurring more or less simultaneously in the literary, philosophical, and medical discourses of the fin de siècle, of the consequences, *avant la lettre,* of the signifier at odds with the signified and of the insistence (rather than the presence) of meaning as a process dependent on the structures of signification. The term *Decadence* thus turns out to be usefully dependent on connotation after all: what "falls away" in this literature are the conventions of everyday language that keep the signifier safely apart from the troubled pools of the childhood unconscious. What falls away are the veils from the eyes of the mind.

Lacanian Semiotics

A great deal of what I am proposing here depends on the rereading of Freud undertaken by the French psychoanalyst Jacques Lacan. I do not intend to take Lacan literally as the last word on Freud. What interests me rather is the process of reading that Lacan imposes on the textual surface and the marvelous suitability of the Lacanian hypotheses of language and the mind to the structural oddities and high self-consciousness of the Decadent text.

In *The Interpretation of Dreams,* Freud discerns two particular "disguises" through which thoughts and desires unacceptable to the conscious mind (or psychic "censor") can find expression (or, in terms closer to Freud's, a necessary discharge of psychic tension) in the dream. These processes are *displacement,* by which the forbidden object is replaced with a contiguous one, and *condensation,* by which a single dream image reveals a multitude of associated thoughts and images, each too threatening to be expressed in its own right. Their operations are characteristic of what Freud calls the "primary process," the prerational and prelinguistic operation of the unconscious, freed by dreams and mental illness from the repressions and logical arrangements imposed on it by the censorship of the "secondary process" or "secondary revision."[3] A font of unresolved desire, the primary process does not recognize the difference between yes and no, between reality and desire, between that which is and that which is not. It has no way of expressing hypotaxis, no ability to represent either/or alternatives. It is the secondary process, basis of social intercourse, that imposes these types of choices on the speaker; since the choices imposed by the secondary process necessarily reshape the undifferentiation of desire into their socially acceptable (i.e., sufficiently repressed) expressions, the operation of the secondary process is equivalent, as we shall see, to a symbolic castration. "Taming" the primary process, "socializing" it, the secondary process forces us to choose between yes and no, between that which is and that which is not, between this and not the other, in order to carry on our conversations.

Lacan's originality was to combine the structural linguistics of Ferdinand de Saussure and Roman Jakobson with Freud's revolutionary approach to the unconscious through its symbolizations, deriving first "a semiotic Freud" (as Robert Con Davis calls him in "Lacan, Poe, and Narrative Repression" [984]) and second a psychoanalytic theory of meaning that makes metaphor and metonymy the elemental figures of the unconscious as well as of language. In defining linguistic value, Saussure had suggested that difference is a fundamental mode of consciousness, which perceives two terms not in themselves but as a function of the difference between them (163). For Jakobson, all language could be said to function along one or the other of two main axes of communication: that of metonymy (for sequence and contiguity, or the flow of language across time) and that of metaphor, which allows for the substitution of one term for another within a paradigm of synonymous or similar words. Jakobson's famous definition of poetic language is based on this concept of the two axes of expression. For Jakobson, poetic language deflects the axis of metaphor onto that of metonymy so that sequence is created not by contiguous advances (as with a plot) but by a continual substitution of terms from within a single paradigm. In "Linguistique et poétique," Jakobson writes, "the poetic function projects the principle of equivalence from the axis of selection onto the axis of combination" (220). That is, the axis of paradigm or metaphor is projected onto the axis of sequence or metonymy. In poetic language, the two axes share in each other's properties: in poetry, Jakobson continues, "where similarity is projected onto contiguity, every metonymy is lightly metaphorical, every metaphor is a shade metonymic" (238).[4]

Lacanian theory analogizes Saussure's function of differentiation to the action of repression in the Freudian scheme. Furthermore, metaphor and metonymy, Jakobson's two axes of language, are considered equivalent to condensation and displacement, respectively. For Lacan, the unconscious is formed within the Oedipal resolution of the competing claims of the primary and secondary processes. Forcing the child, under threat of castration, to give up his mother as an object of desire, the Oedipal resolution imposes differentiation on the undifferentiated desire enjoyed by the primary process. The unconscious is formed then as a structure of *lack* (of mother, the object of desire) in opposition to the existence of *desire* itself. More accurately, the Oedipal capitulation to the secondary process means that desire gains a language from which it can be taken account of, but by which it can never be fully expressed. That part of the infantile subject that coincided entirely with the maternal body in a soft cocoon of mutual desire is forever lost when that subject begins to say "I" and to speak. However, that loss remains present within the subject as the *trace* of what once was. This is why the signifier can float free in Lacan: the unconscious takes shape only when the signifier (S) splits off from the signified (s), repressing the latter, along with desire for the mother (and the mother's desire for the child), to install the two autonomous registers (signifier/signified) on which the sign depends.

Lacan's formula S/s indicates that both the signifying system and the subject that realizes itself only within that system are founded in a process of meaning inherent, or "insistent," within the displacements and condensations that make up the signifying chain. When Lacan speaks of the signifying chain, he intends the image to be taken literally: the relationships of all signifiers to all other signifiers of the language resemble "rings of a necklace that is a ring in another necklace made of rings" (*Ecrits: A Selection* 153). The circular intersections of language and the unconscious also describe new functions for metaphor and metonymy. No longer to be thought of as replacement terms available in succession along a syntagm or by selection from a paradigm as in Jakobson, they are for Lacan fundamental operations of the unconscious.

Freud's studies of dreams convinced him that hysteria is only a point on a continuum of mental functioning: "well" and "unwell" people think and desire in fundamentally the same ways. Following this principle, Lacan treats all signifying structures as resistant to meaning, available only in disguise. Metaphor and metonymy in Lacan therefore have to do with whether and how the "barrier of resistance" (the /) between signifier and signified is "crossed" (or not) in the act of meaning. (This unaesthetic plethora of quotation marks is unavoidable; since the original repression of the Oedipal phase cannot be undone, the "barrier of repression" and the possibilities of "crossing" it must themselves be understood metaphorically.) Like Freud, Lacan considers the unconscious a master of disguise, remarkably adept at expressing itself in figuration. The two processes of disguise—condensation and displacement—can be likened to the signifying processes of metaphor and metonymy. Both become for Lacan actions of the signifier "sliding over" the field of the signified:

> *Verdichtung,* or condensation, is the structure of the superimposition of the signifiers, which metaphor takes as its field. . . .
>
> In the case of *Verschiebung,* "displacement," the German term is closer to the idea of that veering off of signification that we see in metonymy, and which from its first appearance in Freud is represented as the most appropriate means used by the unconscious to foil censorship. (160)

Metaphor, in other words, allows a "crossing" from signifier to signified. This crossing can occur not because metaphor has any special power to "dredge up" the latter from the prelinguistic, pre-Oedipal realms in which it lies buried but because of the action of metaphor on the signifier. In a pun on the German *dichtung* for poetry and *verdichtung* for condensation or metaphor, Lacan describes metaphor as "the substitution of signifier for signifier [in which] an effect of signification is produced that is creative or poetic" (164). That is, the implicit term of the comparison on which metaphor depends (the literal meaning of the word used metaphorically) functions as a signifier itself subjected to repression; metaphor operates by "pushing" this implicit signifier down into the range of the signified and replacing it with the expressed signifier that carries the force of the metaphor.[5]

By contrast, metonymy remains always "above" the barrier of signification. A figure of contingence, metonymy retains within itself the split of the signifier from the signified that originally formed the unconscious. Reaching back across the chain of language to the original (maternal) object of desire, metonymy encounters only one signifier after another; it "makes do" with substitute objects, as indeed it must, since the formation of the unconscious as a linguistic structure entails both the renunciation of (unbounded) pre-Oedipal desire and the experience of the self as a construction of the symbolic order of language. The child who says "I" is separate from the mother, but it has paid for that troubling autonomy by renouncing the pleasures of the primary process in favor of the socializing censorship of human language.

Consequently, metonymy contains within itself the structure of desire and loss on which language depends and which determines the intensity of the subject's object relations as they inevitably relate to the lost desire of and for the mother. In Lacan's definition, the elision from signifier to signifier that characterizes metonymy "permits the elision in which the signifier installs the lack-of-being in the object relation, using the value of 'reference back' possessed by signification in order to invest it with the desire aimed at the very lack it supports" (164). In other words, metonymy's progression from signifier to signifier repeats the succession of objects that, past the pre-Oedipal stage, stand in contiguously for the original and irrecuperable object of infantile desire; lined up as if in a row, metonymy's signifiers lead one to the other in a never-ending procession away from the lost object. The maintenance of metonymy above the barrier of repression thus speaks more eloquently of repression's role in signification than does the companion figure of metaphor, in which that barrier is represented as crossed. Metonymy is invested with unfulfilled desire; it constantly re-

12

creates the desire and the structure of lack in which language and the unconscious are formed.

Decadent Narrative

Combining structural linguistics with classical psychoanalysis, the Lacanian rereading of Freud has opened up the Freudian corpus to new usefulness for literary criticism. It is perhaps an odd useful-ness, for the procedures and theories of psychoanalysis as critical tools can now be shown to be susceptible to sabotage; in a discus-sion that equates the slipperiness of language with that of the unconscious, psychoanalytic and textual procedures can be shown to backfire, to become reversible. If the unconscious is structured like a language, and if the unconscious relies for its functioning on figures like those of rhetoric, then the processes of mind themselves as defined by psychoanalysis can also serve rhetorical purposes within texts. As much as they can *explain* texts, psychoanalytic concepts can also *be explained* by textual procedures.

Concentrating on the semiotics of the Decadence is a way to do just that, to rebound from concept to text and back again in such a way as to point up the self-referentiality of both Decadent and psychoanalytic discourse.[6] Neither, after all, gives us the "real world": both are a set of conventionalized ways to think and talk about how we think and talk. Decadent and psychoanalytic lan-guage make us sit up and take notice because they challenge our "real world" experience: Do all little boys wish to marry their mothers? Do all little girls perceive themselves as castrated? Are bullfrogs really the monsters that Jean Lorrain describes in "The Masked Figure"? Two peacocks, two cats, and a goat are an extraor-dinary menagerie, even for a fledgling author in Proust's "Death of Baldassare Silvande"; and chateaux do not appear and disappear as they do in Rachilde's "Hermetic Chateau," any more than women are frogs as they are in "The Frog Killer."

The language is what counts. Decadent discourse shines the spotlight of desire directly on the signifier; it is language in its high neurotic mode. More important, the rhetorical use of basic concepts of psychoanalysis in Decadent fiction shows us how neurosis can create meaning in narrative. It is, in this sense, not enough that desire be inscribed in the sign, irrevocably figurative of loss and compensation. The question opens onto the larger system of narrative, of the figurative capability of the building blocks of fiction: character, plot, description, and point of view. Technical features of narrative can be shown in Decadent literature to derive directly from neurotic dysfunction. Fetishism is not simply a theme in Proust's earliest stories; it creates and solves actual problems of plot. The return of the repressed determines the descriptive processes and grotesque effects of coherence in Jean Lorrain, while the hysterical resistance of the female body to language is the sine qua non of storytelling in Rachilde, the premise without which there are no stories to tell.

I have chosen to work here with three collections of short stories. John Reed, whom I mentioned earlier, has proposed a distinction between Decadent fiction and fictions of decadence based on what he calls "reconstitutive atomism" (34). "Decadent style," he writes, "invites primitive impulses but confines them in a strict and openly artificial form. It is as though the Decadent novel as artifact represents a victory over its subject matter" (60). Thus Reed judges a work of fiction "Decadent" by the degree to which it strays from the demands of plot and sequence imposed by the realist tradition and substitutes recurrent moods, images, or associative networks — the implicit model being Jakobson's definition of poetic language. So the plotlessness and cataloguing by which *Against the Grain* proceeds make it an exemplary Decadent novel, whereas Lorrain's *Monsieur de Phocas,* despite its gruesome ghoulishness, has far too strong a plot line to be anything more for Reed than a novel of decadence.

This distinction holds better, Reed himself suggests, for the novel than for the short story; unless they are read in collection, short stories offer simply too little to go on to allow the critic to perceive "the relationship between details of style and the larger radical design of the fictional whole" (64). The short story is just not long enough to provide for the succession of catalogues, the polyphonous themes, or the assault on plot that Reed praises in *Against the Grain,* Gabriele D'Annunzio's *Il fuocu* (*The Flame*), or James Joyce's *Ulysses.*

But the short story's brevity may also be its greatest virtue. Concise and rapid, polished to a brilliant finish by obsessive Decadent hands, each story is a set piece of the kind Reed discovers one after another within the "atomized" Decadent novel. Listen, for example, to the contrast Claude Dauphiné detects, in *Rachilde: Femme de Lettres 1900,* between the style of Rachilde's short stories and the more breathless pace of her novels:

> It seems that the talents of the author of *Monsieur Vénus* were, indeed, particularly well cast in the mold of the short story. The brevity of this literary form, which more than any other demands perfection, constrained her to an attention to style that, unfortunately, she hated and which is cruelly lacking in her longer works where, on the other hand, there is no lack of inspiration, imagination, energy, force, color. (52)

What Reed does not mention is that stories in collection are a bastard form of fiction. Neither novel nor nonnovel, the short story collection ignores sequence and chronology; the reader may begin reading wherever, end wherever, and stop at will; there is no compelling necessity to consider any one story in the light of any or all of the others. But that is what we do. We force the stories to make new meanings by setting them off one against the others. The covers of the book itself, the physical object, impose their tenuous closure on the collected stories, transforming (or not) the aria sung by each individual story into the diffuse and sometimes discordant chorus of all of them taken together. Moreover, they make us wonder about what has been left out, about the stories not included, about what the author chose *not* to say in this particular place. Like the case study (particularly in collection), the short story (in collection) is an excellent place to seek out and study neurosis.

I take a certain malicious pleasure in uniting under one cover Proust, Jean Lorrain, and Rachilde (Marguerite Vallette). At least until Rachilde's marriage to Alfred Vallette and the founding of the review and publishing house *Mercure de France,* Lorrain and Rachilde ran in the same literary circles; they were often to be found together in outrageous disguise at literary and other masked balls. But Proust and Lorrain came to blows over Lorrain's snide insinuation in a review of *Pleasures and Regrets* that Proust and Lucien Daudet were lovers. Two shots were exchanged in the early morning in the Bois de Boulogne, with no serious injuries other than to pride. Proust and Lorrain continued to dislike each other, however, with the ironic result that in his *Journal* for 1921, André Gide remarked how much the bedridden and unwell Proust resembled his former nemesis: Proust "is fat," he wrote, "or rather puffy; he looks a little like Jean Lorrain" (qtd. in Jullian 262).[7]

But more than malice unites these three authors. Though I began by their common notes of Decadence—their sense of ennui, their tedium and exasperation, their yearning for apocalypse—I am much more interested in their recourse to neurosis as a structuring principle of narrative, as a determinant of particular technical features of each story. Thus in the 1896 *Pleasures and Regrets,* his first real venture into the literary world, Proust uses antecedent literary texts in the manner of a fetish to establish his narrative authority. That authority, however, is undercut by the hallucinatory or hysterical moments experienced by Proust's protagonists; by throwing into question the real basis of neurotic trauma, these moments challenge the ability of the narrative flow to maintain itself without the support of fetish—without, that is, extraordinary inter-ventions on the part of the author who runs time after time into problems of plot. In the course of the work, mastery of the fetish—Proust's ability to transfer its fascination from himself to his pro-tagonist—will be tantamount to a mastery of plot and will give the measure of a narrative voice approaching a Flaubert-like disap-pearance behind the realist surface of the text.

While Proust thus works toward the realist illusion, the force of desire propels Jean Lorrain away from it. His *Masked Figures and Phantoms* (*Masques et fantômes*) demonstrates the pervasiveness of the return of the repressed in descriptive technique. Lorrain's is a world of childhood trauma continually reduplicated by the shifting signs of the spitefully, frightfully fantastic. Under these conditions, metonymy inflates from a figure of contingency to dominate the entire perceptual fields of the stories. At the same time, Lorrain's deliberately effaced referent draws us deeper and deeper into the circular (non)logic of the primary process. As we shall see in two of his best stories, "The Student's Tale" and "Sea-Green Eyes," coher-ence is created through repetition in fiction only if we consent to the point of view of the psyche driven by a desire it has never had any hope of understanding.

Finally, Rachilde's *Stories (Contes et nouvelles)* and *The Demon of the Absurd (Le démon de l'absurde)* are studies in displacement. What at first glance seems to be her poetry of metaphor turns out to reveal the fate and functions of the female body, displaced on the natural world in a literary corpus ripe with sexual danger and the suspension of meaning. Rachilde's fiction then brings us once again to our point of departure. "I should without question," Freud wrote of Dora, "consider a person hysterical in whom an occasion for sexual excitement elicited feelings that were preponderantly or exclusively unpleasurable" (7:28). In Rachilde, hysteria makes its meaning in just this shadow world between the body and language; "story"— that very thing which one tells—lies somewhere between the two. Rachilde's fiction speaks the horror of the *yes* and the pleasure of the *no* that give Dora and hysteria reason against the discourse of reason and culture. Interpreters once more beware, she suggests: desire appeased, aborted, or brought to an end, can only be desire in its most egregious *mis*interpretation.

2

Common Ground

Freud and the Decadence

Charcot's Soirée and Freud's Obituary

In the late 1880s, Freud was studying in France as a fellow in neuropathology at La Salpêtrière, just outside of Paris. His purpose in traveling to La Salpêtrière was, as he related in his eventual report to his fellowship committee at the Faculty of Medicine in Vienna, to form his own opinion on the advances in neuropathology coming out of the French school headed by its renowned specialist in the field, Doctor Jean-Martin Charcot. "The French school of neuropathology," Freud wrote in his report,

> seemed to me to promise something unfamiliar and characteristic in its mode of working, and moreover to have embarked on new fields of neuropathology, which have not been similarly approached by scientific workers in Germany and Austria. In consequence of the scarcity of any lively personal contact between French and German physicians, the findings of the French school — some of them (upon hypnotism) highly surprising and some of them (upon hysteria) of practical importance — had been met in our countries with more doubt than recognition and belief; and the French workers, and above all Charcot, were obliged to submit to the charge of lacking in critical faculty or at least of being inclined to

study rare and strange material and to dramatize their
working-up of that material. (1:5–6)

In the light of the objections to his own theories that Freud
would later encounter, his comments on the German reception of
the French school seem oddly prescient and more than a little
sympathetic. At La Salpêtrière, Freud was most impressed by
Charcot's personality and authority, as well as by his approach to
hysteria, even if it was one with which Freud would eventually
disagree. According to Freud, Charcot redrew the boundary between the somatic and the psychosomatic. "Charcot used to say,"
Freud reported to the medical faculty, "that, broadly speaking, the
work of anatomy was finished and that the theory of the organic
diseases of the nervous system might be said to be complete: what
had next to be dealt with was the neuroses" (1:10). Not coinciden-
tally, this distinction between the two etiological registers was
already part of Decadent literature by the time of Freud's report.
The doctor brought in at the end of *Against the Grain* to treat Des
Esseintes's physical collapse solemnly "informed Des Esseintes that
he had done his utmost in re-establishing the digestive functions
and that now it was necessary to attack the neurosis which was by no
means cured" (317–18).

Freud particularly appreciated Charcot's careful description of
the symptoms of hysteria. Charcot, he recalled in 1893, "gave a
complete description of its phenomena, demonstrated that these
had their own laws and uniformities, and showed how to recognize
the symptoms which enable a diagnosis of hysteria to be made"
(3:20). He disagreed with Charcot, however, on two key points: the
role of the *condition seconde* and the importance of heredity in the
etiology of hysteria.

For Charcot as for others at the time, the *condition seconde* —
literally, a "second" or other condition of consciousness — expressed
the sort of mental trance, or dissociative state, into which the
hysteric was thought to enter at the time of the hysterical attack.
Freud granted passing credibility to the theory in the "Preliminary
Communication" prefacing his 1893 collaborative work with Josef
Breuer, the *Studies on Hysteria*. He did not, however, make use of it as
an explanatory principle for any of the case histories he described
there. In the obituary Freud wrote of Charcot in 1893, his appraisal

19

of the *condition seconde* suggests the direction his own inquiry would take into repression and the ever-vigilant "psychic censor" that would present neurosis as a fact not of dissociative but of associative behavior. In a useful précis of the bewildering problems involved in dealing with neurosis psychologically, Freud wrote:

> if I find someone in a state which bears all the signs of a painful affect—weeping, screaming and raging—the conclusion seems probable that a mental process is going on in him of which those physical phenomena are the appropriate expression. A healthy person, if he were asked, would be in a position to say what impression it was that was tormenting him; but the hysteric would answer that he did not know. The problem would at once arise of how it is that a hysterical patient is overcome by an affect about whose cause he asserts that he knows nothing. If we keep to our conclusion that a corresponding psychical process *must* be present, and if nevertheless we believe the patient when he denies it; if we bring together the many indications that the patient is behaving as though he *does* know about it; and if we enter into the history of the patient's life and find some occasion, some trauma, which would appropriately evoke precisely those expressions of feeling—then everything points to one solution: the patient is in a special state of mind in which all his impressions or his recollections of them are no longer held together by an associative chain, a state of mind in which it is possible for a recollection to express its affect by means of somatic phenomena without the group of the other mental processes, the ego, knowing about it or being able to intervene to prevent it. (3:19–20)

In hindsight, Freud was not far here from recognizing repression as the process by which the patient could both suffer from and claim not to remember the traumatic causes of his or her hysteria. The theory of repression would, in turn, make it possible to reassemble the associative chain Freud momentarily presents as broken. But also present in the passage is the methodological problem of whether the patient actually deserves to be taken at his or her word: can the analyst really believe the claims to un-knowledge of the weeping and raving patient? So the sticking point becomes the problem of knowing just how "special" is the "special state of mind," or *condition seconde.*

As Freud worked his way through his early case studies, it became increasingly obvious that the somatic phenomena of hysteria were understandable to the measure that their extremes of expression could be traced back, through association, to the traumatic experience at their origin. In *The Interpretation of Dreams,* he gave the names *condensation* and *displacement* to the two most important of these associative principles. The result of the associative method then was ultimately to illustrate that hysteria is less a *condition seconde* of the psyche than a means to understand the *condition première* —first or normative condition—of psychic life. No longer to be thought of as an aberration or dissociation in the life of the mind, hysteria is simply a point on the psychic continuum along which both the mentally healthy and the neurotic are subject, if in varying degrees of intensity, to the same processes of repression and associative displacement. These processes are simply more pronounced and troublesome in the case of the neurotic, whose claims not to know what is wrong with him or her can finally be taken seriously.

Freud likewise discounted the importance of heredity and congenital neuropathology in the etiology of hysteria. In the notes to his German translation of Charcot's consultation lectures known as the *Leçons du mardi de la Salpêtrière (1887–88)* (Charcot's Tuesday lessons at the Salpêtrière during this period), Freud objects to the reigning emphasis on hereditary factors in hysteria, suggesting instead that "sexual noxae . . . constitute the most important and only indispensable aetiological factor" (1:142). He returns more discretely to the charge in the Charcot obituary, suggesting that "the etiological theories supported by Charcot in his doctrine of the *'famille névropathique'* [the neuropathological family], which he made the basis of his whole concept of nervous disorders, will no doubt soon require sifting and emending" as medicine continues to whittle away at neurosis (3:23). The point has particular importance for the literary theory of Decadence, as neither Freud nor Charcot was unaware of the peculiar French reputation for degenerescence, or nervous degeneration along family lines. According to

Freud, Charcot "was very sensitive about the accusation that the French were a far more neurotic nation than any other and that hysteria was a kind of national bad habit"; as a man of science, the French neuropathologist was convinced that his observations would be confirmed in other national groups as well. He was especially pleased, Freud noted, to diagnose a case of hysteria in a Prussian grenadier (3:22)! The most Freud would ever say was that heredity might determine a predisposition to hysteria in a given patient; by itself, it was not sufficient cause for hysteria (1:102–4).This became a kind of backhand compliment to the French Decadents, who, convinced that their blood was bad and their nerves were worse, went right on populating their novels with examples of congenital neurotics.

Freud broke from Charcot when, leaping from physiology to psychoanalysis, he became convinced that the neuroses were best dealt with as meaning-full phenomena, subject to the same processes of signification that govern dreams, humor, memory lapses, and slips of the tongue. Yet even then Freud credited his predecessor with letting out the real secret of hysterical behavior. A now-famous passage from *On the History of the Psycho-Analytic Movement* (1914) attributes the revolutionary essence of psychoanalytic theory to an offhand remark made by the master and overheard by Freud. Describing the hysterical symptoms of a young married couple in his care, Charcot, Freud recalls, "suddenly broke out with great animation: '*Mais dans des cas pareils c'est toujours la chose génitale, toujours . . . toujours . . . toujours*'" (14:14). Freud quotes the remark in its original French; it means, "In these cases, it is always the genital thing, always . . . always . . . always."[1]

The psycholiterary structure of this scene at Charcot's soirée has been wonderfully analyzed by Neil Hertz in his article on the Dora case and the status of knowledge in psychoanalysis, "Dora's Secrets, Freud's Techniques." Hertz notes that this scene is but one of several in Freud's writings in which he claims to have forgotten the odd, offhand remark made by another—until his own later discoveries returned it to him, fresh and retrospectively endowed with the power of prophecy. Hertz thus reads in the Charcot scene Freud's quick passage from the structural position of the hysteric, who in Freud's own words is "paralyzed with amazement" as sexual secrets are tentatively and alluringly revealed, to that of the professional man of medicine who has bested his former superiors by his courageous development of the very ideas they had intimated but never pursued. In Hertz's perceptive reading, then, Freud's coup is to organize his own experience as an explicit validation of the epistemological problem of neurosis, namely, that one can indeed know and not know something at the same time. Served up as his own experience, Hertz concludes, repression takes the place Freud wills for it as the "corner-stone" of psychoanalytic theory (14:16).

The scene of Charcot's soirée, however, also validates Freud's use of narrative as therapy. This narrative method, or talking cure, was, as Freud reports in the *Studies on Hysteria*, based on the fact that there always exists "an intimate connection between the story of the patient's sufferings and the symptoms of his illness" (14:61). In the scene of Charcot's soirée, Freud returns the full compliment that the Decadents had paid him in advance when they adopted neurosis as their literary theme par excellence. Describing the history of psychoanalysis as the history of his own repressions and retrievals, Freud ties the knot between the scientific and the literary—from the point of view of the scientific. He thereby returns to answer the old charge laid at his door in his earliest case studies: "I have not always been a psychotherapist. . . . it still strikes me myself as strange that the case histories I write should read like short stories and that, as one might say, they lack the serious stamp of science. I must console myself with the reflection that the nature of the subjects is evidently responsible for this, rather than any preference of my own" (2:160).

Reading Freud Reading Neurosis: The Case of Elisabeth von R.

In the *Studies on Hysteria*, Freud came gradually to understand the manner in which the neurotic symptom functions as a type of rhetorical figure in a dimly perceived grammar of psychic life. Like the rhetorical figure, the symptom stands out against a tacitly held norm; it is not quite what one would have expected to encounter in some "normal" or routine functioning of language or the body. The symptom, then, is a heavily marked sign that calls attention to itself by the pain or displeasure it produces, much as in poetic language figures of speech stand out against an assumed background of literal language and draw attention to themselves by the surprise, pleasure, or perplexity they occasion in the reader.[2] It was the discovery of Freudian psychoanalysis that, as with literary figures or the codifications of dreams, such symptoms cried out not so much to be "fixed" as to be interpreted, with the happy corollary that if the interpretation were done correctly, the "fixing" would take care of itself.

Literary semiotics uses the term *hypersign* to refer to those signs that show more clearly than others the nature of sign. When such a sign can be shown to cover two simultaneous and contradictory meanings, it is called an *antithetical hypersign*.[3] Used as a broad semiotic term, *antithetical hypersign* would seem a particularly useful — if somewhat cumbersome — description of the type of sign Freud encountered in his first neurotics. The hysterical symptoms his patients displayed were, as he discovered, capable of covering completely opposite and simultaneous meanings. As described earlier, the great mystery of early psychoanalysis was how the patient could know and not know what was wrong, could wish and still not wish to tell what was wrong, could want and still not want to be cured. Solving the problem of opposites would bring Freud closer than even he perhaps suspected to the grammar of psychic life. Not only could symptoms cover opposite meanings, but the very refusal of the psyche to recognize contradiction would eventually define the primary process.

This second meditation on contradiction would have to await *The Interpretation of Dreams.* The earlier *Studies on Hysteria* elaborates a bedrock theory of hysteria based largely on Freud's perception that the semiotic canniness of hysterics is an equal match for his own — and then it complicates the issue wonderfully by showing us Freud upping the ante of canniness to take on the prejudices of traditional medical science. Freud's willingness to confront contradiction in the patients and his own ability to mean in myriad directions at once place a mirror in front of the sign system of hysteria and determine an approach to neurosis that is rigorously and compellingly *textual,* built on interplay and subterfuge, allusion and elusiveness. The Dora case is clearly one such textual battle of wits: Dora leaves uncured and unconvinced — or, more accurately, unconvinced and thus uncured. An earlier case from the *Studies,* however, whose narrative rhetoric is almost as interesting an example of Freud's attraction to the potentials of contradiction (his own and the patient's), is his "first full-length analysis of a hysteria" (2:139), the case of Elisabeth von R.

A young woman of cultivated family and lively spirits, Fräulein Elisabeth von R. suffered from severe leg pains that made walking, sitting, and occasionally even lying down extremely unpleasant. These pains had come on two years after the death of her beloved father, whom she had nursed through his final illness, and in the wake of a series of subsequent family crises. Elisabeth nursed her mother through an operation, her eldest sister married a man Elisabeth did not not like and subsequently moved to a distant city, and her second sister also married and died unexpectedly of complications during pregnancy.

Two facts about Elisabeth's case led Freud to suspect that he was dealing with a neurotic exaggeration of a physically real rheumatism. In the first place, Elisabeth described her physical pains with a remarkable complacency, as if, Freud notes, "her attention must be dwelling on something else, of which the pains were only an accessory phenomenon." Moreover, he thought he could detect more than a trace of sensuousness in her reaction to pressure on the painful areas, leading him to conclude that she was responding "probably more in harmony with the subject-matter of the thoughts which lay concealed behind the pain and which had been aroused in her by the stimulation of the parts of the body associated with those thoughts" rather than to the physical pain itself (2:137).

Freud decided to treat Elizabeth's physical symptoms by electrotherapy, as much for his faith in the method as to build Elisabeth's confidence in his doctoring. The simultaneous treatment of the neurosis through narrative, however, would be directly and deliberately confrontational. Not only does Freud take on the patient's reluctance to identify the psychic conflict that has given rise to her illness (this is the first case in which he treats patient resistance as a signifier in the grammar of the psyche), but he must also defend his procedures in the case against the prevailing views on hysteria held by the scientific establishment.

In the case of Elisabeth von R., the dual polemic clearly addresses the nature of symbolization in hysteria. Thus, after Elisabeth has duly recited what Freud calls her "wearisome" life story, "made up of many different painful experiences" (2:139), his first concern is to contrast the questions answered by the patient's story (the anamnesis) with the new questions that that story raises. He begins, disarmingly, with an admission of failure, or more accurately, of mystification: "As far as the physician was concerned," he states, "the patient's confession was at first sight a great disappointment" (2:144).

This mystification, however, is more rhetorical than scientific; it is a deliberate effect of Freud's sentence. He does not tell exactly *what* physician was disappointed. At the same time, he allows the logical inference that it *must* be Freud to cloak him with the mantle of science: he is humbly and generically *the* physician, representative of the scientific community that has accredited him as one of their own. However, Freud's sly refusal to differentiate among physicians clouds the issue of the "great disappointment." Just who is disappointed by Elisabeth's tale of woe, and what in any case is there to be disappointed about?

Freud's generic physician goes on to claim that Elisabeth's case is "made up of commonplace emotional upheavals, and [that] there was nothing about it to explain why it was particularly from hysteria that she fell ill or why her hysteria took the particular form of a painful abasia" (2:144). The anamnesis itself thus does little to further the theory of hysteria or to clarify the relationship between the patient's emotional life and her painful psychosomatic symptoms. But close rereading again suggests that "the physician" who claims to have been disappointed with Elisabeth's story must have already expected it to throw some light on both the general theory and the particular illness — and that the only physician who would have brought such expectations to the case must be the one who, despite his vocabulary of solidarity, is already inching out from under the cloak of established practice that disregards the anamnesis: Freud himself. The deliberate ambiguity is carefully maintained in the justification Freud now presents for his new working method, a justification that creates its own discourse of solidarity by maintaining both the first-person plural and an oddly proleptic past tense suggesting that what "the physician" is about to discover in the next few pages has already passed into the canon: "These, incidentally," writes Freud of the anamnesis, "were not the kind of questions that physicians were in the habit of raising. We were usually content with the statement that the patient was constitutionally a hysteric, liable to develop hysterical symptoms under the pressure of intense excitations *of whatever kind*" (2:144; Freud's emphasis). It is sufficient to read "but we are now" for each instance of "we were not then" to grasp the subterfuge of Freud's simultaneous identification with and withdrawal from the mainstream of the medical community.

So the physician who *questions* and leaves himself open to disappointment contrasts with those physicians who *state* (from authority) and who thus, implicitly, cannot be disappointed; "disappointment" thereby takes on a purely rhetorical function. Obviously, as a theorist experimenting with the talking cure, Freud could hardly have been "disappointed" to discover in Elisabeth von R. a subject so willing to talk about her life, commonplace though it was. Nor was he "disappointed" to be able to fit his reaction to her story into the larger scheme that calls for him to constantly validate his methods of treatment as true advances in the scientific study of hysteria. Indeed, writing after the termination of Elisabeth's analysis, Freud knew his methods in the case would be proved successful. Thus, by initially confessing a disappointment that he knows will give way to triumph, Freud superimposes on the lines of opposition already evident in the passage a classic discourse of science as struggle and challenge, fraught with difficulty and marked by setbacks, but from which eventually emerge the noble creations of an intellect that refuses to shrink from trial and error.

Additionally, however, "disappointment" identifies the structural position shared by both patient and doctor as the principal narrators of Elisabeth's case. Freud observes that during the first phases of her analysis, Elisabeth continued to "disappoint" by maintaining many of her hysterical symptoms. Worse yet, her complaints of persistent pain were accompanied by "a sly look of satisfaction at my discomfiture," says Freud, so that "I could not help being reminded of old Herr von R.'s judgement about his favourite daughter—that she was often 'cheeky' and 'ill-behaved'" (2:145). But isn't this behavior by the patient exactly comparable to Freud's with respect to the medical establishment? If Elisabeth is "ill-behaved," and smug about it to boot, she is so precisely because she knows something that another does not (yet) know—just as Freud in this case knows something about hysteria that has yet to become accepted medical doctrine.

This "bad behavior" is the key contradiction of the narrative, revealing how firmly grounded it is in antithesis. If Freud and

Elisabeth are "ill-behaved" as narrators, they are so because they willfully disappoint; they refuse to get to the point. However, anyone who appreciates a good story—and this would include Freud, Elisabeth, and any sympathetic readers beyond the medical establishment—will readily understand that this sort of bad behavior is exactly what is expected of a narrator. Failure to get to the point maintains suspense, and so "disappointment" in this sense is really good (narrative) behavior. This is all the more true here because Freud already knows the end of Elisabeth's story and will eventually equate her illness not with cheekiness, nastiness, spite, or other manifestations of misconduct but with her highly developed moral character. Elisabeth, he will conclude, had allowed herself to fall ill rather than admit she was in love with her brother-in-law. And she was, we remember, her father's favorite daughter.

Elisabeth's tale is "disappointing" in at least one other way as well: the heroine is allowed to solicit only a limited amount of sympathy. On the one hand, Freud admits, "we cannot refrain from deep human sympathy with Fräulein Elisabeth," but to do so, we must "put greater misfortunes on one side and enter into a girl's feelings" (2:144). On the other hand, this obvious condescension is meant to shore up the claims of objective science against those of sympathetic narrative, as Freud goes on to describe himself as "a stranger who received [Elisabeth's story] with only a moderate sympathy" (2:144). This is clearly not true: there is too much at stake for Freud to remain so detached from his patient-narrator, particularly since he has just described her plights and perils in terms virtually guaranteed to elicit pity.

So the reader is left with a reserve of sympathy in the text. If sympathy is not to be granted to Elisabeth, and if Freud is not to be the apparent giver of sympathy, the rhetoric of equivalence between patient and doctor strongly suggests that the reader transfer all his sympathy to none other than Freud himself. The equivalence between the two becomes undeniable when Freud finally makes Elisabeth's "bad behavior," her smugness about her secret obsession, an index of truth: "But I was obliged to admit," he concludes, "that she was in the right" (2:145). And so, too, the text insinuates, is Freud, who expected not only a "cure" from Elisabeth's story but insight into the very nature of hysteria. Both stories, after all, have a happy ending: Elisabeth gives up her hysterical symptoms, and

Freud will succeed in imposing his methodology on accepted medical practice.

The point in all of this is not simply to demonstrate all over again what contemporary literary criticism delights in discovering in Freud: that he is an uncommonly gifted writer, canny, witty, disingenuous, and manipulative. Rather, it is to illustrate the intimate connection between narrative rhetoric and the theory of neurosis that characterizes Freud's earliest ventures into the signifying properties of the mind. Weaving his texts through the loopholes of language, Freud assumed his neurotics did exactly the same with their symptoms. They meant what the hysteric wanted them to mean, but also—and this is where the psychoanalyst would step in with superior powers of interpretation—what they did not want them to mean as well. Maybe, one can almost hear Freud surmising in the *Studies,* the method to the madness was essentially the same as that used for reading and writing. When one is already so skilled in language as Freud was, it is but a short step from "text" to hysteria as an *organization* of symptoms that would surrender their fullest meanings, like linguistic signs, by their relation to each other and to the "norm" from which they depart—requiring, not least of all, the physician as chief rhetorician.

The Decadence as Semiotics: Taine's Tree—and Lacan's

It would have been impossible, of course, for Freud to refer to "sign systems" in writings predating modern linguistics. Yet as we have seen, his writings point directly to the concept of symptom as sign, to reading as active interpretation. A similar anticipation marks the aesthetic theory of one of the chief critics of the Decadence, Hippolyte Taine. In his writings on philosophy and art, Taine gives clear expression to both the historical and organic models of Decadence. His railings against the cultural and aesthetic hypertrophy of his nineteenth-century France can also be shown, however, to anticipate a semiotic understanding of Decadence that can now benefit directly from the Lacanian reformulation of language in Freud.

Taine's concept of hypertrophy maintains that decadence is to be considered the result of the overdevelopment of any part of a unity at the expense of its whole. At only one point along the entire curve of civilization has there been achieved the ideal balance between body and mind, barbarism and culture, that Taine considers capable of producing great art. This shining moment was the Italian Renaissance, the moment of organic unity toward which all preceding moments had been tending and from which all successive moments have been declining. The Renaissance had balanced barbarism and culture, physical nature and intellectual life, instinct and idea. This balance, in Taine's view, had come completely undone by the nineteenth century. Taine complains in his *Journey to Italy* (*Voyage en Italie*) that as the centuries produced greater physical comfort and ever greater intellectual stimulation, "the human mind has been emptied of images and filled up with ideas" (1:176).[4]

"Image" is the hallmark of the balance and harmony Taine attributes to the Renaissance. Taine praises the Italian painters for their ability to create the image, that is, for their ability to harmonize form and color within the "interior logic" of each individual work (*Journey* 1:174). The "image" can thus be superimposed, at the exact midpoint, on the curves traced by the development of the physical body from barbarism to culture and by the history of art as an organic unity. The image is what is lost along the sloping curve leading away from the Renaissance, since, as Taine again states in *Philosophy of Art* (*Philosophie de l'art*), "the definition of extreme culture is the gradual effacement of images in favor of ideas" (1:151).[5] The passage from image to idea is degeneration or decadence, as the body loses force in inverse proportion to the overstimulated, hypertrophied mind.

Taine supports his argument with the verbal sign *tree*. "Pronounce . . . the word tree before a modern listener," he challenges in *Philosophy of Art*, and that listener "will assign that sign to a distinctly labeled pigeonhole in his head; today that is what we mean by 'understanding'" (1:152). What Taine objects to in this type of understanding is its highly abstract nature: we who have read too much, argued too much, learned too much, and understood too much now have our minds "populated by abstract signs," he claims, and thus "we can only half-glimpse fragments of colored forms, they do not stay with us; they take only vague shape on our inner canvas; they fly right away" (*Philosophy* 1:152).[6] For Taine, comprehension by "idea" could not be further removed from the ideal of comprehension by "image":

Heard by minds that are still simple and healthy, this same word *tree* will immediately provoke the vision of the whole and entire tree, with the round and moving masses of its luminous leaves, with the black angles that its branches sketch against the blue sky, with its rough, deeply furrowed trunk, with its feet stuck firmly in the soil against wind and storm, so that instead of being reduced to a notation and a cipher, their thoughts will provide [these healthy minds] with a complete and living spectacle.[7] (1:153)

Or will it? The high point of communication from which all else is falling away is nothing less than the myth of plenary signification, of meaning not only independent of linguistic value but ignorant of the resistance to signification effected by repression in the formation of the sign. Taine would like to believe that there *was* at least one moment in intellectual history, midway between "instinct" and "idea," barbarism and culture, image and idea, at which signifier and signified enjoyed a perfect and simultaneous correspondence that permitted the exact transmission of meaning between sender and receiver of the artistic sign. At that magic moment, no gaps, no lapses, no distortions existed within the circuit. Painting "like a horse runs, like a bird flies, spontaneously" ("comme un cheval court, comme un oiseau vole, spontanément"), the Renaissance masters engaged even their public within this smoothly functioning, organically guaranteed circuit, since, Taine writes,

> when spectators contemplate [these colored forms] in a fresco or on a canvas, they have already seen them in themselves, they recognize them; [these forms] are not foreign to them, returned artificially to the scene by some archeological mixture, willfullness, or artistic convention; they are so familiar to them that they carry them with them into their private lives and into their public ceremonies.[8] (1:153)

This gapless circuit depends on the physical body made coextensive with its physical and semiotic functions: the horse is that which runs, the bird that which flies, the painter he who paints, and the spectators they who recognize. But this strategy is bound to fail for the immediate reason that Taine himself, a nineteenth-century Parisian restating the perception of the Renaissance spectator (with all the differences inscribed between him and them by the vagaries of his own heredity, historical moment, and environment, or in his more famous formula, *race, moment,* and *milieu*), has unwittingly introduced the first of many gaps into the communicative circuit: his *tree,* so willfully imagistic and "complete," is in fact a highly conventionalized list of signifiers.

Despite what he thinks, Taine does not go back to nature for his Renaissance "image"; he goes instead to what Lacan calls the "treasury of signifiers" that do his thinking, do his gazing in his place. The place of the "other" in Lacan is

> the locus of the signifier's treasure, which does not mean the code's treasure, for it is not that the univocal correspondence of a sign with something is preserved in it, but that the signifier is constituted only from a synchronic and enumerable collection of elements in which each is sustained only by the principle of its opposition to each of the others. (*Ecrits: A Selection* 304)

Catherine Clément paraphrases, "The point . . . is that there exists a—purely fictive—reservoir in which all signifiers of a language slumber in anticipation" (177). Norman Bryson is more explicit in his assertion that all gazing, all seeing, depends on the mediation of culture. "[W]hat the painter deals in is *representations, not perceptions,*" he writes, "and even as he is recording for the first time an aspect of nature that has eluded all his predecessors, for his image to be recognised it must participate in the economy of signs. . . . the recognition of signs can never occur in presence" (21).

Lacan's *tree* in the *Ecrits* thus comes much closer than Taine's to inscribing gap or opening within the relationship between signifier and signified:

> For even broken down into the double spectre of its vowels and consonants, it can still call up with the robur and the plane tree the significations it takes on, in the context of our flora, of strength and majesty. Drawing on

all the symbolic contexts suggested in the Hebrew of the Bible, it erects on a barren hill the shadow of the cross. Then reduces to the capital Y, the sign of dichotomy which, except for the illustration used by heraldry, would owe nothing to the tree however genealogical we may think it. Circulatory tree, tree of life of the cerebellum, tree of Saturn, tree of Diana, crystals formed in a tree struck by lightning. (*Ecrits: A Selection* 154)

One can only imagine with what cries of "Décadence!" Taine would have greeted this exposition of the multiple and variant meanings that metaphor and metonymy can give to the one signifier *tree*. But that is exactly the point: Lacan's series of playful evocations on the word reveals the slippage of the sign glossed over by Taine's "spontaneous" and unanimously evocative image. The sliding of the signifier over the signified suggests that the "meaning" of the word *tree* depends largely on where one stops the list of potential associations; no longer the spontaneous image emblematic of organic unity, *tree* is the sum, and then some, of all of its stated and unstated rhetorical possibilities. Hence the importance of the "points de capiton"—"upholstery buttons," "anchoring points," or momentary "punctuations"—in Lacan. They put a temporary stop to the sliding of the signifier in order for provisional meaning to be established, as demonstrated in the example of the sentence: "The diachronic function of this anchoring point is to be found in the sentence, even if the sentence completes its signification only with its last term, each term being anticipated in the construction of the others, and, inversely, sealing their meaning by its retroactive effect" (*Ecrits: A Selection* 303).

Characterized by a totalizing rhetoric that imposes on past cultures a single-mindedness of vision and symbolic intent, Taine's discussions of the past are infused by an acute nostalgia for this sliding signifier *not* to be the case; his preference, evident in the opposition between "image" and "idea," is for an impossible sign stable as two sides of a coin. The semiotic concept of Decadence that follows from this preference for the linguistically impossible is then synonymous with the signifier detached from the signified, with the insistence of meaning that plays havoc with "image" by giving free rein to "idea." It is the deliberate and self-conscious anarchy of the signifier decried by Taine. It is signification flaunting its propensity to excess, as a deliberate sign of neurosis. It is Proust covering one text by another, Lorrain breaking description into tiny bits of horror, and Rachilde spitefully imagining a guilty procreation everywhere in nature. It is the double wellspring of neurosis and semiotic extravagance that Huysmans ushered into narrative with *Against the Grain;* it is the entire range of successors to that novel that proclaim in styles from the rarefied to the grotesque to the sublime a double unrepression of desire and the signified. To speak of a semiotic Decadence, then, is to give the Decadents credit for the single most happy discovery inspired by their faith in neurosis: that hypertrophy is a built-in advantage of the process of language itself.

3

Plotting the Fetish

Proust's *Pleasures and Regrets*

The Text Fetish: All the Premature Deaths

The significance of *Pleasures and Regrets* in Proust's literary career has yet to be fully appreciated. Published at the author's expense by Calmann-Lévy in 1896, the work brought together in a single elegant volume a number of short pieces Proust had already published in such literary magazines as *Le banquet, La revue blanche* and *La revue hebdomadaire,* with several others composed expressly for the volume. Prefaced by Anatole France and lavishly illustrated by society hostess Madeleine Lemaire, the book also featured poetry and music: Proust's eight poems, the "Portraits of Painters and Musicians" ("Portraits de peintres et de musiciens"), which were accompanied in the original edition by the piano scores for the "Portraits de peintres" composed by Proust's friend Reynaldo Hahn.

Reviews of the book were mixed, and sales were disappointing. Paul Perret, in *La liberté* of 26 June 1896, noted the bittersweet air of the book, the "toedium vitae" that recalled the Romans of the decadence. In the August 1896 *Revue encyclopédique,* Charles Maurras praised the easy brilliance of Proust's talents and the "exquisite taste" of his poetic language. Jean Lorrain's comments in *Le journal* (3 February 1897), we have seen, provoked the young author to a duel. Proust himself would later downplay *Pleasures and Regrets* as immature, although in the throes of the procrastinations and hesitations that finally led to *Remembrance of Things Past,* he would continue to appreciate the style and the relative facility of the earlier work. "I would find it deplorable," he wrote to Gaston Gallimard about a proposed new edition of *Pleasures and Regrets* in 1921, "that . . . a work of my youth, written in secondary school, before my military service, should appear before I have finished *A la recherche du temps perdu*" (*Correspondance générale* 4:39).[1] In fact, *Pleasures and Regrets* was completed after Proust had finished both his schooling and his military service.

Thematically, *Pleasures and Regrets* is close in spirit to *Remembrance of Things Past.* The work abounds with volatile personalities, shameless social climbers, and disappointed lovers. The affinity with Proust's masterpiece accounts in large part for the general critical neglect that has surrounded the earlier work—excepting, of course, those studies that are specifically concerned with the evolution of Proust's masterpiece from his earliest writings.[2] In terms of Proust's career, however, *Pleasures and Regrets* represents an important first gamble: it is Proust's concerted attempt to convince his parents, particularly his father, of the feasibility of a literary career.

In the fall of 1893, Marcel's future was under heated discussion in the Proust household. Proust wrote to his father in September:

> I have kept hoping that I would finally be able to go on with the literary and philosophical studies for which I believe myself fit. But seeing that every year only subjects me to more and more practical discipline, I prefer to choose at once one of the practical careers you have suggested. . . . I still believe that anything I do outside of literature and philosophy will be just so much time wasted. But among several evils, some are better and some worse. (*Selected Letters* 57–58)

This same period sees him engaged in serious consultation with a certain Charles Grandjean over the choice between the School of the Louvre, the School of Paleography and Librarianship, museum employment, or "a career whose name I don't know that leads to inspections in the Beaux-Arts, and in the meantime involves writing reviews of different exhibitions, performances, etc." (*Correspondance*

1:257).[3] It also finds Proust announcing to his friend Robert de Billy the imminent publication of a literary work. "I am really at a loss," he wrote to Billy in September 1893, "because, my father insists, I have to make up my mind about my career" (*Selected Letters* 56). Two months later he informed Billy, "This year I am publishing a collection of short pieces [*Pleasures and Regrets*], most of which are known to you" (*Selected Letters* 61).

Pleasures and Regrets did not in fact appear until two and a half years later. In the meantime Proust had gotten himself accepted, and more or less dismissed, as an unpaid assistant at the Bibliothèque Mazarine; he had also begun his social climbing in earnest. His heart, however, was still with his book, his chosen response to parental pressure to settle on a career. Narrative authority, then, will respond to paternal authority: the book to be written will not merely settle the question of the son's career but will also assert the son's autonomy by proving the validity of his original choice. The laws of narrative will take over for the law of the father; the "short pieces" of the son—in the original French the "petites choses" or "little things"—will be thrown into the balance against the weight of the father's demands.

The outstanding physical feature of the book *Pleasures and Regrets,* this offering made to appease the father, is its lavishness. With the illustrations and the music, the original edition stretches out over an impressive 271 pages of large type and large margins on thick, glossy stock. The edition included fifty numbered copies, twenty of which featured silk bindings and a signed watercolor by Madame Lemaire. The retail price was thirteen francs, fifty centimes, about four times the usual book price of three francs, fifty centimes. Publishing at his own expense, Proust lost money on the venture. In 1903 he wrote to Edmond Jaloux, "I am still a little surprised that anyone has read *Pleasures and Regrets.* My editor assured me that no one had ever asked him for it. He has to be exaggerating a bit" (*Correspondance* 3:457).[4] By June 1918, nearly 1200 of the original 1500 copies were still gathering dust in a storeroom at Calmann-Lévy's (*Correspondance* 2:219 n. 4).

As Maurice Bardèche observes in *Marcel Proust romancier,* nearly everything about *Pleasures and Regrets* contradicted Proust's ambition to be taken seriously as a literary newcomer, labeling him instead as a "rich amateur" for whom literature was merely a "divertissement" or "diversion" (32). But the book is a diversion in a deeper sense. The overdecorated text, paid for by an author still financially dependent on the father from whom the work is supposed to be a liberation, represents the surplus of contradictory erotic energy that commonly distinguishes the fetish object. In this obsessive attention paid to the work of art, Proust was abundantly in keeping with the aesthetic principles of the fin de siècle: the twisting and spiraling decorativeness of Art Nouveau and the elegant bindings of Des Esseintes's rare editions suggest amply that the point of art was not so much to do as to overdo. An overdone physical object, however, *Pleasures and Regrets* calls on the fetish to serve as a narrative principle as well. Proust's work of liberation is, physically and rhetorically, the answer to a command to choose; in this sense, it becomes his protection as well against the specter of premature death.

In its least complicated sense, the fetish is an intersection between two contradictory libidinal impulses. An initial impulse leading toward an object of desire is interrupted, or diverted, by a contradictory and simultaneous impulse leading away from that object: fear, repulsion, guilt, dread. This ambivalence toward the object of desire drains off into the fetish. A type of lightning rod that attracts the conflicting libidinal impulses and merges them into a compromise object—the shoe, the nose, the glove, the walking stick—the fetish is at once sufficiently evocative of the original object and yet far enough removed from it to satisfy the conflicting demands of the hesitant libido.

The source of these contradictory movements that converge in an idiosyncratic object choice is, according to Freud, the male child's anxiety over the perceived "castration" of his mother. Her absent penis, he explains in his 1927 essay "Fetishism," is so dreaded a replica of the boy's own potential castration that he is unable to surmount this dread and resolve his anxiety through normal psychological development. He thus invents the fetish as a substitute for the missing organ. Substituting for what is presumed to have been destroyed, the fetish object simultaneously acknowledges and denies the horror of castration; "affection and hostility in the treatment," Freud asserts, "run parallel with the disavowal and the acknowledgement of castration" (21:157). The compromise solution is an important one, for it enables the fetishist to proceed as if all were well with his erotic life after all. In fact, as Freud observes at the beginning of the essay, the compromise usually provides a completely satisfactory erotic outlet: "for though no doubt a fetish is recognized by its adherents as an abnormality, it is seldom felt by them as the symptom of an ailment accompanied by suffering. Usually they are quite satisfied with it, or even praise the way in which it eases their erotic life" (21:152).

In her critique of Freud's writings on femininity, *The Enigma of Woman,* Sarah Kofman capitalizes on the faint uneasiness perceptible in Freud's analysis of the fetish. Kofman asks more seriously than Freud why it is that fetishism is not a widespread practical response to the castration anxiety that Freud calls on the existence of the fetish to prove. If the fetish, according to Freud, "saves the fetishist from becoming a homosexual, by endowing women with the characteristic [i.e., the resupplied phallus] which makes them tolerable as sexual objects" (21:154), Kofman wonders why more men are not homosexual or fetishists. If the horror of the castrated woman is as great as Freud makes it out to be, Kofman observes that "far from being 'pathological,' either [homosexuality or fetishism] would be the *normal* destiny of the masculine libido. Under these conditions," she continues, "what becomes *abnormal* is heterosexuality. We then have the problem of understanding how many men, if not all, manage to overcome their horror and even experience pleasure in sexual relations with a woman" (84).

Freud was content to leave this mystery a mystery. "Probably no male human being is spared the fright of castration at the sight of a female genital," he affirmed, adding, "why some people become homosexual as a consequence of that impression, while others fend it off by creating a fetish, and the great majority surmount it, we are frankly not able to explain" (21:154).

But Kofman maintains that Freud's phallocentricity has skewed the question from the outset. As her reading draws out the consequences of Freud's assumptions of "normal" psychological development, it becomes increasingly evident that the theory of penis envy in women is Freud's way of tiptoeing around the "mystery" by assuming a male route around castration anxiety: "Because it signals the fact that man still possesses intact the penis that woman no longer has (she once had one, but her father cut it off), because it signals woman's loss of omnipotence, woman's penis envy increases man's power and allows him to overcome the inhibiting horror; as if 'penis envy' restored woman's value as sexual object by exhibiting—negatively, as it were—man's still intact and complete sexuality" (85).

In other words, woman's envy is the sign of male wholeness and the proof of her own loss of castrating power. But the power of Kofman's analysis is her displacement of "fetish" from referent to rhetoric. As a psychical device, the fetish covers over the horror of a semirepressed absence with a reassuring phantasm of presence. We can observe from Kofman's study that, rhetorically, it does the same in Freud's essay: it protects the writer against the gaps in his text created by what he cannot say. And what Freud cannot say, Kofman asserts, is the enigma of feminine sexuality; unexperienced by him and merely surmised from the biased viewpoint of the male, feminine sexuality is the significant absence that threatens the willed coherence of the Freudian text. The fetish that simultaneously acknowledges and protects against this damning silence is the (too) oft-evoked concept of penis envy. Freud's appeal to this concept serves rhetorically to protect his own text against the gaps opened in it by the pervasive mystery of the feminine.

Pleasures and Regrets responds to the threat of castration (the demands of the father that threaten to cut short Proust's literary ambitions) by offering itself as the fetish object or penis substitute. The son's symbolic surrender of his "little pieces" wards against the real loss that he fears would occur if his gift should be rejected. The stakes are enormous, involving nothing less for Proust than his life—or his premature death—as a writer. Behind the symbolic castration there looms the reality of death; at this early stage, Proust might not actually come to exist as a writer. It is against this unfaceable absence that the fetish of literary representation appears in *Pleasures and Regrets* both as content and as narrative strategy.

Proust dedicated the book to Willie Heath, a young English friend of his who had died in October 1893. Proust's original intention had been to dedicate *Pleasures and Regrets* to another friend as well, Edgar Aubert, deceased in September 1892 at the age of twenty-three. Proust explained to Robert de Billy his attraction to the manner in which each of these young men had met his death: "After a most distinguished life, [Heath] died with a heroic resignation, which, if he had not died in the Catholic faith, having converted when he was twelve . . . would be identical to what you wrote to me about Edgar's death" (*Selected Letters* 62). Proust went on in his letter to ask Billy to intercede with the Aubert family for permission to dedicate the book to Edgar; as that permission was apparently not forthcoming, he settled for the single dedication to Heath.

Or perhaps "settled for" is an understatement. Overblown and grandiloquent, the dedication stretches out across five full pages of the original edition. Its critical history has centered mainly on the extended metaphor of Noah's ark by which Proust describes the experience of illness and claustration that enables him to understand, like Heath, how illness is a "Trêve de Dieu," or "divine truce," a "'Grace' . . . that brings us closer to the realities that lie beyond death" (7). Declaring as a matter of principle that "the sick feel closer to their souls" (7),[5] Proust rhapsodizes over the virtues of the sickroom/ark:

> When I was a little child, no person in sacred history seemed to me to have a more miserable fate than Noah, because of the flood that kept him shut up in the ark for forty days. Later, I was often sick, and had to also spend long days in the "ark." I understood then that Noah never saw the world better than from the ark, even though the ark was closed and the earth was dark.[6] (6)

Proust had written to Billy that the purpose of the dedication was to bring to the attention of his readers the exemplary character and dignified ends of Heath and (presumably) Aubert. Whatever its merits, Proust explained, the book was assured of at least a certain reputation through the name and social connections of its illustrator. "Mme Madeleine Lemaire is going to illustrate my little book," he informed Billy. "Consequently it will find its way into the libraries of writers, artists, and persons of standing in all walks of life, who would otherwise have remained unaware of it and who will keep it only for the illustrations" (*Selected Letters* 62).

There is no guarantee, however, that this appeal to the intellectual and social elite was anything more than a smoke screen for Proust's own snobbish desire to be taken seriously by the Parisian society in which he had begun to make his way. Indeed, the society portraits he paints in *Pleasures and Regrets* give the lie to this project of remembrance by exposing in the elite the same egotism, the same superficiality, and the same pursuit of pleasure at any cost that would later drive the aristocracy of *Remembrance of Things Past*. Nor does the will to remember resist the young author's own disabused philosophizing: when the young Alexis in "The Death of Baldassare Silvande" ceases to be troubled at the thought of his uncle's fatal illness, Proust comments that "because [Baldassare] had once made him cry as we cry for the dead, Alexis behaved toward him as we behave toward the dead: he began to forget him" (15). He likewise overestimated the value of Madame Lemaire's languorous flowers and vines, which were greeted by Jean Lorrain with withering sarcasm: "Never has Mme Lemaire's ingeniousness allied itself so closely to an author's talent," he wrote in his February 1897 review.[7]

It is more likely that what Proust was aiming for in his dedication was the symbolic value attaching to a young person cut down in his prime—the value that confirms the importance of the literary project itself. "All the lovely beings who soon are going to die" ("Tous les êtres beaux qui vont bientôt mourir") is later identified in the poem on Van Dyck in the "Portraits of Painters" as the triumphant subject of Van Dyck's court painting (81); in the dedication, Proust explicitly compares Heath to a condemned royal captured by the brush of the Flemish painter:

> It was in the Bois [de Boulogne] that I often came upon you in the morning, having espied me and waiting for me beneath the trees, standing, but relaxed, like one of those lords that Van Dyck painted, and whose pensive elegance you shared. . . . Everything around you, moreover, contributed to this melancholy resemblance, even the background of leaves in whose shade Van Dyck often halted a king's promenade; like so many of those who were his models, you would soon die and in your eyes as in theirs, one could see the shadow of presentiment alternate with the soft light of resignation.[8] (5–6)

That this resignation is as premature as the death itself is further confirmed in the dedication: "more serious than any of us," Proust writes of Heath, "you were also more of a child" (7).[9]

Proust's identification with Heath thus extends beyond the common experience of illness on which the Noah's ark conceit is based. In the lightning moment of visual exchange in which Heath, posed in the Bois like a Van Dyck painting of early death made legible, is said to look back at Proust, the writer perceives once again the specter of his own premature death. Conjured away by a pretense to age—"[These pages] are only the idle froth of a restless life, that is now, however, calming down" (7–8), writes Proust at the ripe old age of twenty-three—the specter is more properly exorcised by the fetishized book itself, an excess of presence erected against the unfaceable absence of the writer who might not have been. "I give you this book," Proust writes in conclusion to Heath, invoking the tomb as protection for the gift that wards off death: "You are, alas! the only one of my friends whose criticism it need not fear" (8).[10]

"The Death of Baldassare Silvande"

The first short story of *Pleasures and Regrets*, "The Death of Baldassare Silvande," makes literary representation—the ability to create a literary text or exploit the possibilities of a preexisting one—into the fetish object standing over and against the threat of premature death.[11] As overdone thematically as the book object of *Pleasures and Regrets* is overdone physically, "Baldassare" packs into a few short pages a walloping number of the psychological insights that will be the later hallmarks of *Remembrance of Things Past:* the volatility of the personality, the force of habit to dull even the most delicate conscience, the nostalgia for childhood. The sheer number of narrative and psychological reversals crowded into this brief story reduces its many "events" to their purely demonstrative value and creates the undeniable impression of a very young author at work, overanxious to get all that he knows about life on paper lest he never get the chance to write again.

The degenerative physical illness from which Baldassare suffers is directly attributable to his nerves; like Marcel's asthma in *Remembrance of Things Past,* it lessens in severity when he is treated well by those around him and redoubles its attacks when they are less attentive. Proust's first step in "Baldassare," then, is to establish

43

the necessary connection between nervous illness and the figurative language that will allow his fiction to proceed under the attractive, inspirational power of death; his second, for both Baldassare and himself, will be to call on prior texts as fetishes, as uncovering covers for death.

It is not only its thematic profusion that marks "Baldassare" as an early work; a break in the point of view divides the story into two distinct and unequal halves. The first part of the story is told from the point of view of the young Alexis, Baldassare's nephew, who disappears after the third chapter, yielding his viewpoint to that of his uncle. In "La composition des *Plaisirs et les jours*,"—Bernard Gicquel attributes this split—in reality, a technical error—to the thematic concerns of the entire work; Gicquel reads the difference between Baldassare and his nephew as the difference between life and death.

> While Baldassare Silvande makes his way toward death, Alexis, his nephew, walks toward life. . . . It is seemingly he who—under different names, masculine or feminine—will be taken in by the force of habit, like Violante [in "Violante; or, Worldly Vanities"], who will traverse while playing his own role, the spectacle of Italian comedy proposed by society or bourgeois life [in the "Fragments from Italian Comedy"], who will like Mme de Breyves [in "The Melancholy Summer of Madame de Breyves"] know the pain of an imaginary love, and then, regenerated by the revelation of art [in the "Portraits of Painters and Musicians"] will renounce sensuality, like the suicidal maiden [of "A Young Girl's Confession"], and turn away from the world to dedicate himself to the contemplation of the supra-individual realities that men and society conceal and reveal—like Honoré [of "The End of Jealousy"]—to attain with death to the definitive possession of ultimate truth. (253)

Gicquel was certainly right to oppose Alexis's preference for life to Baldassare's orientation toward death. His identification of Alexis with each and every one of the protagonists in the succeeding stories, however, is less convincing. It owes more to the demands of the circularity Gicquel wishes to read in *Pleasures and Regrets* than it does to any real textual evidence that it is indeed Alexis who appears in different guises throughout the work on his way to philosophical maturity. Combined with the need for a single narrator who will "learn" his detachment from the world through the revelation of art in the "Portraits of Painters and Musicians" that Gicquel equates with the revelations of *Time Regained* (the last volume of the *Remembrance*), this circular pattern seems too indiscriminately borrowed from the architecture of *Remembrance of Things Past* to be a wholly satisfactory account of the disparate and much earlier texts of *Pleasures and Regrets.*

Replaced within the context of Decadence, Alexis's preference for life becomes a negative force that must be eliminated. Because he is dying, Baldassare represents the superior world of representations that Proust extolled in the Noah's ark/sickroom metaphor. Alexis, in other words, is far too healthy for his Decadent author, the narrative fetishist who conceived him.

At the beginning of the story, Alexis is passably neurotic. It is the morning of his thirteenth birthday, and he is crying abundantly at the prospect of visiting his uncle Baldassare, whom he knows to be dying. The promise of the horse his uncle is expected to give him for his birthday is barely sufficient to console him. Nor can his preceptor's assurance that he will not cry be of any help, since the very thought of *not* crying in the presence of a confirmed moribund provokes another round of weeping. One interesting consequence of this hysteria is the warped sense of time by which Alexis makes Baldassare's death more and more premature with each turn of the page. First he credits his uncle with three more years to live; he next gives him two years at most, before finally wondering whether Baldassare would survive just a few more months to celebrate his thirty-seventh birthday (3–6).

Baldassare's promised birthday gift to Alexis capitalizes on these neurotic tendencies to initiate the adolescent into the figurative language that is the privilege of those touched by illness. The pony offered for his thirteenth birthday turns out to be the first in a series coextensive with the remaining years of the giver's life: "I know that you would like to drive a carriage and pair, my little Alexis," Baldassare explains. "A horse will be brought to you tomorrow. Next year I shall complete the pair, and in two years I shall give you the carriage. But perhaps this year you will learn to ride" (8). It is clear from the delay attaching to his gift that Baldassare intends to take for himself the full three years of his doctor's original prognosis. Moreover, the metonymic sigificance of the single horse in token of the completed gift and the metaphorical character of the horse and carriage representing the remaining time of his uncle's life are not lost on Alexis. He leaves his uncle's presence appropriately traumatized by "the universal scandal of human lives, not excepting his own, that walked toward death backward with eyes turned toward life" (11).

The horse determines what happens next. Riding it improves Alexis's physical health at the expense (Taine be praised!) of his neurosis.[12] The horse as pony instead of metonymy rebalances Alexis's body and mind, cures his neurasthenia, and thus severely limits his susceptibility to the approach of death.

> When Alexis, on his fourteenth birthday, went to see his Uncle Baldassare, he did not, as he had expected, feel any of the violent emotions of the preceding year. His endless rides on the horse his uncle had given him, while developing his strength, had dissipated all his morbid susceptibility and quickened that continuous sensation of perfect health that youth enjoys, like an obscure consciousness of the depths of its resources and the power of its joyous alacrity. Feeling his chest swelling like a sail in the breeze awakened by his galloping, his body burning like a fire in winter, and his forehead cool as the fugitive branches that whipped him as he rode by, and later, when he returned, the glow of his body under the cold shower or its languorous relish during the savoury pleasures of digestion, he would glory in all this power of life within him which, after having been the tumultuous pride of Baldassare, had left him now forever to rejoice younger souls whom it would in turn one day desert. (14–15)

The realignment of body and psyche resulting from Alexis's physical health inevitably entails the loss of his sense of figurative language. When, for Alexis's fourteeth birthday, Baldassare advances by a year his gift of the carriage, the nephew—who should have been painfully alerted to the metaphorical significance of this advance—is no longer moved:

> When his uncle said to him that day: "My little Alexis, I am going to give you the carriage at the same time as the second horse," he understood that his uncle had thought: "Because otherwise you are in danger of never having the carriage at all"; and he knew that this was an extremely sad thought but without *feeling* that it was sad, because actually there was no room in him for profound sadness. (16)

At this point Alexis virtually disappears or, more accurately, is dismissed from the story. His one parting relapse into hysteria, prompted by a metaphorical connection, is rapidly resolved by his horse and his physical health. Having chanced on a story of "a villain who remained unmoved by the heartbreaking tenderness of a dying man who adored him" (16), he allows himself to worry during one sleepless night whether he himself wasn't the unfeeling scoundrel about whom he had read. But the next day, "he took an exhilarating ride on his horse, worked well, felt such tender affection for his living parents that he was soon enjoying himself without scruple and sleeping without remorse" (16).

What was a passing adolescent phase for Alexis is a permanent condition for Baldassare. Having provided the original inspiration for the figurative gift of the horses and carriage, the approach of death, told now from Baldassare's point of view in the second half of the story, opens a continually widening gap between signifier and signified until the act of figuration itself—presented specifically as *literary* representation—takes over as the fetish object.

Baldassare is the first Proustian hero to be graced with anything like the phenomenon of involuntary memory. At the moment of his death, a sound of distant bells evokes a sequence of childhood memories. "During his whole life, whenever he heard the sound of distant bells, he always remembered their sweetness on the evening air when as a tiny boy he used to come home to the castle across the fields" (29). Even this demonstration is simultaneously rudimentary and overdone, characterized by a dilation of the point of view; romantically accumulating Baldassare's last impressions of life on earth, Proust once again tries to take in too much. Baldassare's view from his window open on the sea allows him not only to identify at the end of a boat "a handsome cabin-boy, fifteen years of age perhaps, [who] leaned far out over the water" (28), but even to take note of the young sailor's "salty lips" (28).

Equally dubious is the sentimental unity that Proust attaches to the cool evening air: "And the same breeze that swelled the sail came in through the open window cooling Baldassare's hot cheeks, and sending a paper fluttering around the room" (28). Moreover, extraordinary atmospheric conditions are required to bring in the bells at just the right moment: "It was the sound of bells coming from a distant village, which, thanks to the limpidity of the atmosphere that evening and the propitious breeze, had reached him across leagues of plain and forest and been caught by his faithful ear" (29). Finally, the entire memory sequence is eclipsed by the more elaborate contrast between the rapid objective time of the living and the slow subjective time of the dying: "All this he saw," recounts the narrator at the end, "yet not two minutes had elapsed since the doctor, listening to his heart, had said, 'This is the end!' Then, rising, 'All is over'" (30).

As a neurotic, Baldassare deals primarily in what Freud calls in *Totem and Taboo* a "neurotic currency," the condition that makes affect a more important signifier in the neuroses than external reality. The "omnipotence of thought" is thus a common experience within the neuroses. "In all [neuroses]," Freud writes in *Totem*, "what determines the formation of symptoms is the reality not of experience but of thought. . . . only 'neurotic currency' is legal tender; that is to say [neurotics] are only affected by what is thought with intensity and pictured with emotion, whereas agreement with external reality is a matter of no importance" (13:85, 86).

Baldassare's involuntary memory is a relatively minor episode within this overall neurotic tendency to the omnipotence of thought, rooted in an instance of metonymy. As the bells stand in for Baldassare's entire childhood, literary representation is put to use as the fetish that guards against absence, against the threat of death.

Baldassare's death scene is prepared by an example of the omnipotence of thought framed as artistic creation. Baldassare's farewell to the Duchess Oliviane is not merely an imagined scene but a projected narrative text of which Baldassare is the author and which he takes great delight in "reading" at will. Oliviane has been Baldassare's "cherished but platonic friend over whose drawing room he had reigned, even when the greatest noblemen, the most glorious artists and wits of Europe were assembled there" (17). With this illustrious company proposed as the readership for his text, Baldassare's reverie becomes an advance, romanticized obituary for himself. As Baldassare contemplates his farewell to Oliviane,

> He seemed already to be *reading* the account of their last meeting:
> ". . . The sun was setting and the sea, visible through the apple boughs, was mauve. Light as light faded garlands and persistent as regrets, little pink and blue clouds floated on the horizon. A melancholy row of poplars was plunged in shadow, the resigned heads in a churchly rose; the last rays of the sun, without touching their trunks, tinted the branches, hanging garlands of light on these balustrades of shade. The breeze mingled the three odors of sea, wet leaves and milk. Never had the landscape of Sylvania more voluptuously tempered the melancholy of the evening." (17–18; my emphasis)

Naturally enough, the details of this necrology cluster around an allusive vocabulary of death: "light faded garlands" "regrets," "shadow," "churchly rose," "last rays," "balustrades of shade," "evening." The imagery is just enough to be melancholy, not enough to be morbid. An apparent metaphor for the fading of so superlative a creature as Baldassare, the sun has set (or more accurately, will have set) that evening in an exemplary manner, creating a bittersweet pleasure heretofore unheard of in the country. That same exemplary pleasure is repeated in the projected text of the farewell interview, in which the Duchess's regrets at not having done enough to prove her chaste love for Baldassare are—or will be—met with his tender protests to the contrary:

> I loved you with a tenderness whose delicate sagacity no carnal pleasure ever spoiled. And in exchange have you not brought me an incomparable friendship, such lovely tea, a conversation by nature richly graced and how many

fragrant roses! You alone, with your maternal and ex-
pressive hands, knew how to soothe my fevered brow,
drop honey between my parched lips, fill my life with
noble images.

Dear friend, give me your hands that I may kiss
them. (18)

But, of course, even in such an early Proustian text, things do
not turn out as Baldassare had imagined. When Oliviane finally
does come to call, it is morning, not evening, the weather is bad, and
Baldassare is in a foul mood. The Duchess's repeated requests to see
her cherished platonic friend are thus testily and repeatedly denied.
Refusing to see Oliviane, however, Baldassare demonstrates the
manner in which affective representation has become his superior
reality. He substitutes the previous texualized scene for the real one
he now refuses to play out. Rather than receive Oliviane, Baldassare
reprises his earlier necrology:

It was ten o'clock in the morning, it was raining in
torrents. A carriage stopped in front of the chateau. It
was the duchess Oliviane. Once he had thought to
embellish harmoniously his death-bed scenes:
". . . It will be on some limpid evening. The sun will
have set and the sea, visible through the apple boughs,
will be mauve. Light as light faded garlands and persistent as regrets, little pink and blue clouds will float on the
horizon." (23)

The shift of affective level is legible in the tenses of the two
versions of the scene. Initially, Baldassare referred in the past tense
to what he imagined would be the case at some later date; at that
later date, however, he calls on the future to express circumstances
clearly in contradiction with the present but capable of continued
repetition. In consequence, the "real" farewell to Oliviane counts
for nothing in comparison with its figurative version, which both
absents Oliviane and more than makes up for her absence in
Baldassare's mind. Behind Oliviane, however, is the present absence
or absent presence of death itself. Repeated with primary reference
to itself and promising, by its future tense verbs, to keep on

repeating, Baldassare's narrative of the farewell to Oliviane absorbs the contradictory impulses of his attraction to and fear of death. Functioning as a fetish, representation takes over as the substitute object of desire. This process has also occurred, confirming the fetishization of representation, during Baldassare's vigil over his sister-in-law's sickbed, after which he congratulates himself that "it was death now he looked at, face to face, and not the imagined settings of his own death" (22). In fact, Baldassare is once again paying homage to the fetish, since his sister-in-law is only another possible representation of death that he interposes between himself and his own demise.

As the title announces, that demise is the point of the story. Unsurprisingly, however, Baldassare "misses" the moment of his death. The death scene is not simply elided through the supposed episode of involuntary memory evoked by the bells. Baldassare's death is revealingly covered over by the most striking instance in the story of literary representation—this time, prior and "sure"—pressed into service as the fetish.

In "*Les plaisirs et les jours:* Chronologie et métempsychose," Anne Henry observes the debt that Proust owes to Tolstoy for the ending of "Baldassare." The gathering of family and servants around Baldassare's deathbed, his revolt against death giving way to resignation, his reminiscences of childhood, and the doctor's stark pronouncement, "All is over!" can all, she maintains, be traced to similar death scenes in *War and Peace* and "The Death of Ivan Ilyich" with which Proust must certainly have been familiar at the time he wrote "Baldassare." However, where Henry finds that "a commonality of convictions" (85), combining idealism and vitalism, realism and romanticism, prompts Proust's attraction to Tolstoy, his use of a borrowed scene to conclude "Baldassare" has in fact much more to do with death and the fetish. The end of the narrative, after all, is the end of the narrative voice, the silence that threatens to undermine the writing project Proust is elaborating against his father's authority.

Borrowing his death scene from previous literature, Proust as author takes over for Baldassare as the narrative fetishist. While Baldassare is busy missing his death by re-representing his life in the metonymy of the bells, Proust is busy copying Baldassare's death from Tolstoy. Concealing the prospect of Proust's death as a writer while calling attention by its placement and its content to the reality of that death, the prior text from Tolstoy serves as Proust's own fetish object. Should the son's "little pieces" come up short against the father's, the text from Tolstoy is reassuringly available as a phantom of presence to guard against the thrilling danger of absence. In "The Death of Baldassare Silvande," the text from Tolstoy is the substitute object for the whole of *Pleasures and Regrets* — the substitute object for the book itself as the substitute object of desire.

Plodding Plot Lines: Hallucination and Happenstance

Substitute objects are an important means by which three other protagonists of *Pleasures and Regrets* — Françoise de Breyves in "The Melancholy Summer of Madame de Breyves," the Young Girl of "A Young Girl's Confession," and Honoré of "The End of Jealousy" — create and maintain desire. Like Baldassare Silvande, all three suffer from their neurotic imaginations; all three deal in the omnipotence of thought. Yet in their increasingly sophisticated use of the fetish, these stories represent a technical advance over "Baldassare." In these stories, fetishization occurs at the level of the characters: it is they who both fear and invite absence, they who create its uncovering covers. The distance Proust maintains from his characters is thus much greater than that by which he tried unconvincingly to remain aloof from Baldassare.

However, the stories are not free of intrusion from the narrator. Indeed, narrative intrusiveness is largely responsible for their appeal as examples of narrative rhetoric based on neurotic trauma. To demonstrate how each character's subjective representations are at odds with external reality, Proust will now deliberately cast doubt (in a way he did not do for Baldassare) on the origins of their traumatic experiences. Each protagonist, in other words, will be made to wonder whether the precipitating event of his or her obsessive representations has occurred anywhere but in his or her own imagination. As event thus slips into hallucination, Proust as narrator shoulders an additional burden of plot: the characters' neurotic uncertainties about what has or has not happened to them will reflect a series of hesitations and discrepancies in the narrative voice that orders their respective fictional worlds. These stories, then, are all about plot, about the problem of making things happen.

Françoise de Breyves is among the best examples of the neurotic imagination at work in *Pleasures and Regrets*. Her story is fairly simple and straightforward. At one of the last social events of the season, she refuses the innocent request of her friend, Geneviève de Buivres, to present to her a young man who has asked to meet her, a certain Jacques de Laléande. "Besides, he's rather ugly and vulgar-looking," she explains, "in spite of his beautiful eyes" (173). Geneviève agrees but cannot resist teasing Françoise about her obvious conquest: "she added, laughing, 'Unless, of course, you'd like a more intimate acquaintance—in that case you're missing a fine opportunity.' 'Yes, a fine opportunity,' said Françoise, already thinking of something else" (173–74).

Like the better-known Proustian lovers who will follow her, Françoise can oppose no resistance to the attractive force of the desire she perceives in the other. Flattered, and "for no reason, for the pleasure of it, the pleasure of being charitable, the pleasure of vanity too and of futility" (174), she flirts discreetly with Laléande across the room, finally arranging to leave the party at the exact moment that he heads for the vestiary. There she finds herself momentarily alone with him; Laléande seizes the occasion to make his move: "He passed close to her, lightly rubbing his elbow against hers, and while still touching her, his eyes very bright, and still pretending to be looking for his cane, said, 'Come to my place, 5 Rue Royale'" (175).

Inasmuch as "Madame de Breyves" has attracted any critical attention, it has chiefly focused on this particular scene. Maurice Bardèche relates Laléande's invitation to the "most unseemly things" (*Pleasures* 89) that older boys whisper into young girls' ears in several of the work's pieces. For Bardèche, it is significant that Proust's heroines are first introduced to sexual temptation by these obscene little whisperings that hint at the forbidden world of sex (54–55). For Maria Paganini, the setting itself is the significant part of the encounter. In both *Pleasures and Regrets* and *Remembrance of Things Past,* she observes, the vestibule functions as unclaimed territory; as a place of public dressing and undressing, the vestiary is particularly full of the potential for sexual encounter (147).

Françoise herself hardly knows what to make of Laléande's invitation. So stunned is she by the "obscenity" that she can never be sure that the violent passion she conceives for Laléande is not wholly a creation of her imagination: "she was never able to decide later," comments the narrator, "whether it was only an hallucination or not" (175). To be fair, it takes Françoise some time to get to this later point of wondering. In the days that follow their initial encounter, she resumes her indifference to Laléande. This indifference, however, perversely feeds the hallucination, since, having dismissed Laléande's words for the social unseemliness that they represented, Françoise "decided she must have heard them as in a dream" (175).

Françoise sees Laléande one more time, at the very last gala of the year; he leaves, however, before she can arrange to meet him. A subsequent attempt to arrange a meeting through a mutual friend also fails, and Françoise learns to her chagrin that Laléande has left for Biarritz with no intention of returning to Paris before the following winter. The extent of her disappointment makes it clear to Françoise that she has fallen passionately in love:

> Until then, preoccupied as she had been in imagining all sorts of romantic ways of meeting and knowing [Jacques], believing that she could realize them when she wished, she had been, perhaps unconsciously, living on this desire and this hope. Deeply implanted in her, they had sent down a thousand little imperceptible roots and started a new mysterious sap coursing through her. And now, all at once, they were uprooted and thrown into the discard. She suffered the agonizing laceration of that hidden self suddenly torn up by the roots. Now she saw clearly through all the lies that hope and desire had held out to her, and, at last, from the depths of her grief came suddenly face to face with the reality of her love. (179–80)

And that concludes the "events" of the story's plot. In the second half of the story, chapters 4 and 5, Françoise's activities are subordinated to the extended demonstration of her deteriorating mental state as she gives herself over more and more resolutely to fantasy. In Trouville, for example, when an unnamed prince gallantly asks how to win her favor, the incident has purely descriptive importance, enabling Françoise to feel "all the concentrated and bitter irony of the contrast between the great and difficult things always being done for her, and the one little thing, so easy and so impossible, that would have brought back peace, health and happiness to her, and the happiness of those dearest to her" (182). By the end of the story, the events of her life have been so subordinated to her psychological state that they become completely interchangeable: "Whether Madame de Breyves takes a walk with a poet or lunches with an archduchess, whether she is alone and reading or talking with a cherished friend, whether she rides horseback or sleeps, the name, the image of M. de Laléande is always over her, deliciously, cruelly, inevitably as the sky is over our heads" (188).

Like the literary "text" of his farewell to the Duchess Oliviane that Baldassare reads and rereads in his mind, Françoise's representations are characterized as narrative fictions; her early schemes to meet Laléande are so many "novels" in which she believes uncritically. Varese translates Françoise's schemes for getting to know Laléande as daydreams of "all sorts of romantic ways of meeting and knowing" him. Yet in Proust's original wording, these schemes are unambiguously *romans,* or "novels." It is also clear from the failure of her "novels" that Françoise's love for Laléande is based on an absence, an absence that the narrator takes great care to establish. Laléande appears twice in the story and speaks only once, to proffer his ambiguous invitation. No physical description is given of him; he is seen only through the eyes of Françoise and Geneviève, and even Françoise will eventually be unable to recall just what he looks like. This absence, then, is Laléande and is not Laléande. As she has had no chance to find out whether Laléande is intelligent or mediocre, faithful or faithless, Françoise consoles herself that "it is then really himself she loves, not his merits nor his charms, which can be found to as high a degree in others" (186), only to be countered by the narrator: "*Himself,* does she know what that is? except that it is something that has caused her such shudders of desolation or felicity that the rest of her life has counted for nothing, nothing else has mattered" (186–87).

Françoise's representations are thus once again made to serve as a fetish; they conceal and announce an absence that is both too horrible to accept and too attractive to renounce. But this story differs from and improves on "Baldassare" by the narrative use Proust makes of the representation fetish. Rather than fetishize narrative representation as blocks of text, as he did with the repeating text of the farewell to Oliviane and the ending borrowed from Tolstoy, he now distributes the function of the fetish across a number of objects connected to Laléande by their metonymic allusiveness.

A photograph of Biarritz, in which appears a shadowy walking figure that Françoise decides must be Jacques, is one such object. So is the very name *Biarritz*, since Françoise "has even reached the point, she who always detested Biarritz, where she finds in everything connected with that city a touching and painful charm" (188). So are her servants, whose "respectful and grieved silence spoke to her of M. de Laléande" (182). So, too (announcing Vinteuil's sonata in *Swann's Way*), is a phrase from Wagner's *Die Meistersänger*, which, since it had been on the program the evening of her single encounter with Jacques, becomes for Françoise "the *leitmotif* of M. de Laléande" (184).

This use of metonymic allusion creates a more convincing narrative rhetoric for "Madame de Breyves" than was the case for "Baldassare Silvande." Attributed to metonymic objects within a represented world of neurotic imagination, the fetish here is consciously used and manipulated as an element within narrative representation, rather than as its justification. The neurotic Françoise is shown in submission to the fetish objects which are recognized and presented by the narrator as such, but which remain unanalyzed by her. All she sees is that they serve her desire; in fact, they serve it so obviously, from her point of view, that she professes astonishment that with all those who "[hear] her talk continually about all the things surrounding her secret, no one has guessed it" (188). The clear delineation of distance between the narrator's world and that of Madame de Breyves contrasts with the use of narrative representation as fetish in "Baldassare Silvande." "Madame de Breyves" is not a story that makes a fetish out of the very notion of "story" in order to allow the narrator to proceed. Instead, it brings the fetish within the domain of narrative and subjects it to the rules of the story, using it objectively and dispassionately as part of the narrative demonstration, and from a perceptible distance of narrative authority.

Yet this very distance creates a problem of plot. The profusion of fetish objects with which Françoise is finally surrounded serves to trap her in an eternal present of pleasure-pain; paralyzed by these two contradictory yet complementary currents, she becomes stuck in narrative time, unable even to want to get over the torment of her impossible love for an unknown man. "She would revile herself for having so artfully measured the doses of pleasure and pain of her love," comments the narrator, "which she had been powerless to reject at once as an invidious poison, or later to cure. . . . Her sorrow can begin again, and it is now almost a joy" (184, 189).

Whereas the death knell of the ending was something to be artfully evaded in "Baldassare," Proust's problem here becomes more properly *how* to end, how to extricate himself as narrator from the subtle psychological web that the fetish objects have woven around his heroine. He needs to get out of the story without destroying the illusion of Françoise's constantly recycled complicity with her neurosis. The solution, similar to but not identical with the one devised for "Baldassare," is the introduction of an ancillary narrative voice. In this case, it is the narrator himself who intervenes as a first-person observer: "I have just come across Madame de Breyves again here at Trouville. I have known her in happier hours. Nothing can cure her" (186).

This seemingly authoritative statement should be sufficient to conclude the story. Having known her before her debilitating passion for Laléande, the first-person narrator is qualified to speak for just how far she has fallen from her previous happiness. Further, the recent past tense of "have just come across" updates the story of Françoise's sufferings to a narrative present which, close to the lived time of both the narrator and the reader, implies that Françoise's obsessive representations of Laléande have indeed stopped time for her. Finally, the narrator knows much more about Jacques de Laléande than Françoise does and can thus be objectively aware of the abyss that separates the real Laléande from what Françoise imagines him to be: "Certainly M. de Laléande, who is probably leading a very banal life on the beach at Biarritz, indulging in harmless dreams, would be very much astonished if he knew of this other existence of his . . . in Madame de Breyves' soul" (187).

However, and again as in "Baldassare," the abrupt shift in point of view recommends a closer look at the problem of the ending. Indeed, even as it confirms the gap between Francoise's representations and the objective reality of Jacques de Laléande, the new knowledge that the first-person voice contributes to the story is sufficient reason to challenge it. Later, in *Remembrance of Things*

Past, Proust might get away with extending the prerogatives of the *I* to include omniscience over his entire cast of characters, but that is chiefly because the sheer bulk of his material provides ample camouflage for the sleight of hand (or voice). In the much shorter "Madame de Breyves," the first-person voice comes from nowhere. The first-person epilogue reads like a tacked-on speech whose effect is really to contradict the omniscient narration it seeks to resolve.

The effect of this opposition of voices—the omniscient voice revealing the workings of Françoise's mind and the personal voice that tries to pass judgment on her—is to return the reader to the role played by hallucination in Françoise's dilemma. Françoise's psychological double bind stems from an event whose reality she questions; it focuses on an eternal absence. By the end of the story, the psychological double bind is a narrative double bind as well, as if the hallucination were reaching out to overwhelm even the objective narrator, the *I* who began his intervention by measuring the distance between Françoise and the world around her. This narrative double bind is evident in two moments. In the first, the narrator avows no knowledge of the probable consequences of Françoise's passion. "How will Madame de Breyves endure her return to Paris, from which, until January, he will still be absent?" he asks. "What will she do from now until then? What will she do—what will he do—afterwards?" (189). In the second, he resigns himself to never knowing, since the power of Francoise's pleasure-pain is ultimately greater than his ability as narrator to break her out of the cycle by making something happen. "A dozen times I have been on the point of going to Biarritz to bring back M. de Laléande. The consequences might well be terrible, but speculation is futile, since she will not hear of it" (189).

And so nothing "happens." The imagined love affair takes precedence over the real one that could ensue if the narrator were granted leave—by the character!—to do what he could to further the plot. If no new "actions," however, are invented by the narrator, a final drawn-out fantasy scene at least introduces a new pronoun: *we.* The narrator once again is speaking of the romantic pictures Madame de Breyves sees in her head:

> Often she imagines that he will come to Trouville, come
> up to her, tell her that he loves her. She sees him; his eyes

shine. He speaks to her in that colorless voice of dream which prevents our believing, while all the time forcing us to listen. It is he. He speaks the words that intoxicate even though we hear them only in dreams, when we see, radiant and touching, the divine and confident smile of two destinies uniting. (190)

The introduction of the first-person plural strongly suggests the narrator's capitulation to the power of the fantasy. He is now among those who succumb to the power of affective perception, he who recognizes the superiority of "plot" as an *absence* of events, sequence, and resolution. Thus resolution becomes a matter of fitting one absence to another. The absence of a proper ending corresponds to the confused sources of Françoise's trauma; to the hallucinatory encounter in the vestiary responds the dream, shared by the narrator, of the picture-book happy ending. And are not things better that way, at least from the writer's point of view? One of the advantages of pleasure-pain, after all, is to indefinitely stave off the end.

The Moral Nondemonstration: "A Young Girl's Confession"

In "Madame de Breyves," Proust relinquishes narrative control of the plot in favor of a continued obsession with absence. "A Young Girl's Confession" reasserts the right of the narrator to make things happen. In fact, "A Confession" overcompensates in narrative control for the complacency of the narrative voice and the run-down nonending of Madame de Breyves's tale of woe. Under the pressure of an intended moral demonstration, "A Confession" features a heavy-handed plot based on a lockstepped series of coincidences that eventually backfire and turn the demonstration against itself. Once more, the precipitating cause of neurotic trauma is thrown into doubt, and in such a way that the narrator once again finds himself wrestling with the protagonist for the final word in the story.

Of all the short stories of *Pleasures and Regrets*, "A Confession" has probably enjoyed the best fortune in Proustian criticism, owing principally to its presumably autobiographical deep structure. Henri Massis's doctrinaire reading of *Pleasures and Regrets* makes the work the record of Proust's slow descent into sexual sin, in which "A Confession" figures as the "final echo of a breaking voice: the last resonance of a soul awakening far from him, out of him, never to be heard from again" (76).

Constitutionally incapable of resisting sexual temptation, the Young Girl holds herself responsible for her mother's death when the latter surprises her in the throes of sexual passion. Overcome by remorse, she shoots herself—inexpertly enough, however, to gain at a least a week of death agony during which to tell her tale, to "reconstruct the horrible chain of events" (31) that has brought her to this protracted moment of confession. Proust's matricidal heroine has thus been considered an easily recognizable stand-in for Proust's guilt-ridden overattachment to his own mother, an attachment that requires his sexuality be kept secret from her in dread of the consequences should she ever find out. Moreover, the Young Girl is a clear forerunner of the waffling and indecisive—thus morally deficient—Marcel of *Remembrance of Things Past*. She articulates the paradox of the absence of will every bit as lucidly as does Marcel: "What grieved my mother," she recalls, "was my lack of will. . . . To wish to possess a will was not enough. What I had to do was precisely what I could not do without a will: to will to have one" (37, 38).

The Young Girl is tempted first by a young cousin already "very depraved" for his fifteen years and who, repeating the ploy of obscene whisperings, "told me things which instantly made me shudder with remorse and voluptuousness" (34). She is saved from further misbehavior in this occurrence by the fortuitous appearance of her mother in the park at Les Oublis, their country home. However, at the age of sixteen and on the heels of "a period of nervous depression which affected my health" (38), she has the misfortune to fall in love with a young man particularly "depraved and evil," who "initiated me to depravity almost without my realizing it, then accustomed me to encourage the evil thoughts that awoke in me and which I had not the will to oppose" (38–39). This seducer proves merely the first of a series. "When love died," she explains of her new promiscuity, "habit had taken its place, and there was no lack of immoral young men to exploit it" (39). Finally, her mother's illness, the Young Girl's engagement to a respectable and chaste young man, and a heartfelt talk with her confessor set her back on the path of good conduct. She perseveres until the night of a dinner party, at which champagne is served to celebrate her upcoming marriage. It is after this dinner that her mother, chancing on the Young Girl in the arms of a lover, drops dead.

The Young Girl's attempt to bare her soul in a flashback confession is, as Walter Kasell has shown in "Writing and the Return to Innocence: Proust's 'La confession d'une jeune fille,'" a literary project doomed from the start. For her confession to truly exculpate her, Kasell suggests, she must somehow find an unambiguous language in which to confess the full extent of her corruption and restore her lost innocence. "If the primacy of appearance is the hallmark of corruption," Kasell writes of the Young Girl's happy bewilderment at being taken for a model of filial piety even at her most promiscuous, "then the recovery of innocence will be a return to an appearance fully and immediately itself: a transparent language, entirely free of deception" (37). But this return to a transparent language, of course, is impossible, especially for one who has learned, as has the Young Girl, how the appearance of virtue can add spice to the practice of vice. Her language can never account for the perverse contribution that remorse has already made to her sexual pleasure; intended as a pure expression of regret, her confession fails because she will not allow herself to admit the pleasure she took in her sins.

But this is only one reason why the Young Girl is unable to "reconstruct the horrible chain of events" that leads to her confession. The only first-person narrator of the stories in *Pleasure and Regrets,* she is in effect outmaneuvered by a superior causal world that controls events behind her, as it were, in the story. The Young Girl cannot reconstruct—in the original French, *re-saisir,* or "seize again"—the sequence of events because she has never had hold of them in the first place. In this story about the failure of will, she never has a chance to be will-less or not, thanks to a shadow narrator who takes over for her and makes things happen in her stead.

A closer examination of the plot reveals clearly the presence of this superior order, manipulated by the shadow narrator. This order is what saves the Young Girl from more serious damage than a good fright at Les Oublis. Usually, she spends these vacations in the country away from her mother, to whom she is, naturally, overattached, and who "would take me to *Les Oublis* toward the end of April, would leave again after two days, spend two more days there in the middle of May, then, in the last week of June would come to take me away" (32). The occasion of a visit by the young cousin who whispers seductively into her ear falls outside of one of these two-day grace periods when the Young Girl's mother could be expected to be present. When, freeing herself from her cousin's embrace, the Young Girl runs into the park and calls for her mother, "whom I knew, alas! to be in Paris," the latter appears as an hallucination come to life: "Suddenly, as I was running past a vine-covered arbor, I saw her sitting on a bench, smiling and holding out her arms to me" (34).

Her mother's kiss and their reassuring conversation become a pledge of tenderness that frees the Young Girl's mind from the turmoil of her recent temptation and protects her, so she believes, against all those yet to come. Her mother's departure the following day "was more cruel than all those that had preceded it. It seemed to me now, having once sinned, that together with happiness, strength and the necessary succor were abandoning me" (35).

But the question is, of course, just what her mother was doing there in the first place. It is evident that her main function is to serve as exactly that prop of whose departure the Young Girl so presciently complains. Her uncles had known that her mother was coming, she finds out later, but had not told her about it so as not to aggravate her neurasthenia. This may be motivation for the secret, but it does not explain the mother's arrival. The appearance of the mother at a critical moment in the tragedy slows down the Young Girl's fall from grace; their tender scene together in the park makes that fall all the more tantalizing for having held the Young Girl one moment longer over the abyss. But none of this is the doing of the ostensible narrator, the Young Girl. It belongs instead to the causal order elaborated and manipulated by the shadow narrator, an order that is curiously predicated on coincidence. The Young Girl's highly fortuitous "redemption" by her mother's sudden appearance rivets her moral world to the power of happenstance; from now on, her "goodness," or lack thereof, will depend on the concurrence of optimal circumstances that are entirely beyond her control.

One of the most breathless passages from the ending of *Time Regained* has Marcel reflecting on the long sequence of coincidences that has led him, finally, to the project of his book. Had he not known Swann, he muses, he would never have gone to Balbec, would never have known Albertine or Charlus or been introduced into the circle of the Guermantes. Thus, without Swann, he would never have written his novel.[13] Coming at the end of the massive *Remembrance of Things Past*, the reflection on coincidence builds to a powerful crescendo, sounding at once most of the different themes of the novel. In "A Confession," however, Proust once again has so much less to work with that the dependence on coincidence becomes embarrassingly evident. More seriously, by basing the moral demonstration on a superior causal order itself based on coincidence, he robs the Young Girl of any real chance to "prove" herself either moral or immoral. By offering her only the narrowest of circumstances and the most elaborate of props, the shadow narrator in effect does not leave the Young Girl much chance to be "good." Her "badness" is no more "bad" than her "goodness" is really good.

This narrative duplicity is particularly evident, and particularly unsettling, at the climax of the story, "the very evening" (43), the Young Girl calls it, "when *all was accomplished*" (43; Proust's emphasis). The setting is a dinner and the circumstances are extraordinary. In the first place, the Young Girl's fiancé, who "because of his remarkable intelligence, his gentleness and energy [was] just the young man to have the happiest influence over me" (42) is (conveniently) absent; in his place has been (inexplicably) invited the young man "who was principally to blame for my past sins" (43). The Young Girl's mother, in the late stages of mourning for her husband, is at the far end of her own convalescence from a weakness of the heart that, the doctor has (pertinently) declared, needs to continue only fifteen more days before she can be pronounced (definitively) out of danger.

During the dinner, the assembled company toasts the coming nuptials. Usually abstemious, the Young Girl is encouraged by an uncle—the same who did not tell her about her mother's unexpected arrival—to drink a glass of champagne. The Young Girl's relapse gathers momentum: the champagne is excellent, "so cool that I drank two more glasses" (45), the Young Girl recalls, and its effect is so ennervating that, by the end of the dinner, "my head grew heavy, I felt a need to rest and, at the same time, to expend my nervous energy" (45). It is no surprise, then, that when her former lover suggests they go read his poetry together, "I understood that I was lost and I was without power to resist" (45).

Retelling this sequence, the Young Girl attempts to identify the exact moment, the precise act of consent that precipitated the tragedy: "It was when I uttered those words, or perhaps, even before, when I drank my second glass of champagne, that I committed the really responsible act, the abominable act. After that I did no more than let myself go" (45). Yet as in the earlier scene with her mother in the park, the real mechanism of the dénouement escapes her. The story's real climactic moment is her mother's appearance on the balcony outside the Young Girl's room at the very instant that she has stopped to contemplate herself and her lover in the mirror. There is no narrative justification for this event other than the shadow narrator's desire to have things turn out this way. Her agonized reflections to the contrary, the Young Girl's tragedy is the result of one supremely unlucky coincidence.[14]

The split in the causal order of the story, opposing the sincere if limited first-person narrator to the superior world of coincidence arranged behind her back, strips the moral demonstration of whatever effectiveness it might have had in exposing the dire consequences of a failure of the will to be good. If the Young Girl needs *so* much to be good—the right fiancé, her mother's presence, no champagne, and certainly no unscrupulous dinner companions—then it can only be said she has no will of her own. But in this case, then, why care about her? It seems that Proust's marksmanship is no better than that of his suicidal heroine, for he has considerably overshot his target. Excessive narrative control, too great a concern for making just the right things happen at just the right time in the story, creates a heroine who is so much a literary character that she becomes, at the climax of her story, nothing more than that. With no will of her own, she offers no return to the "real" world in which her story could have exemplary value. The moral demonstration of a will-less heroine who is given no choice but to fail turns inside out and is no moral demonstration at all.

However, all is not lost for the Young Girl. As in "Madame de Breyves," doubt about the moment of trauma gives her narration a chance to reestablish its authority against that of the shadow narrator in a conjunction between language and sight. The precipitating moment of trauma is the exchange of glances between the Young Girl and her mother in the mirror. Perceiving her own face disfigured by desire, the Young Girl also perceives behind her "my mother looking at me aghast" (46). The death agony that is the pretext of the story is thus not simply a verbal act; it is also and more compellingly a visual replay of the exchange of glances: "I may stay like this another week," the Young Girl repeats at the end of her confession, "and during all that time I shall be unable to stop trying to grasp the beginnings . . . never stop *seeing* the end" (46; Proust's emphasis).

But the visual replay is not exact; under the force of trauma it distorts the original image—her mother's horrified face in the mirror—even as it repeats it. Denying that her mother could really have seen her and yet entertaining the possibility that she did, the Young Girl abandons herself to an hallucinated version of events that, like Madame de Breyves's imaginings of Jacques, becomes a tolerable, indeed attractive, pleasure-pain complex: "I should rather my mother had seen me commit still other crimes, and even that one too, than that she should have seen that look of joy on my face in the mirror. No, she could not have seen it" (46–47).

As in "Madame de Breyves," the pleasure-pain complex over-whelms the story's "objective" narrative voice (that of the shadow narrator), leading the Young Girl to surmise the role played by coincidence in her story. "It was a coincidence," she decides of her mother's appearance on the balcony, "she had had a stroke of apoplexy a moment before seeing me . . . she did not see [my face]" (47). Stumbling on the malleable truth of coincidence, the Young Girl reasserts her voice as a match for that of the shadow narrator. After all, the role of coincidence has been such throughout the story that there is no good reason for apoplexy *not* to have intervened at just the opportune moment. The Young Girl has discovered the narrative trick by which she was tricked and put it to work in her own behalf. Assuming then the truth of her own "coincidences," the Young Girl cancels out the manipulations of the shadow narrator who has dogged her throughout the story. But this does not make her any less overdrawn as a literary character. As hallucination takes over for happenstance, the moral demonstration definitively col-lapses. It yields to the continuous play and replay of the figurative force of desire, to the Young Girl's languorous, amorous refusal to accept or dismiss the precipitating moment of trauma.

The Body Fetish: "The End of Jealousy"

The concluding story of *Pleasures and Regrets*, "The End of Jealousy," ties up a number of the threads left dangling in the earlier stories. From "Baldassare" there is the protracted death scene in which the subjective, dilated time of death is contrasted to the objective time of the spectators. From "Madame de Breyves" and "A Confession" there is the obscene remark that precipitates trauma and whose "truth" can never be ascertained. Along with the auditory hallucination of the obscenity, "The End of Jealousy" further develops the visual hallucination introduced in "A Confession": as stimulus for his pleasure-pain complex, the protagonist, Honoré, imagines he is spying on his mistress as she makes love with another.

What advances the story over the preceding ones is the resolution of the plot and voice difficulties that broke "Baldassare" into two parts, that situated the narrator both within and without the mind of Françoise de Breyves, and that forced the failure of the moral demonstration of "A Confession." By entrusting questions of causality entirely to the consideration of the characters, the narrative voice in "The End of Jealousy" achieves an appropriate distance from the story and manages thereby to create a fairly convincing realist illusion. More important, hallucination in "The End of Jealousy" is accompanied by a breakdown in the complementary signifying orders of language and the body so that each—particularly the body—becomes a fetish, a locus of simultaneous truth and untruth.

In this story, Honoré is passionately in love with the young widow Françoise Seaunes, who returns his desperate and clingy affection. Their affair, kept secret from those around them, is presented as a careful equilibrium between two overly delicate nervous systems; each reacts to the other in voluntary harmony with their delicate susceptibilities. Their idyll, however, is once more interrupted by "obscenity": a certain M. de Buivres chances to remark to Honoré that Françoise Seaunes is sexually "easy" and that she has been the mistress of François de Gouvres, who, M. de Buivres assures, "had quite an affair with her" (198). As will Swann and Marcel after him, Honoré allows this suspicion of Françoise's infidelity to fester within him.

> Even if he had acquired the impossible certitude that she had never given herself to anyone but to him, the un-known pain which had visited his heart the night that M. de Buivres had accompanied him to his door, not a

kindred pain, or the memory of that pain, but that very pain itself, would not have ceased making him suffer even if he had been incontestably shown that it was without cause. (201)

The causal sequence that incites Honoré to fantasize that Françoise has been unfaithful benefits from a more motivated preparation than Proust has managed in the preceding stories. Honoré himself sets it in motion by questioning Buivres about the Princesse d'Alériouvre; it has already been established that Honoré has not always been faithful to Françoise and that in the case of the princess, "without being in love with her, Honoré would have enjoyed possessing her, if he could have been sure that Françoise would not find out, not be made unhappy" (198). For his part, Buivres is a man of the world who chides Honoré, "You're young" (198), when the latter protests he has heard nothing negative about Françoise.

For his part, though, Buivres has been out of circulation for some time, so his information may be less than reliable. The fateful soirée after which he and Honoré have their conversation had been held precisely to welcome Buivres back from a long sojourn out of the country. Moreover, not only is the one person who *could* verify the rumor—this François de Gouvres who had supposedly nearly ruined himself for Françoise—kept out of the story, two equally plausible (and similarly unverifiable) explanations are given for Francoise's practice of leaving social gatherings early. According to Honoré, she wishes to avoid scandal (and knows that Honoré can discreetly join her later), while Buivres maintains, "I'll wager that she's enjoying herself at this very moment. Have you noticed how she always leaves any affair early?" (198).

The highly contingent nature of this causal sequence contributes to the ambiguities of Honoré's ensuing trauma. It will eventually become less important that he know whether or not Françoise *has* cheated than that he prevent, by his continual presence at her side, any possibility of her ever escaping him again. This, of course, has the ironic effect of advertising the liaison that the lovers had taken such pains to conceal, but Honoré is unable to see beyond his own need for Françoise's material presence. He is thus aptly compared to "those people suffering from hallucinations whom sometimes one succeeds in curing by having them touch the armchair or the living person occupying the place where they thought they saw a phantom, and thus chasing it from the real world, curing them by reality itself, which leaves no room for phantoms" (205–6).

And so Honoré uses Françoise's body to cover a threatening absence that, if revealed, would jeopardize the precarious security he has finally worked out for himself. This use of Françoise's body as fetish, however, is only apparently reassuring. The simultaneous truth/untruth of the fetish object, which, in the Freudian view, conceals and reveals the misperception of the mother's penis, serves here to contaminate both the body and language as reliably truthful signifiers.

From the very beginning, Françoise and Honoré make use of a private language by which they reveal their passion for each other while concealing it from those around them. The story's opening lines are an outpouring of this language: "My little tree, my little donkey, my mother, my brother, my country, my little God, my little sea-shell, my lotus flower, my little stranger, my darling, my little plant, do go away and let me dress," Françoise cajoles her lover; "and I'll meet you, Rue de la Baume, at eight o'clock" (192). Like a neurotic symptom, this language/exhibits an extraordinary capacity for absorbing contrary meanings. Reflecting on their language, Honoré recognizes that it has indeed been "stretched" beyond the bounds of ordinary communicative intent:

> Returning home, Honoré kept repeating to himself, "my mother, my brother, my country—" He stopped. "Yes, my country! . . . my little tree, my little sea-shell." And he couldn't help laughing as he said these words which they had so quickly adopted as their own, seemingly so empty but that for them were filled with infinite meaning. (193)

From a simple stretching of meaning, the language gradually engulfs categories of opposites. Everything that Françoise and Honoré say to each other, from pet names to tender accusations, is invariably readable as an expression of their desire; this inflation of the signifier imitates the equation of positive and negative, yes and no, imposed on the hysterical symptom by the contradictory impulses of repression. It is also, as we have seen, characteristic of the (nondiscriminatory) primary process. Within the complicated code of amorous transgression and punishment reflected in the lovers' private language, guilt and innocence in particular lose their significance. Françoise knows, for example, that Honoré cannot resist kissing her if she pouts and shakes her head in a certain way; when he responds by calling her "Naughty! Naughty!" (197), thus blaming her for his own inability to resist her, she accepts the accusation as a compliment. Likewise, when Honoré "transgresses" by appearing to let his thoughts wander away from her, Françoise knows that her accusation, "So that's it! You weren't thinking of me at all!" (197), will be praised as a clever lie, on the assumption that she ought to have known that Honoré is always thinking of her. So she once again becomes a "transgressor," the guilty party chided as "Little liar!" (197) by an original "transgressor" now pretending to be a "victim" (149).

These reversals of language serve the couple well so long as the only referent they need is their own desire. The contamination of truth, however, becomes a serious matter when Honoré needs language to ascertain Françoise's real guilt or innocence according to the new grammar proposed by M. de Buivres. Honoré's problem is that he and Françoise *have* no language in which reliable confession or disavowal might be made. The terms of the code by which Françoise is "naughty" and capable of clever lying have already been used up, exhausted, as signifiers of affection; they are therefore unavailable to help Honoré make sense of Buivres's allegation. By making "negative" signifiers indistinguishable from "positive" signifiers, their private language leaves nothing left over that might serve as an index of truth.

Honoré's quest for truth through *language* plays itself out primarily as a relationship between two physical *bodies* already tainted by the ambiguity of the fetish. Honoré's own tendency to infidelity is presented as a strict matter of the body, as he recalls "those pleasures that only my body enjoys away from [Françoise]" (197). Thus Honoré's initial attempt to provoke Françoise's confession by attempting to confess himself receives only an ambiguous gesture in response:

> It was one evening while they were walking along the
> Champs-Elysées that he tried to tell her he had been

unfaithful. He was terrified to see her turn pale, sink powerless on a bench, and worse still when, gently and without anger, as he held out his hands to her, she pushed him away. For two days he thought he had lost her, or rather that he had found her again. (201)

If the language of gesture is contaminated by the equation of truth with falsehood, this is because the body itself is a signifier of both truth and untruth. In an earlier moment, Honoré had explained to Françoise that their two bodies were independent witnesses to the truth of their love:

> Even if you objected . . . , there would still exist between your neck and my mouth, between your ears and my mustache, between your hands and my hands, little personal understandings. I am sure they would go on even if we stopped loving each other, just as my valet, since my quarrel with my cousin Pauline, for all I can do, continues to go to see her maid every evening. It is entirely of itself, without my consent, that my mouth goes toward your neck. (192–93)

But if Honoré can cheat on Françoise only in his body while professing to remain faithful to her in his heart, the body is equally a locus of falsehood. Honoré's awareness of this facile dichotomy between love and the body cannot help but spill over onto his perceptions of Françoise and the bodily "truth" he had previously explained to her:

> When, having yielded to a purely physical desire for another woman, and remembering how many times before he had indulged such passions and had been able to lie to Françoise without ceasing to love her, [Honoré] no longer thought it absurd to suppose that she also lied to him, and that to lie to him it was not even necessary for her not to love him, and that before knowing him she had thrown herself on others with the same ardor that now so excited him. (200)

Thus, like the lovers' language, the body that attempts to signify everything ends up signifying nothing. Honoré's "solution" to his dilemma, to his need to know, is less a decision than an evasion. Denying the right of language or the body to make him choose yes or no, Honoré cultivates an hallucination of Françoise in bed with another as a result of his own machinations: "Taking advantage of the fact that his liaison was not known, he longed to make wagers with other men about her virtue, make them test her virtue to see if she would yield, try to discover something, to learn everything; thought of hiding in her room (he remembered having, when younger, done such a thing) to see" (203).

Honoré's hallucination of the *something* he would discover were he to act on his fantasy is ultimately bound up with the childhood world of idiosyncratic sexual interpretation. The imagined scene of Françoise being spied on while making love explicitly recalls—"he remembered having, when younger, done such a thing"—the classic primal experience of the parents observed by the child. This primal scene is important for Honoré not only as a source of pleasure but as a type of knowledge. The something he would learn by repeating the scene with Françoise is also everything. The knowledge to be derived is both nonspecific and all-inclusive; it is not a choice between right and wrong, truth and untruth, fidelity and infidelity. Rather, Honoré will be no further advanced in his knowledge of Françoise's sexual activity than is the child who observes confusedly that what his parents are doing is both something unknown and everything attractive.

In *The Subject of Semiotics,* Kaja Silverman describes the cinematic process of *suture,* by which the viewer is drawn into the images on the screen, as a castrating entry into the symbolic. The viewer enters into the discourse of the film by casting away all other possible discourses available at that moment. Consequently, Silverman explains,

> cinematic coherence and plenitude emerge through multiple cuts and negations. Each image is defined through its differences from those that surround it syntagmatically and those it paradigmatically implies ("this but not that"), as well as through its denial of any discourse but its own. . . . This castrating coherence, this definition of a discursive position for the viewing subject which necessitates not only its loss of being, but the

repudiation of alternative discourses, is one of the chief
aims of the system of suture. (205–6)

Honoré's hallucination is a paradoxical and psychologically
regressive attempt to view while avoiding suture. His fantasy represents a tentative return to the free signifiers of childhood desire,
precedent to the (castrating) choice between yes and no fixed by
convention and paternal law. The fantasy allows him a return to the
free signifiers of his early idyll with Françoise, before the obscenity
of Buivres's remark that brought him up short against the need to
define what really is or is not there in front of his eyes. Honoré's
decision never to let Françoise out of his sight is therefore not a
guarantor of truth; it is an evasion of the need to decide, a refusal of
the threat of castration. Like the shadow narrator of "A Confession,"
Honoré will simply not give Françoise the opportunity to behave or
misbehave on her own; the knowledge he chooses is a *something*
conscientiously inflated to an *everything*. Both truth and untruth,
Françoise's body-made-fetish "restores"—in the Freudian scheme of
things—the phallus to the mother and "cures" Honoré of his
obsession with the truth.

This fantasy of childhood freedom, however, is decisively countered by the end of the story. Causality in the epilogue represents an
ultimate experience of limit, a cutting off that now proves unavoidable. The final chapter of the story begins with a flashback announcing that "Madame Seaune has entertained extensively this season
and the season before, but her salon was closed during the three
preceding years, that is, during the years following the death of
Honoré de Tenvres" (207). Besides being a more sophisticated use
of chronology than Proust had hit on for "Baldassare," "Madame de
Breyves," or "A Confession," the technique is a forerunner of what
Brian G. Rogers has termed the "double vision" of *Remembrance of
Things Past,* by which a later vision in time is superimposed on and
alternates with a vision rendered in experiential time (103). In "The
End of Jealousy," this vision gives the reader in advance the answer
that Honoré avoided right up to his death, namely, that Françoise
had been a faithful mistress who would prove her love by grieving
long and publicly for him.

Yet as a reflection on causality, the ending replaces coincidence
with a more realist dependence on "precise timing." Precise timing

is the single most striking element of the dispassionate, almost clinical, account the narrator gives of the events of Honoré's death:

> It was hardly two months after [Honoré's] restoration that the accident of the Avenue du Bois-de-Boulogne occurred in which he had both legs broken by a runaway horse. The accident took place the first Tuesday in May; on Sunday peritonitis set in. Honoré received the last sacraments Monday, and died that same Monday at six o'clock in the evening. But from Tuesday, the day of the accident, to Sunday night, he alone knew there was no hope. (297)

While the Young Girl is able only to intimate coincidence *in extremis*, Honoré contemplates and measures the chain of events in which he has been an active participant. Like the Young Girl, Honoré has an obsessive need, rooted in loss and desire, to play and replay the fateful sequence. However, contrasting what actually happened with what might never have happened *if*. . . , he repeats the ambiguity of the fetish as the site of both truth and untruth. Like Buivres's remark, the accident was an obscenity, a traumatic cut in the action, a symbolic castration:

> At a certain moment he had glanced at his watch, had retraced his steps and then . . . then it had happened. In a second the horse he had not seen had broken both his legs. It did not seem to him that that particular second must inevitably have been like that. At that very second he might have been a little farther away, a little nearer, or the horse might have deviated a little, or it might have rained and he would have gone home before; or if he had not looked at his watch he would not have retraced his steps and would have continued his walk to the cascade. (208)

It is a brisk and clever *mise en abyme* that Honoré trips the fatal sequence into being by stopping to look at his watch; that he accepts responsibility for the dénouement provides the authorial distance from the chain of events necessary to convert "coincidence" into "narrative control." That Honoré dies as a result of the accident reasserts the necessity of the either/or choice he had avoided in his fetishization of Françoise's body.

Thus the temporal cutoff at the end of the story, the split second in which all the rest is decided, restores the primacy of castration over the attempts of the fetish to (un)do it. In Proust's own later opinion, this story that pointed most reliably toward *Remembrance of Things Past: Swann's Way* was, he wrote, "very different from *Pleasures and Regrets. . . .* however one part resembles (only is so much better than) 'The End of Jealousy'" (*Correspondance générale* 4:99).[15] Yet it also, by the precision of the cutoff that is the precision of the ending, remains firmly grounded in the young Proust's fears of literary impotence and premature death.

It is hardly coincidental that Honoré's death scene is once again overlaid with borrowings from the original text fetish, Tolstoy. Anne Henry writes: "This is Honoré's story, but Tolstoy depicted at length in *Ivan Ilyich* the scandal of the fully living being who cannot conceive of this negation of the self, and *War and Peace* told in an even more hallucinatory fashion of the little grenade spinning in the sunlit grass, so exterior to Prince André, and which abruptly becomes the reality of the painful gangrene in his stomach" (90).

On his deathbed, Honoré discovers his indifference to all that is not a universalized love for humanity participating in divine love. This totalizing vision that puts an end to the castration drama— "And this was the end of his jealousy," the narrator concludes (221)—represents the final attempt of *Pleasures and Regrets* to forestall choice through recourse to the fetish. The willful transcendence of this ending is thus the correlative in narrative to the erotic overabundance that marked the physical fetish object of the book itself. An investment against loss, each bespeaks Proust's gamble for immortality, as the "little things" of the son become the something and the everything required by the father. It is a gamble that will be paid off—in so much better a way—only by the later masterpiece.

4

The Return
of the Repressed

Lorrain's
Masked Figures
and Phantoms

Repetition and the Return of the Repressed

Jean Lorrain's *Masked Figures and Phantoms* (*Masques et fantômes*) is a collection of short stories originally published in such papers as *L'écho de Paris, Le courrier français,* and *Le journal;* they were collected in book form between 1891 and 1905. The titles of some of these early collections reveal the hallucinatory atmosphere and the tremulousness of the soul that pervade them: *Drinkers of Souls* (*Buveurs d'âmes,* 1893), *Feelings and Memories* (*Sensations et souvenirs,* 1895), *Possessed of the Devil* (*Un démoniaque,* 1895), *Stories of Masked Figures* (*Histoires de masques,* 1900), *The Wandering Vice* (*Le vice errant,* 1902), *Paints and Poisons* (*Fards et poisons,* 1904), *Stories of Simple Souls* (*Propos d'âmes simples,* 1904), and *The Crime of the Rich* (*Le crime des riches,* 1905). Lorrain's literary world is permeated by the occult and the ambiguous. In his fiction, ghosts rise from the dead, ether addicts encounter terrifying new worlds of sensation and fear, and the masked revelers of Mardi Gras are simultaneously male and female, alluring and repulsive, dead and alive.

Ambiguity, as Tzvetan Todorov has shown in *The Fantastic,* is the single most important element of the genre. For a story to be truly "fantastic," it must compel the reader to believe and disbelieve it simultaneously; the elements of the "unreal," in other words, must be as convincing as the elements of the "real," which must in turn be of dubious credibility themselves. Not only do Lorrain's short stories, like those of Edgar Allan Poe or E. T. A. Hoffmann (both important pre-texts for Lorrain), fulfill this requirement in truly disconcerting ways; *Masked Figures and Phantoms* also offers tantalizing glimpses into the psychoanalytic trauma of the equivocal sign at the tangled root of it all. Specifically, Lorrain's work is a celebration of neurosis manifested in the return of the repressed, again both as thematic material and as narrative strategy.

In his 1920 essay *Beyond the Pleasure Principle,* Freud addresses the contradiction inherent in the fact that certain neurotics seem to take pleasure in their compulsive repetition of neurotic trauma. The neurotics in question were soldiers who had suffered grievous mental trauma in World War I and who reported repeating in their dreams the very conditions under which they were traumatized.

These reports flew in the face of two essential tenets of psychoanalytic theory: first, that dreams are always to be understood as wish fulfillments, and second, that the pleasure principle works to spare the mental apparatus the unpleasantness of mental excitation by repressing those wishes and desires contrary to one's consciously held system of beliefs and values. In *Beyond the Pleasure Principle,* Freud explains what the *Studies on Hysteria* had presented as the "constancy principle" of mental functioning:

> The facts which have caused us to believe in the dominance of the pleasure principle in mental life also find expression in the hypothesis that the mental apparatus endeavors to keep the quantity of excitation present in it as low as possible or at least to keep it constant. This latter hypothesis is only another way of stating the pleasure principle; for if the work of the mental apparatus is directed towards keeping the quantity of excitation low, then anything that is calculated to increase that quantity is bound to be felt as adverse to the functioning of the apparatus, that is as unpleasurable. The pleasure principle follows from the principle of constancy: actually the latter principle was inferred from the facts which forced us to adopt the pleasure principle. (18:9)

The soldiers who still dreamed about the war were repeating just the opposite of what dream theory and the pleasure principle thus predicted. Obviously, a compromise solution, one between pleasure and unpleasure, repression and the return of the repressed, was necessary.

Freud derived this compromise solution by looking more closely at the relationship between pleasure and the repetition of the trauma. "If we are not to be shaken by our belief in the wish-fulfilling tenor of dreams by the dreams of traumatic neurotics, we may argue that the function of dreaming, like so much else, is upset in this condition and diverted from its purposes, or we may be driven to reflect on the mysterious masochistic trends of the ego" (18:13–14). Since neither dream theory nor the pleasure principle was to be discarded, these "masochistic trends" must have to do with pleasure.

Indeed, that is the direction Freud took in his observations of his grandson's *fort-da* game. The game consisted of the toddler throwing away his toys and crying "o-o-o-o" for "fort" or "gone" and then recovering them with a joyful cry of "da" or "there." It was clear to Freud that greater pleasure was attached to the recovery of the toys than to their being thrown away, even though "the first act, that of departure, was staged as a game in itself and far more frequently than the episode in its entirety, with its pleasurable ending" (18:16). Thus it had to be concluded that the "fort" part of the game also entailed pleasure, though of a different sort from the lowering of mental excitation assured by the pleasure principle.

Freud predictably surmised a connection between the toys and the toddler's mother. By throwing away his toys, the tot repeated his mother's departures; retrieving them, he repeated her returns. The pleasure of the "fort" was therefore more than a masochistic tendency of the ego. It was for the pleasure of mastering the unpleasant in his own (symbolic) terms that the child acted out his mother's absence, with its heightened tension, more frequently than her returns. "It is clear," Freud concludes, "that in their play children repeat everything that has made a great impression on them in real life, and that in doing so they abreact [bind or defuse] the strength of the impression and . . . make themselves master of the situation" (18:16–17).

What is more interesting, however, is that the *fort-da* game figures in Freud's essay as an instance of bad behavior. The little grandson was generally recognized as being a "good boy," as Freud notes with more than a little pride:

He did not disturb his parents at night; he conscientiously obeyed orders not to touch certain things or go into certain rooms, and above all he never cried when his mother left him for a few hours. . . .This good little boy, however, had an occasional disturbing habit of taking away small objects he could get hold of and throwing them away from him into a corner, under the bed, and so on, so that hunting for his toys and picking them up was often quite a business. (18:14)

Here again, as in the case of Elisabeth von R., bad behavior opens onto truth. This time, however, it is less readily excusable than when it involved Freud's rhetorical stance as the narrator-doctor of the *Studies on Hysteria*. In that earlier work, Freud as narrator had to align himself with the "bad behavior" of his patient for the sake of the case to be made against accepted medical practice. By 1920, however, dream theory and the pleasure principle had attained the status of psychoanalytic dogma; conflicting empirical evidence had somehow to be recast in their mold. Thus the soldiers' failure to repress their traumatic experiences in obedience to the pleasure principle implies that they, too, like Freud's grandson and despite what they will eventually add to psychoanalytic theory, stand at least temporarily accused of wrongful behavior.

It is no wonder, then, that Freud's attempts to go beyond his compromised theory of the pleasure principle lead into murky waters. At midpoint in his essay, a flight of fancy takes over from the discussion of traumatic dreams. "What follows is speculation," Freud begins, "often far-fetched speculation, which the reader will consider or dismiss according to his individual predilection. It is further an attempt to follow out an idea consistently, out of curiosity to see where it will lead" (18:24). The idea is that the pleasure principle, contradicted by the compulsion to repeat traumatic experience, may not be so fundamental after all.

But that, of course, would be intolerable. After proving its worth in case after case up to *Beyond the Pleasure Principle*, the doctrine cannot simply be discarded as Freud attempts to go "beyond" it. As Freud picks his way through psychobiology to arrive at the death instincts, the will to self-extinction alleged to lie beyond the pleasure principle is not implausibly readable as Freud's clever projection of reproach toward the misbehaving (unrepressing) children and soldiers. The "death instincts" do nothing more than confirm the original theory: that is, the pleasure principle is so fundamental, so interested in keeping the level of excitation low, that it in effect wills the organism to death. Guarding against overstimulation, it keeps the organism on the right path to that most lowered of all energy states—nonbeing:

> The hypothesis of self-preservative instincts, such as we attribute to all living beings, stands in marked opposition to the idea that instinctual life as a whole serves to bring about death. Seen in this light, the theoretical importance of the instincts of self-preservation, of self-assertion and of mastery greatly diminishes. They are component instincts whose function it is to assure that the organism shall follow its own path to death, and to ward off any possible ways of returning to inorganic inexistence other than those which are immanent in the organism itself. We have no longer to reckon with the organism's puzzling determination (so hard to fit into any context) to maintain its own existence in the face of every obstacle. What we are left with is the fact that the organism wishes to die only in its own fashion. (18:39)

Beyond the Pleasure Principle calls on "some system of aesthetics with an economic approach to its subject-matter" to explain how "even under the dominance of the pleasure principle, there are ways and means enough of making what is in itself unpleasurable into a subject to be recollected and worked over in the mind [with] a yield of pleasure as their final outcome" (18:17). Freud makes a great show of dismissing these artistic creations as *too* exemplary of the pleasure principle to merit discussion. Artistic creations, he insists, "are of no use for *our* purposes, since they presuppose the existence and dominance of the pleasure principle; they give no evidence of the operation of tendencies *beyond* the pleasure principle, that is, of tendencies more primitive than it and independent of it"—such as the death instincts (18:17), which do, in fact, demonstrate the pleasure principle pushed to extremes. After all, this is only speculation, a nice, safe way to wish contradiction out of existence and to punish with the threat of death "bad" behavior that refuses to go by the books.

In the Dora case, bad behavior, or the return of the repressed, goes by the name of "transference." But of course Dora, who did not wish to be cured, is a notoriously bad girl in Freud. Artists may fare better. In *Psychoanalytic Criticism,* Elizabeth Wright suggests that "Freud's fascination with art is due in part to his admiration of the artist for his ability to control the return of the repressed" (16). This repression, in accordance with the pleasure principle, is the proper behavior toward which Freudian theory and therapy aim.

In this case, Jean Lorrain is a very bad boy indeed. *Masked Figures and Phantoms* are far less concerned with the *control* of repressed material than with its riotous repetition. Lorrain's narratives express an excess, not an economy, of pleasure, as they return again and again to the disruptive childhood game that threatens to swamp the pleasure principle by an overload of dread. The equivocal sign of the childish imagination maintains the psyche in that heightened state of tension that the pleasure principle is supposed to counter. In Lorrain, neurosis governs narrative as a repetition of the repressed and a resistance to its resolution.

The Childhood Signifier

Hidden behind a satin domino or swathed in a voluminous cape and cowl, the masked figure is the phantasmagoric figure par excellence in Lorrain's stories. "You cannot see their face," Lorrain writes of the "attractive and repellent mystery of the mask" in "One of Them; or, the Soul of the Mask" ("L'un d'eux; ou, l'âme du masque"):

> Why not blood-sucking ghouls beneath these wide capes, framing faces frozen in velvet or silk? Why not emptiness and nothingness beneath these ample clown smocks draped like shrouds over sharp-angled tibias and humeral bones?
> The mask is the troubled and troubling face of the unknown, it is the smile of the lie, it is the very soul of perversity that corrupts while it terrifies.[1] (21–22)

The Return of the Repressed

The masked creature "beyond nature and beyond the law" ("hors la nature et hors la loi" [22]) is intimately related to repressed material. The mask is that which has not been abreacted by the psychic apparatus; it is the release into full consciousness of the netherworld of unrestricted desire expressed by the primary process. As we have seen, the primary process is prerational: "The alternative 'either-or' cannot be expressed in dreams in any way whatever," Freud writes, adding, "'No' seems not to exist so far as dreams are concerned. . . . Dreams feel themselves at liberty, moreover, to represent any element by its wishful contrary; so that there is no way of deciding at a first glance whether any element that admits of a contrary is present in the dream-thoughts as a positive or as a negative" (4:316, 318). Kaja Silverman restates succinctly, "Whereas the [primary process] maintains no distinction between the original object of a desire and the object which replaces it, the [secondary process] insists at all points on *difference,* upon those features or qualities that separate one signifying element from another" (79–80).

The masked figure thus represents an unrestricted field for the play of the signifier. The masked figure shares its perversity and attractiveness with the drug addict—whose ether-glazed eyes give him or her the same absent quality as the half-hidden face—with the corpse, and with the phantom or ghost. Recurring through the work, all are treated with the same obsessive-compulsive mixture of pleasure and masochism that is indicative of the return of the repressed.

This aspect of the return of the repressed in the figures of the mask, the ether addict, the corpse, and the ghost can be traced to a prescient conviction in Lorrain that childhood trauma is the primary determinant of adult neurosis. Lorrain's protagonists all more or less agree that "the mental organism is so delicate that any incident however fleeting in appearance can bring about the worst disorders" ("The Gloved Hand" ["La main gantée"] 310); they prefer their poetry full of "morose stanzas, anemic with spleen" ("The Visionary" ["Le visionnaire"] 298); they live in ambiguous, sometimes haunted surroundings and cannot look at their fellow humans without falling prey to the most vivid hallucinations. Serge Allitof, a recurring character, explains of his futile attempts to *not* envision the riders on the Paris tramway as so many grotesque animals in a

81

traveling menagerie: "it is within reality that I become a visionary. Flesh-and-blood beings that I meet in the street, passers-by, male and female, the anonymous crowd that I brush elbows with, these all become like ghosts to me, and it is the ugliness, the very banality of modern life that makes my blood run cold and transfixes me with terror" (21–22).[2]

"Magic Lantern" ("Lanterne magique") makes clear Lorrain's resistance to the "cure" and his profound attachment to the action of the repressed on psychic life. During the intermission of Berlioz's *Damnation of Faust,* the narrator reproaches Forbster, the "electrician," for trying to cure hysteria by hypnotism and electrotherapy—hence the electrician as medicine man, guilty, in the narrator's eyes, of smothering humanity's last gasps of imagination and art by slowly converting the race to its belief in science: "You and your kind suppress Folie," accuses the narrator, "this last citadel where a cultivated man, out of patience, could still take refuge! . . .—You suppress it, yes and no. But you cannot deny you analyze it, you explain it, specify it, localize it . . . you cure it, if need be, and by what means! by electricity and therapy. You have killed the fantastic, Monsieur" (329).[3]

To the narrator's surprise, the "electrician" proves remarkably attentive to the manifestations of neurosis—more so, in fact, than the narrator himself. Forbster's professional eye identifies in the fashionable theater audience a veritable witches' sabbath of ghouls and other assorted bloodsuckers, of society ladies "all morphined-up, cauterized, dosed-up, drugged-up with psychotherapeutic novels and ether, medicated, anemic, androgynous, hysterical, and consumptive" (332), of painted women on the make like so many "damnable cadavers escaped from the cemetery and spewn out of the tomb among the living, flowers sprouting on graves to seduce and charm young men and carry them off to perdition" (331), of vapid would-be fiancées who smile and curtsey automatically like barely living reproductions of Hoffmann's wax Olympia.[4]

The role of childhood trauma in the formation of neurosis is alluded to in many of the stories of *Masked Figures and Phantoms.* Childhood trauma in these stories is not merely thematic, preparing the reader to accept a fictional world of unexpectedly grotesque and compellingly repulsive situations and characters. The trauma determines a signifying system of pure equivocation, in which the signifier plays freely between mutually exclusive categories, in which anything can and does come to mean anything else.

In "Three Masked Figures" ("Trio de masques"), Lorrain explores the relationship between childhood and the later mystery of the mask. The story's long preamble describes the terror of the mask as a remainder of the child's fear of the dark—or fear, more precisely, not of darkness but of what it does to ordinary reality:

> All these grimaces floating in the shadows, the ambiguous sneers of stones that watch you, of trees that want to seize you, sudden enlargements of inanimate objects, that come alive in the shadow, that the shadow deforms and whose shadow threatens, whoever has seen these things as a child, will surely find them again in masked figures; masks, this wandering horror of our streets and our museums, be they the ill-fashioned cardboard type sold at discount by toy merchants, or the masterpieces in wax born beneath a sculptor's fingers; for the mask is the laugh that mystery laughs, it is the face of the lie made by the deformation of the truth, it is the deliberate ugliness of reality, exaggerated to hide the unknown.[5] (42–43)

What the child sees in the dark convinces him of the superior existence of these "deformations," of this world of errant significations. In an example bristling with sexual innuendo, Lorrain uses the closed-off rooms of the family country house to suggest how the childhood experience of ambiguity is the repressed that returns to the adult—however seasoned and skeptical, however reasonable he or she may be—with its full original charge of terror and perplexity. For whatever practical reason certain rooms are off-limits to the child, the child imagines they can be forbidden only for mysterious and horrible reasons. Lorrain rhapsodizes on the tenacity of the equivocation thus engraved in the childhood psyche:

> Oh! the great trees rustling in the depths of damp and lonely autumn groves, the interminable corridors of old, half-deserted country houses, attics tall as cathedrals, . . . empty bedrooms in country houses where now-dead grandparents used to sleep, the room you never entered

because something had happened there (a great-great-grand-mother had been locked up in there), but the truth is that fruits and jams were stored there. . . . Oh! all these chateaux of horror now crumbling away in our skeptical souls, but that once held so formidable a place in our frightened and anxious childhood, with what a quivering and icy atmosphere they seemed to fill up for us at nightfall, especially with the return of autumn, in these months drenched in fog and rotted out by unceasing downpours, by torrential rains.[6] (41–42)

The forbidden room is thus endowed with a double signification, such that even when the child finally learns the real reason for the interdiction (that the stores of fruits and jellies were kept there), this reason is forever insufficient to banish his or her primordial belief that the room was haunted. This enduring attraction to the mysterious is also a release of the signifier; this is the point of the adult experience of "deformation" that Lorrain couples in the second half of "Three Masked Figures" with the example of the forbidden room.

In the second half of the story, the narrator recounts a lugubrious costume ball sponsored by the management of a vacation hotel to distract its guests from the sempiternal rains that have spoiled the season. The hotel rooms recall those of the country house: "oh! the sadness of these hotel rooms on rainy summer evenings" (45), sighs the narrator, bored and slightly nauseated by the seedy spectacle of the second-rate festival.[7] In a second-floor ballroom, however, a waltzing couple attracts his attention:

Between the high wainscotings of the violently lighted room, the so-called Ladies' Salon, a single couple was waltzing; two women, one an enormous fat dump of a woman we could only see from behind, with, in her arms, a beautiful creature sumptuously dressed in a brocaded dress, sleeveless; her exposed breasts, very white, sprang like a flower from a strange bodice . . . , a bodice you'd see on a carnival princess or a fairy queen, since the immense train on the rose dress wrapped twice around the fat lady. . . . Holding a large blue satin fan

84

open before her face, the beautiful one waltzed with wild abandon, sweeping with her her fat, stocky partner; and the dancer in rose had the most beautiful eyes in the world, shiny and soft black hair, twisted into a thick knot at the nape of her neck, tiny feet and delicate hands sheathed in elegant gloves, while her partner, encased in a type of sack in grey silk, displayed ankles thick as a carter's and a neck all in heavy folds of fat, ignominiously red and coarse beneath the yellow hairs of her clown's wig. . . . Sitting cross-legged in a corner amid the cushions of an armchair, a dwarf dressed like a Japanese picked out a tune on a guitar. [8] (46–47)

That the waltzing couple should be composed of two women is a first deformation imposed on the usual arrangement of the male/female dancing couple. The breathless pace of the waltz further contrasts with the hesitant music provided for it, since the dwarf is said to only scratch out the tune on her guitar. Of the two dancers, the more beautiful one is partially masked by the fan held in front of her face; all of the adjectives describing her visible parts are elaborately complimentary and heavily coded as feminine: she has white skin, beautiful eyes, luxuriant hair, and delicate hands. The partner, on the other hand, is particularly heavy and ill-dressed; her markings—the sacklike dress, the thick ankles, and the coarse, stubbly neck—read as a travesty of womanhood.

As the narrator discovers moments later, this unattractive partner is not a woman at all, but a travestied man. The real horror, however, is reserved for the dancer who has been coded female. When she lowers her fan, the narrator perceives

a sapper's beard, a most beautiful brown beard framed this face, waving down into two silky points between her breasts: the lady was bearded like a king of legend.

The lady waltzing so frantically was a bearded lady, her partner a frightfully fat and clean-shaven man, made-up and painted-up and disguised as a woman.[9] (47)

The description is remarkable first of all for the insistence with which the beard, formerly hidden (repressed) beneath the fan, now rivets the attention of the conscious mind. The narrator repeats no fewer than four times that this amazingly feminine female has an abundant and flowing beard; a further excess is the manner in which the beard is opposed to the one "positive" sign attributed to the man: he, at least, is clean-shaven, though in contrast to the woman, grotesquely so. The compulsion to repeat is once more evident in the description of the partner's travesty; he is described in the sequence of barely nuanced synonyms as, "made-up," "painted-up," "disguised as a woman." Moreover, the discovery of the dual travesty continues to couple the vocabulary of the grossest adult reality with that of the childhood world of legends and fairy tales. Her fan held before her face, the waltzing woman resembles a fairy-tale princess; with her flowing beard, she is a king from an illustrated children's book.

This two-step description demonstrates the manner in which the childhood repressed returns in adult perception to determine a migration of signs across normally exclusive perceptual fields: to the ultrafeminine dancer is added the male marker of abundant facial hair and the comparison to the mythical king, while her male partner is grotesquely feminized by the superimposed female markings of his disguise. In language and in phantasm, the world of remembered fairy tales here literally dances before the narrator's eyes. His exit from the room again relates this equivocal scene to the forbidden room of childhood. The narrator has glimpsed these horribly mismarked dancers through a door that has been hurriedly opened and immediately shut. The door marks the boundary behind which adult signifying logic yields to that of the primary process and the free-floating signifier: "All of that seemed evident, reasonable, to us," the narrator concludes, "in the flash of light of a door opened and closed immediately; and yet we had had a moment of stupor, felt we were falling into an abyss, into the absurd, into the impossible" (47).[10]

The fall into the abyss occasioned by the mask is attributed throughout Lorrain's stories to this type of equivocation produced by the migration of signs across mutually exclusive fields. In "One of Them; or, the Soul of the Mask," the narrator describes a representative masked figure left over from the Paris Mardi Gras balls. Like the dancers in "Three Masked Figures," this figure of horror is characterized, or cross-marked, by ambiguous sexual markings:

> He wore [on his legs] a tightly fitting leotard that could
> be seen to sheath him completely, since his cloak had
> come open a bit; but, oddly enough, though his right leg
> wore a woman's stocking clear up to the thigh, a silk
> stocking in a glaucous green, encircled just above the
> knee by a moiré garter, the other foot wore a man's sock,
> an evening-wear sock strewn with a flower pattern, so
> that this masked figure was a double mask, the terrifying
> charm of his ghoulish face coupled with the disturbing
> equivocation of an unidentifiable sexuality.[11] (25)

As if this were not enough, the figure attempts to *double* his equivocal signs: despite the fact that his face remains completely obscured by his hood, he contemplates himself at leisure in a small pocket mirror. The perverted reflection suggests then how the mask creates, in adult perception, the gap between signifier and signified associated with childhood terror. The masked figure opens that space of desire that will be filled by the return of the repressed. And what was repressed is embroidered in silk on the costume of the mask: he wears a giant frog at the place of his heart.

Childhood Trauma Bis: *The Ostrich, the Frog, and Descriptive Technique*

Deformations of persons into animals are one recurrent manifestation of neurosis based on equivocation in Lorrain. Serge Allitof, for example, who is both constitutionally neurotic and addicted to ether, is finally obliged to "leave Paris to escape from the obsession of comparing every human face with that of an animal" ("The Gloved Hand" 310).[12] In this menagerie,

> sumptuous and difficult, modern life gave to men as well
> as to women souls akin to those of bandits or chain-gang
> wardens; envy, hatred, and the despair of poverty give to
> some the hard flattened heads and sharp curved faces of
> shrew-mice and vipers; avarice and egoism give others
> snouts like those of aging pigs with jaws like those of
> sharks.[13] ("The One Possessed" 307)

87

Two specific animals speak to the collapse of signifying logic that marks the return of the childhood repressed: Hoffmann's ostrich and a blinded frog.

"Three Masked Figures" retells briefly a story by E. T. A. Hoffmann in which, according to Lorrain, a couple bringing their young son to the doctor's is astonished to be received by—of all things—an ostrich. With exquisite courtesy, Lorrain's first-person narrator recounts, the animal opens the door, ushers the visitors into the office, and goes off to summon the doctor. The door opened by the ostrich is yet another door onto the contradictory reality of the primary process, since the unexpected presence of the ostrich is alone sufficient to dislodge the couple and their story from the ordinary. "The most extraordinary adventures can now rush in on the town counsellor and his wife," the narrator comments: "the ostrich opened the door onto the supernatural" (44).[14]

Within the structural logic of the story, the ostrich episode links the discussion of childhood experience—whose terrors return in the mystery of the masked face—with the nightmare experience of the cross-marked dancers at the end of the story. The episode is meant to serve as a progression from the mask at the beginning, through "even more appalling human faces" (43), to experiences that are, as in the episode of the travestied dancers, so grotesque that "reason loses its grip, and the very reality of life itself continues in the realm of the nightmare" (43).[15] At the midpoint of this progression, the episode uses a logical ellipsis to suggest how the signifier might break away from the communicative circuit, how it can begin to float at cross-purposes with its wealth of potential signifieds.

The ostrich episode introduces a double shift or slippage into the narrative logic. First, Lorrain's résumé of Hoffmann's story does indeed usher in the world of the fantastic with its extremely simple premise: once one bizarre event has occurred, everything bizarre is possible. In terms of the equivocal signifier, this means that once one signifier has slipped the bonds of meaning, anything can come to mean anything else. The second shift, however, makes slippage itself a process of narrative logic, since the ostrich episode owes its place in "Three Masked Figures" to the narrator's professed desire to connect his experience of the dancers to that of the bewildered couple in Hoffmann's story. He asserts, "Well, but for the ostrich, I myself lived out this summer the story of 'Doctor Cinabre' [*Little Zaches*]" (44).[16]

In other words, with the exception of the ostrich, the narrator has had the same experience as the couple in Hoffmann's tale. But the ostrich was the entire point of the digression into Hoffmann: it was the ostrich that had transformed the everyday experience of visiting the doctor into an adventure into the unreal. By excepting the ostrich from his own experience, Lorrain's narrator cancels its value as logical predecessor. It was the ostrich that made the difference in Hoffmann's story. Lorrain's narrator freely admits that no ostrich exists in his own narration—yet he maintains nevertheless that his story is *identical to Hoffmann's*. Surely, then, the example must be deficient and singularly ill-chosen as the narrative bridge between the childhood and the adult experiences.

Lacan's "Seminar on 'The Purloined Letter'" adds another ostrich to this perplexing menagerie. Lacan's ostrich illustrate the complex intersubjectivity of looking and not seeing, finding and not finding that determines the plot of Poe's "The Purloined Letter": the first look does not see anything; a second look realizes that the first is unseeing but also thinks itself safe from observation; and the third, and ultimately triumphant, look (that of the detective Dupin) sees that the first two are missing the obvious ("'Purloined Letter'" 44). In using Hoffmann's ostrich as the equivalent to his own missing or non-ostrich, Lorrain makes the obvious (and therefore easy to overlook) point that the ostrich can also be its opposite and still "work" within the fantastic of desire. That is, the "real" narrative logic that cries out for Lorrain's narrator to produce his own ostrich to match Hoffmann's counts for nothing in the world of signification inspired by childhood trauma. The freely associative signifier is once again at work, suggesting that narrative logic is dependent here on the connections of the primary process—connections that are by their very nature elliptical, subject to seemingly random displacements and condensations, and, above all, oblivious to contradiction.

In other words, the primary process has no difficulty "reading" Hoffmann's *ostrich* as the exact equivalent of Lorrain's *non-ostrich*. So the example retains its value as a narrative bridge, but only on condition that the reader recognize with Lorrain the "unreal" logic of repressed desire. Childhood trauma returns as a process of narrative, freeing the signifier to create its own ambiguous visions of the sort that the rest of the story will evoke and that Lorrain's descriptive techniques will repeat throughout the *Masked Figures and Phantoms*. Repressed from "Three Masked Figures," the ostrich returns much later in "January Night" ("Nuit de janvier") as the narrator of that story is warned of the dangers of reading Hoffmann. "You will end up seeing fox heads on your friends' shoulders," a friend reproaches him, "unless you risk mistaking my servant for an ostrich, for the gigantic and fallacious ostrich who opens the door to visitors and shocks the Mock family with his exquisite courtesies in 'Doctor Cinabre'" (374).[17]

If the ostrich was playful, the bullfrog is terrifying. In his biography of Lorrain, Philippe Jullian recounts Lorrain's horrified fascination with this species, suggesting he identified unconsciously with it. "Disgust for a body that could inspire desire only in certain perverted persons," Jullian writes of Lorrain's willfully exaggerated homosexuality, continuing, "In his subconscious, [Lorrain] felt close to the pustulous animal with the poisoned blood: the bullfrog. He identified himself with the bullfrog as much for the opprobrium in which his family held his sexual tastes, as for a certain physiological similarity" (167). Jullian notes in particular Lorrain's appraisal of his collection of frog figurines: "The frog is my favorite animal: I have seventeen in my study; first there is an orchestre, absolutely exquisite, of tree frogs made of green stoneware; two in bronze, one in spun glass that comes from London, a painting by Mme Desbordes with three, plus a ceramic by Carriès. There are seventeen in all, and I'm not counting the portraits of women" (167–68).[18]

In "One of Them; or, the Soul of the Mask," the frog is the emblem that qualifies this particular masked figure to represent the essential horror of the mask. The story "The Mask" ("Le masque") indicates why. In "The Mask," a bullfrog is noted as "one of the most agonizing impressions" ("une des plus angoissantes impressions" [233]) of the narrator's childhood. As if unable to evoke the experience in his own words, Lorrain has an imaginary interlocutor cite this childhood horror from a hidden text—Lorrain's *Feelings and Memories*. "In your *Feelings and Memories*," the interposed narrator thus begins,

> you told of a schoolboy's small mishap, not particularly unpleasant in itself, but which made a most horrible and

lasting impression on me. Do you remember? the story of the bullfrog, the sudden appearance in a spring from which you had just drunk, of a fleshy and monstrous batrachian! Aggravating circumstance, the eyes of the unworthy beast had been gouged out, and the water you had just tasted took on in your mouth a hideous taste of blood. . . . even after twenty-five years, you still cannot remember this moment without feeling your heart overturn within you, without tasting an indescribable nausea upon your lips.[19] (233)

The device of the interposed narrator casts Lorrain in the curious role of *receiver* of his own previous experience. Recounted by another, the trauma of the bullfrog comes back to him not as a lived experience but as a narrative that is both a return of a past repressed narrative and an imposition of a new narrative (a new experience with a fresh potential of horror) through the interlocutor's retelling. Such a presentation by an interposed narrator could be said to create above all a distancing effect between the supposedly intolerable tale and its presumed "audience," Lorrain himself, the original author. This argument would start from the fact that Lorrain does not speak in his own name and conclude that he *cannot* speak in his own name: that the only way for him to present the trauma is to attenuate it by making someone else—the interposed narrator—speak it for him.

But the opposite might also be true. The new narrative may be even more horrible than the original, as Lorrain imagines himself subjected to the actions of signifiers that are and are not his own. Figured once by *Feelings and Memories,* and refigured here by the interposed narrator, the experience of the bullfrog is accessible only through metonymy.[20]

The recessive characteristic by which metonymy continually suggests objects contingent to yet other objects in the real world explains in part its usefulness for the realist illusion: from a few leading details, the reader more than willingly completes the picture through the narrative process Mathieu Bénézet succinctly calls the "identificatory phenomenon" ("phénomène identificatoire") between reader and character, between written word and real world, on which realist literature has traditionally been based (95).[21] Yet this same recessive characteristic of metonymy is what makes it the very figure of desire. Progressing ever backwards from intermediary object to intermediary object, metonymy is the inscription into language of the search for the continually displaced (lost) maternal object of childhood desire.

The emotionally and culturally well-adjusted reader, it is assumed, has no difficulty understanding metonymy as a figure of speech. Exhibiting no undue attachment to the figure as figure, such a reader mentally reattaches the sails to their masts and the masts to their ships in the common figure "a thousand sails" or realizes that "Allons boire un pot"—"Let's have a drink," expressed as the literal invitation to drink a pot—is an invitation to consume what's in the pot, not the pot itself, in an instance of metonymy as the use of the container for the contained. The degree of attachment to, or investment in, the figure is the red herring of poetic language: at what point does the language call enough attention to itself to be warranted "poetic"?

The episode of the bullfrog is intensely "poetic" in the sense that it calls unusual attention to its elements. Decadently speaking, it is willfully hypertrophied. Within the episode, metonymic description itself falls under the sway of the obsessive attachment to the signifier that characterizes neurosis in Lorrain. Rather than aiming at a coherent, "realist" whole, the description of the episode breaks apart into a series of successive, intermediary signifiers; rather than asking the reader to complete the picture, the metonymies of the description are overvalued as signifiers in themselves. Thus the elements of the description remain as separate moments of autonomous horror, unrelated to a unified perceptual field.

The description of the frog, a deliberate sequence of details each more horrifying than the last, registers the progressive perception of an observer transfixed by each detail. The passive position into which the interpolated narrator forces the listener, Lorrain, repeats the passive receptivity of the original experience of observation at the same time that it makes reading and listening an imposition of unpredictable and therefore frightening signifiers. "Three Masked Figures" begins with the definition "terror is chiefly the unexpected" (41), and so the interpolated narrator claims still to be suffering from the troubling effects of *Feelings and Memories.* Moreover, he hopes to duplicate those troubling effects for his listener's pleasure-pain: "Well, I also have a bullfrog in my life," he affirms, "and this bullfrog is a story of a masked figure: and since you like them and seem to be collecting them, here is my experience of a costume ball" (233).[22]

The description, jerky and awkward, hammers away at the realist illusion. The narrator's comments on the action and on Lorrain's presumed response interrupt the sequence after each detail; they thus contribute to the impression of horrified contemplation that considers each detail as a complete picture in its own right. This effect is magnified by the leading comments of the narrator, such as the "aggravating circumstance" by which the scene is suddenly shifted to the riveting sight of the frog's empty and bleeding eye sockets. A strategically placed device, repetition of the second-person pronoun appeals to the listener to retrieve his repressed material through active remembering: "Do you remember? The story of the bullfrog?" the interposed narrator begins, "the sudden appearance in a spring from which you had just drunk, of a flaccid and monstrous batrachian!" The placement and repetition of the *you* reinforces the most morbid of the associations said to spring up between the event and its physical and psychic consequences: the *you* is pronounced most often in immediate proximity with the water from which Lorrain has been said to drink: "the eyes of the unworthy beast had been gouged out, and the water which you had just tasted took on in your mouth a hideous taste of blood." Undercut as realist metonymy, the frog displaces the reader's attention onto specific psychic effects: fresh water in the listener's mouth takes on the taste of blood at the sudden apparition of the bullfrog, which is then perceived, in a second horrible moment, to have been blinded.

Thus the scene is never resolved into the coherent whole of realist fiction.[23] The entire passage is, moreover, underscored by a double attack on the processes of vision and identification: the blinded frog who does not see the observer observing him interrupts the visual circuit of the gaze. As with Lacan's ostrich, seeing is equated with nonseeing. Like the mask who studies his hooded face in a pocket mirror, the frog is a dead letter within the communicative circuit. The energy of vision is thrown literally back into this observer's face. In the passage, Lorrain exists only as parts of a face:

he is sight, the taste of blood in the mouth, and the feeling of disgust on the lips.

The extent of the displacement is finally evident in the signification imposed on *frog* as signifier at the end of the episode. Under the influence of his own reaction to both narrations—the one he has read and the one he has told—the interpolated narrator freely borrows Lorrain's signifier *crapaud,* or "bullfrog," as a full and sufficient signifier of horror; the story of the mask he is about to tell is the "frog" he has known in his own life. This conflation of the signifier *frog* confirms the lack of "real world" referents for the metonymies of the description. At the end of the interpolated narrative, itself built as a blockage of realist description, "crapaud/bullfrog" is permanently removed from its real world context to be identified only with the experience of trauma preserved in narration: "I too have a bullfrog in my life, and this bullfrog is a story of a mask" (233).

The Disrupted Perceptual Field: Lorrain's Head Metonymies

The disrupted perceptual field of childhood trauma revealed in the frog episode sets the pattern for descriptive technique throughout the *Masked Figures and Phantoms.* In this technique, the metonymies that ought to be contributing to the illusion of completeness in the "real world" beyond literature are instead presented as a series of obsessive figures that eventually take over as the entire field of signification. Under the impetus of (un)repressed trauma, the descriptions are blocked, the figures are frozen, and the pieces of the puzzle—the blinded frog and the taste of blood—take over *for* the whole, *as* the whole, experience. Not surprisingly, the most interesting and easily traceable of these metonymies continue from the frog episode with a fixation on heads and faces.

The first set of metonymies, most closely related to realist metonymy, consists of what we might call Lorrain's "head metonymies." These metonymies describe persons strictly in function of their hats or hair styles. "Last February," recounts the narrator of "Bad Lodgings" ("Le mauvais gîte"), "at about six o'clock, as I was descending the staircase at I no longer know which editor's, I inadvertently ran into a top hat stuck down into the turned-up collar of a fur-lined coat" (254).[24] The "top hat" so distractedly encountered turns out to be none other than the ubiquitous Serge Allitof. Or, again, the companions of a group of society ladies are simply presented in "The Life-Sucker" ("L'égrégore") as a group of "bald male heads of serious mien" ("calvities mâles à mine grave" [336]).[25] In both examples, the metonymy is intended to evoke the entire person; the technique would be purely realist if "The Mask" had not made it clear that the choice of metonymic detail—the head—is predicated on an experience of trauma centered on that part of the body.

One effect of trauma on the signifying system is to completely banish the referent from the descriptive metonymies. In a development of the basic "head metonymies," the head itself, or some variation on it, takes over as both signifier and signified; it reappropriates to itself the entire perceptual field. Into this category falls, along with the Mardi Gras face mask, the particularly strange device of the killer head mask. In "Masks from London and Elsewhere" ("Masques de Londres et d'ailleurs"), a series of murders committed near the London docks goes unsolved until the police finally discover that the killers have been chloroforming their victims with poisoned face masks that asphyxiate quickly and leave no traces of violence. The technique is repeated in "An Unknown Crime" ("Un crime inconnu"), in which one would-be Mardi Gras reveler punishes his less enthusiastic companion by tying around his face "a glass mask, a mask hermetically sealed without eyes or mouth, . . . filled to the brim with ether, liquid poison" (286).[26] The killer head mask again centers the experience of trauma on the face; showing up in the mystery stories, it is both the signifier of death and the ultimate signified, the solution to the whodunnit.

Even more compelling is the recurrent figure of the decapitated head. In this case, the metonymy is the entire perceptual field; it is not the person that is signified, only the decapitated head. With this figure, the trauma condenses into a single and sufficient signifier; moreover, because it has been severed from the body, the head is free to rejoin the experience of the equivocal signifier.

"The Man with the Wax Heads" ("L'homme aux têtes de cire") is a first example of the obsessive completeness that attaches to this type of metonymy. In the story, the narrator is introduced by his friend Gormas to the eminent sculptor Ringel; he had been attracted to the latter's work by the sculpted head of a woman on display in Gormas's studio. This sculpted head figures in the opening passages of the story as the complete and perfect substitute for the living woman herself:

> She pursued me like an obsession. . . .
>
> Completely molded in wax, she was of delicate coloration and infinite details and in the semidarkness of the studio, where I had entered on the heels of Gormas, this head said no, immobile upon her pedestal, rendered almost supernatural by the intensity of her proud mouth and her lapis luzuli eyes. . . .
>
> Hands crossed behind his back, Gormas focused on the painted wax figure, as I did myself, two eyes made distant by dreamy admiration.
>
> "Yes, that reconciles me to life," he followed up an earlier thought, "and that almost consoles me for how boring life is. We can find similar creatures, and yet can we find them? No, for you could pass Ray of Dawn in the street (that's what we call her) and you would not recognize her. The proof is that you have already seen her one hundred times and you did not even notice her."[27]
> (210–11)

Gormas thus maintains that the sculpted head is superior to the model; reshaped as a work of art, the former is remarkable, while the latter goes unnoticed, obscured by everyday life in the streets. A superior creation and the object of the narrator's obsession, the sculpture signifies itself rather than the model. It is a closed circuit, leading only to and from itself.

As described in the rest of the story, Ringel's work goes even further in asserting the superiority of the sculpted head over its possible real-life referents. Ringel's work invariably reminds the narrator of death; it calls back past eras of bloodthirsty crime. Of the luxuriant figure of a woman contemplating herself in a mirror, the narrator suggests, "If the theory of avatars is valid, Ringel must have encountered this insidious and smiling creature in some tapestry-draped corridor in the chateaux of Blois or Amboise" (213). The robust head of a young man and a pale and terrorized head of indeterminate sex prompt the reflection that in some previous existence, Ringel must either have frequented the medieval torture chambers of the infamous Gilles de Rais or have learned in Florence or at the court of the Valois the bewitching art by which sculpture is said to extract the soul from the body. Ringel must have lived, the narrator ponders, "between Queen Catherine and René the Florentine, in a society completely given over to the science of potions and spells" (215).[28]

It is this second head, the pale and desexualized one, that the narrator decides to buy. The model, Ringel confides breezily, was "a little Italian boy [whom] I met . . . in the street one December evening, shivering, emaciated, almost begging" (216). Brought into the studio for the modeling session, the tubercular child was fated to disappear soon after. "Oh, he's dead all right, our little Antonio Monforti, and in Beaujon, wasn't it, Gormas?" Ringel calls on his friend to testify (217).[29] Attracted by the evocative silence of the head, the narrator is seduced by its stand-alone quality. There is no more body to which it belongs; the decapitated head *is* the entire body. The artistic self-sufficiency of the sculpted head thus easily dispenses with the human life of the model, making the head another example of inflated metonymy.

Implicit within this inflation is the Decadent preference for the formalism of art over the randomness and ennui of life. Lorrain's "Posthumous Complaint" ("Réclamation posthume") concentrates this formalist preference once more on the traumatic image of the severed head, suggesting that mutilation of the work of art is a far more serious crime than the negligent homicide to which Ringel owed his inspiration for the androgynous head of the boy. In "Posthumous Complaint," (un)repression not of the model but of the complete work of art creates a delicious horror in the owner of a severed head. The hallucinatory experience depends not on the return of the model but on that of the fully sculpted figure crying out for the restoration of the perceptual field, crying out for the return of its head.

As the story begins, the narrator is complimented by a friend on a particularly lurid decapitated head of a woman (a "chef de décollée" [273]) displayed on his wall. Pressed to reveal its origin, the first-person narrator confesses with a combination of shame and pride that the early work, that he was admiring so sincerely, was a simple casting from the Louvre that I had deliberately had decapitated, that depriving the bust of its head was my own idea and that I ordered the molder to take off the head and add the clots of blood . . . and that the barbaric colors to the plaster, from the glaucous green of the blinded pupils, to the faded pink of the lips, from the touches of gold in the hair to the dark purple of the blood clots were my own work of art, or rather the inept product of a lazy day.[30] (274)

The friend's reaction is a far greater outcry than the suave complacency with which Ringel recounts the story of the model's death in "The Man with the Wax Heads": the interlocutor accuses the narrator of "every perversion and every audacity" (274) for having willfully mutilated a masterpiece. He predicts, moreover, that the consequences of the narrator's act will be serious. "I have nothing more to tell you," he cautions, "than that mutilating a work of art is a real act of murder, and that that is often a dangerous game" (275).[31]

To reassure himself against this dire threat, the narrator steps momentarily out of character. From a connoisseur of the grotesque, he becomes a spokesman for the wholesomeness of the sculptor's art:

I had been very kind to pay attention to the stupid ideas that had flown into [de Romer's] head on his glimpsing my plaster cast; if he had his way, sculptors' studios would be full of visionaries and the School of Beaux-Arts a branch office for Charcot, while on the contrary all the sculptors that I know just happened to be strapping and bearded *bons vivants,* with clear ideas and clear skin, more interested in physical sensations than in dreams.[32] (276)

The change of character is, of course, a false clue; by the rules of the fantastic, the friend's prediction must, and does, come true. Working alone in his study late one night, the narrator is seized with a sudden sense of presence. To his horror he perceives, protruding beneath the silk drapery covering an unused door, a single bare foot of a woman, "of so smooth and pale a texture it might have been a precious objet d'art" (277). The vision reappears on a subsequent night; this time the entire headless form of the woman is clearly molded beneath the drapery. Frantic, the narrator rips down the drapery to discover the decapitated body in all its gory splendor— "with a red wound between the two shoulders and rivulets of blood flowing from the gaping neck" (279). The body and its lost head, the plaster hung on the wall, exchange a desperate and loving gaze that deprives the narrator of his senses: "[the body's] two feet writhed on the dark carpet, convulsed in a terrible anguish; at that moment the head fixed on me an otherworldly gaze; I rolled on the carpet, my nerves shattered" (279).[33]

The narrator's loss of consciousness at the end makes "Post-humous Complaint" one of the few stories in the *Masked Figures and Phantoms* to forgo a resolution of the traumatic experience into the higher formal demands of narrative. The narrator simply passes out, passing up his chance to evaluate his own story. This ending is in marked contrast to Lorrain's more usual device of presenting indi-vidual stories as part of an ongoing series swapped by a group of storytellers, each trying to outdo the other in the horrific. This device is partially at work in "The Mask," in which the interpolated narrator offers his own story of a "bullfrog" both to top *Feelings and Memories* and to resolve the experience of trauma it recounts into a further narrative structure.

Another variation ends the experience of horror by commenting directly on its narrative form. The narrator calls on his listeners to agree that his experience, while horrible to live through, did make a wonderful story, did indeed produce that "yield of pleasure" of which Freud spoke. This is the case, for example, in "The Mask's Revenge" ("La vengeance du masque"), in which a certain Madame Campalou, driven to hysteria by the crowds of carnival time in Nice, unmasks a reveler so violently that one of his eyes is torn out. At carnival time the following year, the one-eyed victim reappears to bare his ravaged face, curse Madame Campalou, and slip into her hand a cold glass eye. She dies from the shock, "without regaining consciousness, stupid and dumb," leaving the narrator to conclude of his story, "Isn't that a beautiful revenge by the mask?" (134).[34]

None of these framing devices figures in "Posthumous Com-plaint." The reader is left with the image of the evanescent narrator who, unable to comment on his experience or his tale, simply relinquishes the power of speech. The absence here of any of Lorrain's familiar devices for narrative closure speaks eloquently to the seriousness of artistic mutilation. Having tampered with art, the narrator is punished where he has sinned — within his own art. More important, the narrator's loss of speech testifies to the tremendous suggestive power that accrues to metonymy throughout the *Masked Figures and Phantoms*. Depriving the narrator of his ability to narrate, the head metonymy in "Posthumous Complaint" takes over for the "talking head" of the narrator, erstwhile guarantor of authority in the text. It is obviously with no less impunity that one mutilates a signifier than a work of art in Lorrain.

The final, and longest, short story of the *Masked Figures and Phantoms*, "A Man Possessed by the Devil" ("Un démoniaque"), shows how the figure of the decapitated head rejoins the earlier experience of equivocation associated with mysterious doors (one of which also figured in "Posthumous Complaint"), forbidden rooms, and migrating signifiers. As with the crossed markers of the masked figures in "One of Them; or, the Soul of the Mask" or "Three Masked Figures," the decapitated head in its turn begins to migrate; detached from the body and substituting for it as a complete perceptual field, it is free to reattach in any position it chooses. In this sense, the head as a migrating signifier completes the fantasy of reunion sketched out in "Posthumous Complaint"; in "A Man Possessed by the Devil," the head reattaches perversely at the site of the female sex.

"A Man Possessed" abounds in cross-markings, unions of signifiers of opposite fields. Not only is the protagonist, Monsieur de Burdhe, morbidly attracted to the sexually equivocal; he is himself a hybrid form. Although a Parisian, he has tinted his hair with henna to resemble an Oriental; he is human but marked by an "almost feline suppleness"; he is old but appears astonishingly young, such that "everything about this mysterious de Burdhe, like an enigma, set one on edge" (417). The narrator's response to this enigma is the same neurotic ambiguity that attaches to the mask: de Burdhe "was at once a repellent and an attractive being" (417).[35]

De Burdhe's fatal obsession is with a particular type of gaze, first glimpsed in the figure of a head in a Roman cameo. "Roman cameos have an intensity I cannot describe," he writes of his discovery. "The setting of a ring portrayed the head of an adolescent crowned with laurel wreathes, some young Caesar, looking as extenuated and sensuous as he was rapacious and bored, about whom I will be dreaming for many a long night" (424). This expression of desire, which recalls that of the adolescent head in "The Man with the Wax Heads," de Burdhe subsequently rediscovers in an obscure pastel of a face in which "beneath heavy eyelids there shimmers and slumbers so green a water, the gloomy and corrupted water of an unsatisfied soul, the plaintive emerald of a terrifying lust!" (425).[36] This liquid green gaze takes form in de Burdhe's hallucination of a woman who pronounces three names, "Astarté, Acté, Alexandre." Transfixed by the vision's gaze, de Burdhe devotes the rest of his life to recovering it in the pleasure capitals of the Orient.

All of this information is presented in the story as excerpts from de Burdhe's journal, which has fallen into the narrator's hands upon de Burdhe's mysterious demise. De Burdhe's legacy also includes a statue of a goddess with a severed head at the place of her sex; into her eye sockets de Burdhe had inserted emeralds, suggesting that contrary to the evidence of his journal, which bemoans that Astarté had always eluded him, he had managed to recover by metonymy her mysterious and haunting gaze. In fact, that gaze has been fetishized, cross-marked as living and as nonliving by the substitution of sparkling if inanimate stones for the blind gaze of statuary, a gaze which had in any case always seemed to de Burdhe "alive in different ways than our grimacing physiognomies" ("autrement vivan[t] que la grimace de nos physionomies" [423]).

The severed head at the statue's pubis reprises in more evidently sexual terms the obsession with the animate/inanimate gaze. Its archetype is the masochistic male fantasy of the supposedly castrating power of the female sex, the *vagina dentata*. "A Man Possessed," however, goes this fantasy one better by cross-marking and thus realizing it. By dint of his obsession and the impulse to erotic violence that it gradually unrepresses within him, de Burdhe becomes an expert at obscene evocation, one of his favorite scenarios being the decapitation by the French revolutionaries of Marie Antoinette's alleged lover, Madame de Lamballe:

> The air is heavy, reeking with alcohol and with the stench
> of filth and rags, naked arms are waving pikes and with a

great shout I suddenly see a severed head raised aloft against the leaden sky, a bloodless head with extinguished and immobile eyes that drunken men pass from hand to hand, strike and kiss on the lips. Wrapped around his naked arm, one of them is wearing like a bundle of bloody lashes, an entire knot of viscera; he is sneering, his lips adorned with an ambiguous blond mustache just like the curly hairs of a sex . . . and around the fake mustache there are nothing but filthy remarks, scurrilous hoots of laughter; and the head sways back and forth above the crowd, brandished on the tip of a pike.[37] (432)

In this description, the man's moustached mouth is a vagina, as is the decapitated head pierced by the phallic pike. This reciprocity of the sexual markers for mouth, head, and sex is the clue to the mystery of de Burdhe's death. Struck down in midadoration of his death's-head goddess, de Burdhe's corpse reveals only one sign of violence: a hematoma on the neck, "just where the flesh is softest and most white, . . . like a bite or the suction of a long and slow kiss" (421).[38] Thus his own fantasies of sexual violence centering on decapitation are fatally revisited on de Burdhe himself; the signifier of erotic violence it has so pleased him to imagine on others—the wound on the neck by which head and body are severed—returns to his own body by the migration of signifiers that marks the return of the childhood repressed. In this story of the sexual fantastic, there is simply no other way to explain de Burdhe's inexplicable death.

It is, finally, not coincidental that de Burdhe's journal stops long before the moment of his demise. If the aggrandizement of the decapitated head in "Posthumous Complaint" could deprive the narrator of speech, childhood trauma in "A Man Possessed by the Devil" combines the aggrandized head with the equivocal signifier to reveal the full range of its fantasized power to kill. It would seem in this case that, contrary to the interpolated narrator of "The Mask," the embedded narration of "A Man Possessed by the Devil," in which the narrator quotes passages from the dead man's journal, is indeed meant to serve as a distancing device. The narrator hastens to assure the reader that he wanted no part of de Burdhe's legacy; he ceded the grotesque statue almost immediately to a collector and, more important, claims to have edited out (or repressed in his turn) the more "unprintable" passages of the work. The two manuscripts, however, ultimately participate in the same reciprocity of the signifier by which de Burdhe was undone. Whatever comforting distance the narrator may have hoped to establish between them is effaced by the concluding remark, "That was the end of the manuscript" (439), "C'était la fin du manuscrit" (439), which ends not only the journal but also the narrator's frame tale and, fortuitously, this particular edition (Union Générale d'Editions 10/18) of the *Masked Figures and Phantoms* as well.

What Goes Around Comes Around: Narrative Strategy and the Return of the Repressed

The (un)repression of the figures of desire in the *Masked Figures and Phantoms* is written into the structure of Lorrain's narratives as a preoccupation with the double. Reduplication of the hallucinated gaze had fatal effects for the "possessed" de Burdhe; this trauma is traceable to the fragmented perceptual field of the bullfrog episode, presented in "The Mask" as a reduplication of a previous narrative by Lorrain, doubled again by the interpolated narrator's story of his own "bullfrog."

This type of "me too!" narrative is one of the most common means by which the reduplication of the mask is made to serve a formal narrative purpose in the *Masked Figures and Phantoms*. Under the impetus of an antecedent narrative, what was previously repressed returns to the surface of the new narrator's consciousness and becomes a story in its own right. Thus the narrator of "An Unquiet Night" ("Une nuit trouble") is inspired by Maurice Rollinat's description of a stormy night in *La nature:* "'Ghosts creeping around, things brushing up against the soul,'" he recalls from Rollinat. "Well! I who am neither suspicious nor nervous, I have lived such a night of horror in such strange circumstances that, by God, I must tell you about it" (266).[39]

As in "The Mask," the quoted text is not infrequently attributed to Lorrain himself. The narrator of "Janine" begins his story with the reminder "Terror is principally the unexpected, you said in one of your stories," and continues to characterize his tale as "one more story to add to your series about masked figures, since this is truly a story about masks, this adventure in a furnished hotel where the critical moment brought about such a terrible, such an unexpected substitution between persons" (183, 184). This adventure is thus based on a deformed duplication: expecting to find the lithe and lovely Janine in bed with him, the narrator finds her "brother" instead, who pulls a knife and robs him. As is often the case for Lorrain's narrators, however, the story was well worth the fright it had caused him: "You must admit," the narrator of "Janine" concludes, "that it is a beautiful story of a mask" (190).⁴⁰

Other antecedent narratives, credited with unlocking a repressed store of terror, belong to Poe or Hoffmann. In "Green Bean" ("Haricot vert"), however, Huysmans is the predecessor of choice. In this very short story, Lorrain relates a pair of chance encounters between the narrator and a bizarre young man dressed in green from head to toe. This same person, affirms a jeweler of the narrator's acquaintance, was responsible for having incrusted with precious gems the enormous turtle on which the author of *Against the Grain* supposedly modeled Des Esseintes's, a turtle that in turn is thought to have been modeled on one owned and gilded by Proust's one-time mentor, the poet Robert de Montesquiou. Repetition is even more insistently a structural principle in "Green Bean," as the story breaks apart into two distinct episodes, each recounting one of the two encounters. In the first, the narrator visits his friend the Academician and has the satisfaction of seeing himself preferred to the young man in green, who is also waiting for an audience; in the second, he encounters him again at the jeweler's. The two episodes are connected only by the recurring appearance of the young man, the "green bean." It is not by coincidence, however, that the mysteriously styled figure of the man dressed in green turns out to be connected with that other recurring image of trauma in Lorrain: the frog. "It is about him," recalls the narrator about the "green bean," "that, frightened by his greenish complexion and clothes, a poet of the new school wrote this couplet: The frog sees him and calls him sister / And the green bean, from fear, goes greener still" (208–9).⁴¹

The neurotic return of the repressed differs from simple repetition by the figuration imposed upon the repressed material. Freud's grandson's *fort-da* game was both a metaphor of and a displacement for the anxiety caused by his mother's absence; hiding and retrieving his toys played out the tot's anxiety as it sought a symbolic substitute for it. As in dreams, the return of the repressed forms the basis for a subjective system of signification whose deeper meaning the sufferer both knows and does not know.

This type of subjective return is a distinct challenge to narrative structure. Narrative whose system is overly subjective risks dissolving into incomprehensible babble, while narrative with no subjective figuration is fundamentally uninteresting. Ideally, then, the task of narrative would be to elaborate both the repression and its return so that the reader, like Freud in his case studies, has at least a fighting chance of recognizing and interpreting its psychological substructure. Another way of saying this for Decadent fiction, whose claims to high art are no less important than its ability to shock, is that the reader must be both sufficiently pulled into the neurotic logic of the story to participate in its affective complex while remaining appropriately outside of it in order to evaluate and appreciate its artistic structure.

Two stories in the *Masked Figures and Phantoms* are particularly striking examples of neurotic narrative structure based on the return of the repressed. "The Student's Tale" ("Récit de l'étudiant") uses an especially subjective return to create a nightmare climax of barely disguised sexuality. "Sea-Green Eyes" ("Les yeux glauques") constructs a presumption of murder from an antecedent narrative and uses each to prove the other on the basis of a haunting gaze.

"The Student's Tale" is a first-person recollection of the strange doings of a certain Madame de Prack, whose elegance, companions, and ostentatious spending set her apart from the impoverished pensioners in a residential hotel in Paris. The student who tells the story marks it by an extreme interiority; his preoccupation with the mysterious Madame de Prack contrasts sharply with the usual self-absorption to which he freely admits: "I was then only a poor law student," he begins, "little concerned with outside appearance, and so, for this woman to attract my attention, she must indeed have stood out violently against the grey uniformity of the other lodgers in the hotel" (35).[42] It is also abundantly obvious that, beyond her external trappings, it is the student's desire for her, all the stronger for being denied, that makes her stand out so. "More than once," he recalls, "I had happened to rub elbows with her on the stairs in the hotel; . . . and each time I'd tried to brush up against her, slid my hand furtively along the banister in an attempt to meet her own, for that enigmatic shaded smile and those promising eyes cut through me like a knife, but each time my efforts came to naught. I wasn't her type, there was no doubt about that" (37).[43]

One night at the theater, the student overhears two women behind him discussing how one of them might escape her husband's vigilance and go with the other to a masked ball. The timid wife recognizes full well the allure of the mask, as she sighs, "Ah! to wander for an entire night, free beneath one's mask, with the certainty that you would never be found out, rub up against, brush up against all the lewdness, all the vices whose existence you suspect, and all those of which you haven't an inkling" (38). However, her more experienced companion calls her naive for supposing it to be so difficult to elude a jealous husband. "Really, you're too innocent, my little Suzanne," comes the light-hearted reproach. "For my part, don't you see, I allow myself all my fantasies. . . . One doesn't have to be that smart, after all, to rent a room by the month in a furnished hotel, under an assumed name; take me, for example" (39).[44]

Shortly after this incident, the hotel keeper dies, and the hotel's lobby is pressed into service for the wake, with the grieving widow both keeping watch over the body and tending to hotel business as needed. As the student finishes paying his respects in this double-duty room, the mourners are suprised by the sudden apparition of Madame de Prack. She is accompanied by a heavily veiled young woman. Explaining that she wishes to lend some of her costumes to her friend for a masked ball, Madame de Prack insists that the hotel keeper retrieve them right then and there from the closet in the lobby. But the casket is blocking the closet, and so the widow is forced to straddle her husband's corpse in order to reach the dresses. Her arms full of the costumes, Madame de Prack then turns to her companion and asks, "So, Suzanne, are you coming?" ("Allons, Suzanne, tu viens?" [40]).

The repressed name "Suzanne," first pronounced in the theater and then again only in the final line of the story, is the story's connecting thread. Hearing the name, the student immediately identifies the two women in the hotel lobby as the same two he has overheard at the theater. Thus he "solves" the mystery of Madame de Prack: she is an unhappily married woman amusing herself unrepentantly in costume and under an assumed name.

The Return of the Repressed

But there is a catch. For this solution to work, the reader must believe with the student that the Suzanne with Madame de Prack at the end is *indeed* the same Suzanne that he overheard some time before in the theater. While the impulse to narrative closure certainly argues in favor of this solution, the closed psychic world of the student, doubly dependent on the workings of chance and desire, argues just the opposite. It is not "really" probable that Suzanne is the only oppressed wife of that name in Paris or that Madame de Prack is the only woman to have resorted to fake names and cheap hotels (especially since the woman in the theater makes no secret of how easy it is to do so); but the student is, by his own admission, incapable of relating anything outside his own preoccupations. It is therefore his own desire that makes the most of happenstance. Desire valorizes the returned name as a marker of identity and so provides the "solution" to a mystery of the student's own making. Thus the return of the name is a particularly subjective return in the story; it is the student's own desire coming back to him.

The nightmare quality of the final scene betrays just how subjective the return of the repressed is in this story. The description of the widow straddling her husband's corpse to get to the costumes in the closet is insisted on as a perverse sexual disguise, from the detail of the keys that unlock the closet (the forbidden door) to the repeated synonyms for *straddling,* which the imperfect tense of the original French ask us to read as actions that describe an interminable scene: "With some effort, the hotel mistress took up the key ring at her belt, *stepped over* the casket, and, *her legs apart, straddling the dead man,* she opened the cupboard and passed out to her impassive client a huge pile of satins, velvets, and laces" (40; my emphasis).[45]

The impassiveness of Madame de Prack before this scene of metaphorical necrophilia is, of course, easily explained: she is an old adept at the use of disguise in the satisfaction of sexual desire; indeed, her presence in the lobby is motivated by her need for disguise. However, the student's anguish at the scene does not result, as he claims it does, from seeing a wig almost catch fire on a funeral candle. The wig is just one more disguise in the masked ball that suddenly sets to spinning before the narrator. It is an ingenious displacement, since what truly unsettles the student is his own adroitness at having buckled the buckle on his desire by equating the two Suzannes and devising the "truth" about Madame de Prack.

"Sea-Green Eyes" uses a similar type of circular reasoning to return the repressed to the plot in a particularly unsettling way. The eyes of the title belong to the celebrated but aging courtesan Nelly Forah; her charms are the subject of heated debate among a group of gentlemen at the beginning of the story. A forceful variant on Lorrain's head metonymies, Nelly's eyes are a locus of repression. Not only are they never seen by the curious public, since Nelly goes about heavily veiled, but, according to the one gentleman in the group who *has* seen them, the principal narrator Michel Stourdof, they have an uncannily evocative power: "well, they're blue, a lightly pale blue-green. When the sea is high and frothy, it is this color blue, a blue verging on green. Your great painter Baudry used this shade of blue when he painted waves, those waves in which he places, trickling with sea foam, such delectably white women's bodies" (347).[46]

Nelly's eyes evoke an entire complex of repressed narrative. This narrative—or more appropriately, these narratives—form the plot of "Sea-Green Eyes," but with the twist that the story becomes so circular and so subjective as to once again suggest the closed symbolic system of neurotic thought that privileges the relationship of signifier to signifier over that between signifier and signified. The psychoanalytic structure of repressed narrative is marked in the story by a regressive series of embedded storytelling. From the omniscient narrative of the opening pages, the narration passes to Michel, who recounts the death of his friend (Nelly's lover Serge Stréganof), Nelly's version of this event, and the related legend by which Michel justifies his fear of Nelly's eyes. There is, furthermore, an attempt not to have Michel tell his story at all. The dinner bell rings just as he begins, and the group temporarily decides that his story will be far too long to hear right then.

Michel's foreign nationality (he is the only Russian in a group of Frenchmen) and his opinion of Nelly set his narration apart as subjective and governed by desire. Not only does Michel assert that Nelly's charms have outlasted her age; he is the only one of the group to have seen her unveiled. This peek behind the veil of repression, however, does not so much uncover the "truth" about Nelly as it entices the reader into the circular world of Michel's desire, traceable through the series of narratives by which he "explains" how

Stréganof died. The first of these narratives is paraphrased from Nelly herself, who claimed that Stréganof had died in a boating accident one romantic evening on the Bay of Capri. "In the middle of their outing," Michel recalls that Nelly said, "Serge, tempted by the temperature, insisted on taking a swim, that he gave her the oars, undressed, swam for a while behind the boat, joyous and playful in the moonlight, that then to her great terror, he suddenly sank beneath the waves and never reappeared" (348).[47]

Michel is convinced, however, that Serge's death was a murder — one might say "at Nelly's hands" if the real metonymy were not in fact "at Nelly's eyes." His conviction is rooted in the Russian legend that maintains that a woman who has seen "the farewell gaze of the throes of death" ("le regard d'adieu d'une agonie" [348]) in the eyes of a lover who has died watching and desiring her will capture the reflection of that desire in her own eyes and thus remain infinitely desirable. Michel's imagined version of the boating accident therefore differs considerably from Nelly's, as it reprises it now in terms of the legend: "I can see Nelly clearly," he recounts,

> seated at the prow of the boat and gently rowing and pushing the boat along, while, swimming with slow and graceful strokes, there is my friend Serge for whom I mourn; the moon bathes them both in a gauzy light, striating Serge's torso above the water and Nelly's white bodice in the boat; both are very beautiful; they continue this way for an hour, looking in each other's eyes, smiling at one another; then Serge begins to tire, little by little he is running out of breath, he would like to climb back in the boat, he says to Nelly: "Stop," Nelly does not hear him, her lips curled in a smile, her eyes deep in his, she is rowing gently and the boat gets farther away; Serge at first thinks she is teasing. . . . What a beautiful night to die! Serge has understood, he thrashes about in the water, his mouth submerged, he is at his last gasp, but with his eyes fixed on Nelly's, in front of him the boat is rocking. She smiles, still pushing on the oars, and water gurgles in Serge's ears as he enters his death throes, as he clutches in vain at the sea foam and sinks into the green and moonlit shadow of the waves.[48] (348–49)

Michel's description of Serge's death is a thinly disguised hysteria fantasizing female sexual drive as powerful enough to kill. Indeed, the rhythms of Serge's agony are a reversed sexual rhythm; as he tires, she requires greater effort, so that the paroxysm of his love for her is the moment of his real, and not just sexually metaphorical, death.

Michel's hysteria, however, is more clearly evident in the circular logic by which he justifies his narrative. Called on to prove its accuracy, he returns to the "evidence" of the Russian legend he had cited earlier, supposing that Serge had recounted it to Nelly, who had then undoubtedly wanted to test its truth for herself. Surely, then, Serge had been murdered because, Michel insists, "I have ever since that time seen Serge's gaze in Nelly's eyes" (349).[49] Reconstructing his narrative of murder from a previously supposed narrative, Michel snaps shut his hermetic circle of desire. His narrative is said to prove the "truth" of Serge's murder in the same way that the murder proves the "truth" of the previous narrative (the legend) on the basis of which it has been assumed. There is no way of determining which comes first, the narrative or the legend: each is equally unreliable, each equally dependent on the other for its validity.

As in the psychoanalytic case study, Michel's assertion of belief in the events he has recounted is wholly equivalent to the psychic "reality" conferred on them by hysteria. Asked by one of his listeners, a stereotypically cynical French marquis, whether Nelly might not have been more interested in Serge's inheritance, Michel responds disdainfully, "You are slandering Nelly, and besides, one must not make legends lie" (349).[50] It would seem that the neurotic thrust of the *Masked Figures and Phantoms* is exactly this: that the legends of childhood, the phantasms of its traumas, cannot be made to lie. It is these phantasms and legends, after all, that guarantee the aesthetic superiority of the neurotic psyche and provide, at whatever cost, the only shivers of sensuality worthy to compensate for life.

5

The Epithalamic Horror

Displacement in Rachilde

The Hysterical Body: Dora, Simone de Beauvoir, Rachilde

To be a woman writer at the turn of the century, Rachilde maintained, was to assume an unenviable personality. Rachilde's preface to her 1888 *Madame Adonis* assures that the "woman of letters" commits herself to "a god-awful career, the most god-awful career possible." Engaged in by women, this career "is immoral, meaning that it ruins one good marriage in twenty, produces illegitimate children under the specious pretext of excess cerebral activity, leads to unnatural vices for the same reason . . . disrupts the harmony of the household, stains the fingers, and bugs the hell out of magazine publishers" (viii).[1]

Rachilde wrote this preface to counter a personal attack by the press. It seems that the author of *Monsieur Vénus,* whose masculine garb and provocative novels had already earned her considerable notoriety, had actually slapped a journalist, producing cries of outrage against her lack of feminine decorum. If she lacks feminine decorum, Rachilde responds, this is because she was either not enough, or too much, of a woman to abide by conventional notions of gender: "So I am a dog of letters," the preface continues, "to my great regret, an hysteric of letters, and lest one think I merit neither this excessive honor nor this indignity . . . I am an androgyne of letters." (xi).[2]

The experience of the female body underlies Rachilde's fiction in the same way it does the preface to *Madame Adonis*. For a woman, the preface suggests, writing is a corporeal experience: it stains the fingers, produces bastard "children," ruins the sexual relationship between husband and wife. Moreover, it is physically demanding and can result in physical damage:

> It takes on average one year to write a good novel, six months to write a passable one, three months to write a bad one . . . those who write them in a month and a half, like my fellow women writers, belong to the category of hysterics. . . . During the different honeymoons of the *authoress* with her novel, she no longer converses, she takes on the air of a constipated hen, no longer combs her hair, horrible detail, has indigestion and nightmares, or else she scratches her lover.[3] (ix; Rachilde's emphasis)

This description is all the more apt for its representation of Rachilde's own writing habits, which recall the *condition seconde* theory of hysteria. Cranking out her annual novel in a thirty-day frenzy of writing, Rachilde impressed her friend Paul Léautaud as a woman possessed, as one of those writers "whose literary talent comes chiefly from a type of instinct, from an impulsive force that makes them write in a sort of delirium" (qtd. in Dauphiné, *Rachilde* 48). Clearly the urgency of her writing places her in her own "category of hysterics," all the more so that the thirty-day writing cycle is a lunar or menstrual cycle as well. Further bodily effects may result from the finished product of the woman writer. Because the woman of letters writes from what she knows, Rachilde's preface assures, "unsavory rumors are expelled from the shadows, [and] the vindictive woman always uses them to inform Paul that Caroline is cheating on him, to which Jacques . . . is obliged to respond by a duel to the death" (viii).[4]

Claude Dauphiné gives the role of the body its due in Rachilde's life and career. Dauphiné attributes a hysterical paralysis that Rachilde suffered at the start of her career in the early 1880s to a libido at war with itself. Caught between the sexual aberrations she was describing in her works, the bourgeois respectability (despite the male garb) of her personal life as a young woman living alone in

Paris, and the amorous attention being paid her by Catulle Mendès, Rachilde "had clearly what we would call a nervous breakdown that resulted in a temporary paralysis of her legs" (27). It was only after a retreat from Paris to her native Périgord that Rachilde reconciled these competing expressions of desire. Her compromise solution is found, once again, in the preface to *Madame Adonis*, which announces a defiant justification of Rachilde's works by "life": "I wrote some stories. — They are hardly edifying. In that they resemble life. That is even the only contact that they have with life, it seems to me" (xi). Her books themselves, conduits of desire, are in turn desirable objects: they sell and people read them, since "all the critics in the world do not prevent an author from being read if the public likes that author" (xii).[5]

The author-public relationship as Rachilde defines it carries strong overtones of promiscuity. Rachilde brags in her defense that "ten thousand readers" can read her without knowing her, as opposed to the handful of journalists who know and critique her personally but who do not read her (xii). This defense recalls the reasons Rachilde had given earlier in her argument for why impecunious women may choose to become writers; it is an alternative to forthrightly selling one's body for cash or, only slightly better, for marriage:

> General rule: one is wrong to be a woman of letters.
> There is always something better to do.
> For some, prostitution, society's hygiene.
> For others, a husband.[6] (vi)

In *Writing and the Body*, Gabriel Josipovici relates the sense of impotence attaching to language as expression of the body in literature. The body is seen as a discourse opposed to writing; it is that which cannot be said in words. Thus Josipovici asks, "Why this sense of a word that would make all the difference? Why this feeling that words are incapable of expressing the emotions of the body? Why this desire to write and the simultaneous sense that the desire has only to surface to be frustrated?" (65).

The inadequacy of words to express the lived existence of the body opposes the very premise of Freud's "talking cure" at the same time that it acknowledges with him the semiotics of the hysterical body. The long-running antagonism between Freud and Dora can be understood as an opposition of this rational discourse to the prerational or irrational discourse of the body. It is, in other words, an antagonism between secondary and primary processes. Fresh from the insights of *The Interpretation of Dreams,* Freud made it a point of honor in the Dora case to interpret as figurative the least gesture, the least refusal, the least dream image shared by his often reticent patient. Indeed, as he states in his preface to the case, its title

> was originally "Dreams and Hysteria," for it seemed to me particularly well-adapted for showing how dream-interpretation is woven into the history of a treatment and how it can become a means of filling in amnesias and elucidating symptoms. . . . I must once more insist . . . that a thorough investigation of the problems of dreams is an indispensable prerequisite for any comprehension of the mental processes in hysteria and the other psycho-neuroses. (7:10-11)

As is well known, Freud's interpretations in the case are so aggressively couched in a language of triumph that Dora's nos are unhesitatingly understood as yesses and her objections routinely and authoritatively dismissed as concessions made by her unconscious to the principles of the analysis. Thus Freud explains:

> The "No" uttered by a patient after a repressed thought has been presented to his conscious perception for the first time does no more than register the existence of a repression and its severity; it acts, as it were, as a gauge of the repression's strength. If this "No," instead of being regarded as the expression of an impartial judgment (of which, indeed, the patient is incapable), is ignored, and if work is continued, the first evidence soon begins to appear that in such a case "No" signifies the desired "Yes." (7:58–59)

The *yes,* of course, is desired by the analyst, who needs it to confirm the accuracy of his theories of repression and transference. If, however, Freud has to pronounce his treatment of Dora unsuccessful and call her case study a "fragment," it is a failure not only because, as he says, he failed to recognize the impact of transference on the analysis.[7] The analysis also fails because Dora refuses to give up her privileges as a female body. She comes and goes as she pleases; she keeps to her own rituals of place and time; she is attuned to the sexual processes in ways that mystify Freud. As numerous critics have pointed out, Dora is smart enough to figure out the use the men around her (including Freud) have devised for her body: she is to be given to Herr K. in place of Frau K. so that her father and Frau K. can peacefully continue their liaison.

Consequently, the Dora case reveals nothing so much as Freud's attempts to make his (rational) language keep up with the (prerational) physical body as Dora knows and lives it. Having asserted in the *Studies on Hysteria* the happy coincidence between narrative coherence and the cure of the troubled psyche, Freud is obliged in his famous case study to keep changing the plot: first Dora is adjudged to be in love with Herr K., then with her father, then with Frau K., then with her childhood self, and finally, as Freud allows in his discussion of tranference, with Freud himself. Dora's body, in other words, *chooses* hysteria by refusing the entrapment into language that Freud's scientific positivism would propose as its cure. *She* will choose whom *she* will love; in the detective game she plays with Freud, she changes her secrets so often and so skillfully that the louder Freud's claim to understand her, the more hollow that claim rings out.

Dora abruptly ends her analysis by physically removing herself from the field: she stops coming to see Freud. She thereby asserts the superiority of her body, free of the snares of analytic discourse: Freud has not *pronounced* her cured. She reappears at the very end of the study, however; many years have passed since Freud has last seen her and she has married. In one sense, then, the men — Freud, Herr K., and Dora's father — have triumphed: Dora has ultimately submitted to the demand that she marry. The fact of the marriage makes Dora a "whole" body, consistent with Freud's demand that the body acquiesce to sexual gratification in order to be considered "healthy." That refrain is by now a familiar one: "I should without question consider a person hysterical in whom an occasion for sexual excitement elicited feelings that were preponderantly or exclusively unpleasurable" (7:28).

But there is no word from Dora on this arrangement, second best in the eyes of the men, but an arrangement nevertheless. It is precisely Dora's silence, however, that preserves her bodily autonomy: no one is to know for sure whether her acceptance of the marital relationship was the right "answer" to the "hysteria" of her initial refusals. The plethora of commentaries on Dora's case are in large part grounded in this silence, in this suspension of the mystery of the body. Octave Mannoni cleverly and revealingly imagines Dora clinging to hysteria as an experience lived by the physical body opposed to the body of rational or scientific commentaries. The first chapter of Mannoni's *Fictions freudiennes* has an outraged Dora responding to her reading of Freud's "Fragment of an Analysis" in a letter to Frau K.:

> You see, if I wrote to the *Monatschrift* to give *my* version (it would be justified from a *scientific* point of view that I should have my say as well), in the first place they wouldn't publish it, and second they would surely find in it the proof that I am an hysteric. I might very well be an hysteric; what I particularly don't like is that they would say it's not up to me to judge! It's possible that I suffer from a "minor hysteria." So what? You see, up till now they had no use for hysteria. It had to have some purpose. Now that's done: now hysteria is popular, it's a research topic for professors. Do you think that makes things any better?[8] (16–17)

That the female body is *by nature* a hysterical body is one of the unexamined assumptions of Simone de Beauvoir's classic work on the feminine experience, *The Second Sex*. Launching the first salvos in the feminist attack on Freud, de Beauvoir objects to the psychoanalytic definition that understands female sexuality as a deviation from the male. "Freud never showed much concern with the destiny of woman," she observes correctly; "it is clear that he simply adapted his account from that of the destiny of man, with slight modifications" (39). Accordingly, for de Beauvoir the processes of libidinal reinvestment required by woman's "two distinct erotic systems" (the clitoral and the vaginal) is an open invitation to dysfunction: "There is only one genital stage for man [the phallic], but there are two for woman; she runs a much greater risk of not reaching the end of her sexual evolution, of remaining at the infantile stage and thus of developing neuroses" (40).

While de Beauvoir purports to disabuse her readers of Freud's view of woman, which she judges to be reductive and reifying, she nevertheless shows herself to be quite taken with the neurotic manifestations of female sexual development gone awry. It is not function but dysfunction that interests de Beauvoir; while *The Second Sex* treats the hysterical body as an explainable, changeable, product of culture, that body within the work still resists language in the way that Dora resisted Freud. Irrecuperable by language, the ambiguities of the body are the unrecognized conditions for meaning in *The Second Sex*. The missing body undermines de Beauvoir's social argument and reimposes the structure of hysteria on a discourse intended to conform in spirit and in style with rational (male) scientific discourse.

De Beauvoir fills her landmark essay with case studies of women chronically unable to reconcile their experience of themselves with their experience of their bodies. She quotes, for instance, Isadora Duncan's account of her first sexual experience in *My Life:*

> I, too, was aroused and dizzy, while an irresistible longing to press him closer and closer surged in me, until one night, losing all control and falling into a fury, he carried me to the sofa. Frightened but ecstatic and crying out in pain, I was initiated into the act of love. I confess that my first impressions were a horrible fright and an atrocious pain, as if someone had torn out several of my teeth at once; but a great pity for what he seemed to be suffering prevented me from running away from what was at first sheer mutilation and torture. . . . Next day what was at that time no more than a painful experience for me continued amidst my martyred cries and tears. I felt as if I were being mangled. (Qtd. in de Beauvoir 384)

Though literary intent informs much of this overwritten description, de Beauvoir presents it quite literally as evidence of the crisis of sexual union, "even when quite voluntary" (384). For more pedestrian examples, she borrows amply from the files of the psycho-analyst Wilhelm Stekel to illustrate the drama of the female body, as in this example of an unhappy bride-to-be:

> When Stekel met her, she suffered from vomiting, took morphine every evening, flew into rages, refused to bathe, took her meals in bed, remained shut up in her room. She was engaged and claimed to be deeply in love with her fiancé. She admitted to Stekel that she had given herself to him. . . . Later, she said that she had had no pleasure in the act: that she now recalled his kisses with repugnance and that is the source of her vomiting. It was discovered that in fact she had given herself to him to punish her mother, whom she did not feel loved her enough: as a child, she used to spy upon her parents at night for fear that they would give her a brother or sister; she adored her mother. "And now she was to get married, leave her father's house, abandon her parents' bedroom? it was impossible." She gained weight, scratched and mutilated her hands, fell stupid, fell ill, tried to offend her fiancé in every possible way. The doctor cured her but she begged her mother to call off the marriage: "She wanted to stay at home forever, to stay a child." Her mother insisted that she marry. A week before her wedding day they found her dead in her bed: she had shot herself.[9] (*Deuxième sexe* 2:233)

For de Beauvoir the female body is hysterical to the measure that it is discursive. If the female body is radically different from the male, it is so because the female gives bodily expression to the hesitations and conflicts of the psyche or, to be more consistent with de Beauvoir's ontological vocabulary, to the ambiguities inherent in woman's sense of her being-in-the-world. The reluctant fiancée engaged in self-destructive behavior, the wife who turns frigid to punish a husband's infidelity, the mother-to-be experiencing morning sickness, or the woman-child suffering the pain of her first menstrual period—all these unfortunates who populate de Beau-voir's essay are acting in accordance with Freud's theory of hysteria. In other words, the hysterical body wills and wills not, knows and yet does not know. The psychic disorders traceable to the onset of menstruation express the girl's refusal of womanhood even as she ardently desires to leave behind the world of childhood; the adolescent who provokes and then flees men's advances both fears and longs for sexual experience; the wife whose frigidity originates in a disappointing wedding night wishes and does not wish to accept the reality of her married state.

Sexuality is always a crisis for the women of *The Second Sex*. In de Beauvoir's view, the forces of nature that assure the perpetuation of the species guarantee that woman's body is never wholly and completely her own. "Woman, like man," writes de Beauvoir, "*is* her body; but her body is something other than herself" (29). "From puberty to menopause woman is the theater of a play that unfolds within her and in which she is not personally concerned" (27). For most of her life, woman in de Beauvoir's view remains a stranger to the obscure forces of nature churning and burning within her.

It is hardly contemporary, and more than a little disheartening, to consider with de Beauvoir that the physical ailments accompanying the female reproductive cycle demonstrate "the revolt of the organism against the invading species" (30). In fact, feminism has battled mightily to have the physical discomforts occasioned by the female reproductive cycle—from menstrual cramps to morning sickness to postpartum depression—recognized by the medical community as biologically "real" and not hysterically "made-up" phenomena. To take but the latter example, Carol Dix points out in *The New Mother Syndrome* that postpartum depression was considered by the medical profession as simply the manifestation of latent neurosis in new mothers rather than as a disorder with biochemical as well as psychical components. Only in 1984, she notes, did the *Journal of the American Medical Association* report that postpartum depression had not been included in the computer classifications of the *Diagnostic and Statistical Manual of Mental Disorders* (12–13).

Attempting to repudiate Freud, *The Second Sex* in fact follows his lead from hysteria to rational discourse. Hysteria must be "trappable" by language for de Beauvoir in much the same way as it must be for Freud. De Beauvoir's ability to tolerate the antithetical nature of hysteria—its will and will not—is countered by her desire to avoid impugning the existentialist values of choice and becoming that *The Second Sex* spells out for both men and women. Hysteria as a simultaneous willing and unwilling cannot be carried too far in de

Beauvoir, for fear of giving the lie to the existentialist quest. For de Beauvoir, psychoanalysis is wrong because it is determinist; as she states in *The Second Sex,* "Replacing value with authority, choice with drive, psychoanalysis offers an *Ersatz,* a substitute, for morality—the concept of normality" (50). Therefore, women must not be shown to be entirely determined by authority, inaccessible unconscious pulsations and the norm of standard behavior; rather, they must, and this is de Beauvoir's contention, have been forced into their corners by society's preconceptions of their place. *Hysteria* is limited to mean only the way in which woman's body translates the psychical into the physical; it is not irremediable. Given optimum social and economic conditions, even the hysterical woman will eventually conquer her right to her own choices and desires. The hysteric's inability to choose between competing desires is not an inborn trait of womanhood; it is for de Beauvoir a double bind imposed on women by a patriarchal society obsessed with interpreting women's bodies from the cultural (ad)vantage point of the male.

Yet hysteria in *The Second Sex* continues to oppose language to the body as two separate registers of semiotic experience. De Beauvoir's silent debt to Freud belies her attempts to comprehend woman's body fully within a superior, authoritarian discourse. Something important remains not said—and this is the body itself. De Beauvoir's own female body is repressed in the work to become the site of the unsayable; the authoritarian assertions "I have seen," "I have read," and "I have known" by which she introduces her examples and validates her conclusions limit her presence in the work strictly to that of a witness. This is intentional; she means to testify to the general experience of womankind. But it is indeed curious that de Beauvoir is never in her own right a corporeal source of female experience. Unlike Freud, who uses a number of his own dreams to buttress *The Interpretation of Dreams,* de Beauvoir never once counts herself as one of the women in *The Second Sex.* As Mary Evans suggests in *Simone de Beauvoir: A Feminist Mandarin,*

> de Beauvoir's entry into feminism—or at any rate the arousal in her of something approaching a consciousness of the specificity of the female condition—occurred in a cerebral way that becomes apparent in the early pages of *The Second Sex.* Having experienced no disadvantages or

difficulties in her own life that she could relate to her own sex, and having received a considerable amount of help and support from a man in her chosen vocation, de Beauvoir's attitude to women suggests a lack of engagement with and experience of the subjectivity of femininity. (59–60)

Imposing a cerebral distance between her own body, held in reserve outside the limits of her discourse, and the hysterical female body that she describes but does not inhabit, de Beauvoir opposes the willed coherence of her discourse to the radical incoherence of the hysterical body she takes as her subject. Again, Evans notes de Beauvoir's refusal of feminine experience lived within a female body:

> [De Beauvoir's] uncritical belief in what she describes as rationality, her negation and denial of various forms of female experience, and her tacit assumption that paid work and contraception are the two keys to the absolute freedom of womankind, all suggest a set of values that place a major importance on living like a childless, rather singular, employed man. Indeed, a reading of *A Very Easy Death* and de Beauvoir's novels could lead to the conclusion that de Beauvoir's message to her readers is dominated by her view that to live like a traditional woman is to invite unhappiness—far better to live like a traditional man. (56–57)

Determining the extent to which the female body does or does not "return" in de Beauvoir's novels, and particularly in her journals, exceeds the range of the present discussion. What is most useful for Rachilde in *The Second Sex* is the light it shines retrospectively on the novelist's perception of hysteria and the body. Where de Beauvoir would repress hysteria (like Freud) by describing it, Rachilde understands (like Dora) that hysteria is a discourse that must be allowed its say. As the (primary process) incoherence that challenges (secondary process) logic, hysteria is resolutely the domain of the feminine.

Rachilde's codes of feminine hysteria oppose the male to the female not as model to incomplete (castrated) copy but as sign systems whose aesthetic coherence actually depends on their relationship to the female, ultimately maternal, body. For Rachilde as for de Beauvoir, the female body is prey to alienating forces, to the debilitating work of nature that underlies and undermines the conventional appearance of the blushing bride or the bourgeois housewife. Rachilde, however, fully accepts this body as one that both wills and wills not. Under the pressure of the rational discourse by which the body would make contact with the world, metonymy allows Rachilde to preserve the unsayability of the body (its opposition to discourse as a separate register of experience) and to sublimate the internal divisions of that body into the devices of narrative. By an all-encompassing process of displacement, the universe in Rachilde becomes a vast metonymy for the female reproductive functions, bodily functions that are the very source of desire and meaning.

Description and Displacement: "The Harvests of Sodom" and "The Mortis"

Rachilde claimed to prefer *Monsieur Vénus* to all her other novels. In the preface to *Madame Adonis,* she calls it a "work that I do not disavow and that I prefer to my other works, since mothers always prefer their hump-backed sons to their upright ones" (xviii).[10] The breathless quality of *Monsieur Vénus* is created by a profusion of loosely motivated episodes and a constant switching of genders through which the author drives home the perversity of Raoule de Vénérande's masculine love for the feminized Jacques Silvert.

The opening pages of *Monsieur Vénus* thus furnish a splendid example of the workings of displacement in Rachilde. As Raoule de Vénérande enters the dingy attic apartment of the florist Marie Silvert, her senses are assailed simultaneously by the unpleasant smell of apples cooking on the stove and by the sight of the exceptionally beautiful Jacques Silvert, half-covered by the artificial roses he is making at the single table in the room. The point of the scene is to establish as rapidly as possible the intense and contradictory passion Raoule is about to conceive for the young Jacques. The onset of this passion is marked, however, not by Raoule's responses to Jacques himself but by the changes in her response to the odor of the apples. At the beginning, she is categorical: "No odor was more repulsive to her than that of apples" (23); five pages later, however, "Mlle de Vénérande imagined that she could perhaps eat one of those apples without too much disgust" (28).[11]

The connection between the florist and the apples is metonymic in nature. It is based on the golden reddishness of the silken chest hairs alluringly displayed beneath Jacques's half-open shirt. The color that he shares with the apples forms the implicit connection between him and the (classically forbidden) fruit. This displacement of Raoule's pleasure from Silvert's body onto the apples is more than just a clever artistic device allowing Rachilde to engage in a steamy description of the first moments of an unusual passion. The combination of disgust and pleasure with which Raoule reacts to the apples, the "without too much disgust" with which she tempers her desire to taste them, announce the sexual ambiguity that will characterize her future relationship with Jacques: she will be the man, he will be the mistress, and their affair (whose consummation remains in doubt throughout the novel) will be governed by a single "thought in common: the destruction of their sex" ("pensée commune: la destruction de leur sexe" [110]).

The displacement of Raoule's pleasure/disgust from Jacques to the apples preserves the ambiguities of female desire without violating its reserve. Because Raoule is a divided body, because neither attraction nor repulsion is a more "true" sexual response in hysteria, Rachilde preserves in this scene the unsayability of the hysterical body. If that body's *yes* and *no* are equivalent, there is no way to express the body in rational discourse based on the ability to distinguish, precisely, between *yes* and *no,* between that which is and that which is not. Rachilde makes this unsayability, this inability to distinguish, a determinant of the plot. Unlike the changing plot of the Dora case, which can be read as a constant frustration for Freud, Rachilde's plot is a mise-en-scène of her characters' sexual ambiguities. Rachilde is free, as it were, to keep tossing the coin between the competing couples of desire and disgust, male and female. Each successive chapter of *Monsieur Vénus* is based on whichever side of the coin turns up: Raoule as desiring male or disgusted female, Jacques as desiring female or disgusted male, and so on. It is for this reason, perhaps, that Maurice Barrès suggests so enthusiastically in his preface to the novel that "[Rachilde's] creations have a whiff of death about them" (19).[12] When Jacques is killed in a duel arranged by Raoule, it is impossible to determine which combination of male/female traits has been eliminated. The remaining complementary body, Raoule's, is thus properly left unsayable, corresponding to Rachilde's vague hint in the closing pages that Raoule's body has finally found its (necrophiliac) match in this corpse of indeterminate sexuality.

A similar process of metonymy in the short story "The Harvests of Sodom" ("Les vendanges de Sodome"), from the 1894 *Demon of Absurdity (Démon de l'absurde)*, functions again both as stylistic device and as figuration of the unsayable female body. In this story, the body is represented only to be destroyed. Metonymy both announces this process of physical destruction and introduces the displacement of the female reproductive processes onto the world beyond the body that characterizes description and plot in much of Rachilde's short fiction. Moreover, the physical destruction of the female body is presented in this story as its very condition of meaning.

The plot of the story is relatively simple. The males of Sodom leave the city early in the morning to begin the grape harvest, the major agricultural task to which they devote their entire year's worth of saved-up physical energy. During their midday siesta, the men are furtively joined by a naked woman, who eats all the grapes from the basket of the youngest and most comely of the males, Sinéus, and then stretches out next to him in a none-too-subtle attempt at seduction. Her advances to Sinéus, however, awaken the entire group, who, furious at her attempts to divert their virile forces from the harvest, stone her to death. In her death agony, the woman crawls into the vat in which the men have been stomping the grapes: it is in her description of this moment that Rachilde pulls out the stops on metonymy:

> She made herself small, very small, crawled, humbly serpentine, slipped into the vat where the must was fermenting, and, pulling around herself heaps of crushed grapes, she remained inert, *adding to the blood of the grapes all the exquisite wine of her veins.* While she was still in agony, they climbed down into the barrel and *trampled her underfoot,* while there sprang *from the prodigious*

124

black fruits that seemed like so many rolling eyes, a gaze of supreme malediction.[13] (80; my emphasis)

The annihilation of the woman's body is her commingling with the forces of nature and the earth. Her blood is now wine, the wine is her blood, the grapes the men stomp by stomping her stare back at them with the curse reflected in her eyes. From the men's point of view, the annihilation of the female body is only to the good: they so consecrate their entire physical forces to the harvest that all women have long been banished from the city. The destruction of the woman's body at the end of the story responds to this unanimous repudiation of female desire:

> They all surrounded the woman. She was one of these wanderers, skulking around in search of love, that the wise men of Sodom had banished from their city. In a just and formidable anger, certain men of God had joined together to rid themselves of these demented women, who were haunted from dusk till dawn by hankerings after immoral pleasures. Sentencing themselves virilely to several years of chastity so as not to waste their best energies during the harvest on these abysses of sensual pleasure that were the daughters of Sodom, keeping only mothers in labor and old women, they had banished even their wives, even their sisters.[14] (77)

Yet by their entry into nature at the moment of the woman's death, female desire and the female body itself circumvent the interdiction imposed by the men. As Rachilde displaces desire from the body onto the surrounding natural environment, her model and vocabulary are the specifically female ones of the reproductive processes. Her description of the grapevines on the morning of the harvest at the beginning of the story both announces the future commingling of the wine and the woman's body and participates in an elaborately overdone metaphor of rampant sexuality, gestation, and birth.

> At this dawn, the earth was steaming like a vat filled with an infernal must, and the vine, in the center of the

immense plain, gleamed red under an already ferocious rising sun, a purple sun coiffed with glowing embers that began already to ferment the enormous clusters whose grapes, supernaturally large, took on the reflections of rolling eyes, sprung completely black from their orbits. . . . Like an overly fertile beast, who must not be held down by any restraint in the painful hours of her multiple births, [the vine] rolled against the earth in frightful convulsions, throwing out furious bursts of garlands, imploring arms raised toward the sun, seeming both to suffer and to be ecstatic with a guilty yet heavenly joy, while her overheated marrow overflowed from her, flooding her with a dew of thick tears. She gave birth anywhere she could to these prodigious fruits of a shining, velvety brown, mysterious blossoming of the mortal bitumen, which they recalled by their sooty hue, their shade of satanic sugar distilled in the violence of a volcano.[15] (69–70)

The description introduces to the story the unsettling ambiguity toward sexuality that makes up the "epithalamic horror," or the desire and fear of coupling in Rachilde. The displacements effected by her descriptive passages determine her plot: the result of the woman's death is that the men of Sodom, refreshing themselves with deep draughts of the wine into which she has been crushed, turn to each other in the first orgy of homosexual activity that would give their town its irrevocable notoriety. Thus, even as the story moves from a kind of universal parturition to the sterility of homosexual copulation, desire undoes the men's will to chastity by the very agent that the refusal of desire was intended to serve: the wine, which begins and ends as a metonymy of the female body.

In this way, the unsayable body becomes the condition of meaning. The "Sodom" of the title is not the Sodom of the reader's expectation *until* the elaborate physical and semiotic displacements of the story have been completed. It is only after the men drink the woman/wine that they invent homosexuality. Displaced from the city, then, woman inflicts her sexuality on nature and thus denatures desire among the men who once thought to disown her.

126

Rachilde repeats some of this descriptive technique, and much of this sexual displacement, in "The *Mortis,*" a short story from the 1900 collection *Stories (Contes et nouvelles)*.[16] In this story, the female body appears not only in the feminized description of nature but also within the contradictions between the surface appearance of things and the seething world beneath them that strongly recall the alienation of woman from her body that is one of de Beauvoir's most frequently sounded themes.

"The *Mortis*" begins in similar fashion to "The Harvests of Sodom." An elaborate description of the natural setting precedes the entrance of the human protagonists. In this case, there is only one protagonist, Count Sebastiani Ceccaldo-Rossi, who is not only the "last survivor of the powerful house of Ceccaldo-Rossi" ("dernier survivant de la puissante maison Ceccaldo-Rossi" [59]) but also the last survivor of the plague in fourteenth-century Florence. Tormented by hunger, the Count ventures out of the relative safety of his palace into the nightmare world of the city, overgrown now not with massively "parturient" grapevines but with monstruously reproductive roses.

There are no women in "The *Mortis*"; they have been finished off long before, in the early days of the plague, and are alluded to only in retrospect.

> No woman walked through the city, and rummaging through the heaps of putrefying bodies in the public squares, you would not have exhumed the least little scrap of a skirt. The women had disappeared, leaving no memory of their grace. Had they left perhaps from the very beginning of the scourge? Had they been the very first to die perhaps—of fear—before the plague?[17] (59)

Once again the feminine has been displaced onto the natural world; female desire is metonymically described through the profusion of flowers that cover the dying city as both a raging copulation and a superimposition of beauty on corruption. The result is a grotesque reunion of contradictions, simultaneously exalting and repudiating female desire. The flowers of domestic gardens, for example, are described as passionate women escaping from their familial restraints. "Crazy about their bodies, scrambling up the iron grillwrok, overflowing their bronze urns, dropping down from gilded balconies," they are among the first to participate in the universal nuptuals, to "break their last ties to their patrician class to unite themselves with the vagabond [flowers] in monstrous nuptials" (53). At the same time, however, this vast fornication has a seamy underside: the wildly rampant flowers are "on fire with forbidden perfumes, seasoned by the human compost heap" from which they take their nourishment (53).[18]

Thus the silent earth seethes with sexual processes. It is, however, not only by their vocabulary that Rachilde feminizes the descriptions of the earth in this story. Her marked discordances between surface appearance and underside reality are also displacements of the absent female body, paradigmatic site of division and ambiguity.

Through a wildly overwrought and unabashedly sexual vocabulary Rachilde describes the flowers, and in particular the overgrown roses, as participants in a vast cycle of fornication and birthing. The sustained fever pitch of this prolonged description is perhaps its most remarkable quality:

> In the amorous fire of a June sky, along the still-white steps of staircases falling in ruin toward an Arno that had become almost black, [the] most savage [flowers], warriors already accustomed to obstacles, mounted the assault against the city. . . . the wind of revolt entwined branches to branches, wove garlands, hung crowns of flowers, raised arches of triumph, sang the epithalamion in the middle of the great silence of death.
>
> The roses, mouths of embers, flames of flesh, licking against the incorruptibility of the marble surfaces, splashed the long pure columns up to the very top with stains red as wine, purple as blood, and that at night, made round signs, extravasating in brown, marking the skin of the pale monuments with violet shadows, like the traces of fingers deeply inserted. The roses, on all tonalities, from saffron to the dregs of wine, from furious scarlet to the hues of the tender limbs of newborns, screamed out their deliverance. They were mouths tirelessly open, clamoring cries that one surmised with-

out seeing. They shook, above the open graves, their heavy buds feverishly anxious to bloom, buboes filled to bursting with sap, ready to explode in spurts of pus, and the horrible threat was accomplished in torrents of inebriating odors, violent and exasperated like screams. . . .

A clinging type [of rose] having penetrated the bell tower, having thrown in through the rib of an arch, the forest of its ferocious thorns, clung to the length of a rope, made it sway beneath the weight of its young heads, and when the one hundredth [rose] bloomed, full of dew, a chalice heavy with tears, the rope stiffened, shook . . . one could hear the sound of a bell: the roses were tolling the tocsin! To the fire of the amorous sky was joined the furnace of their passionate odors.[19] (53–55)

Rachilde could hardly be more explicit in her evocation of sexual processes through this insistent vocabulary of grasping and clinging, of invasion and introduction, of climaxes offered or refused, or of sensual avidity represented in the nourishment of the roses likened to newborns, their mouths constantly open for nourishment from the *boutons*—which means both "nipples" and "flower buds"—to which yet other roses are compared.

Perhaps less evident, but equally evocative of female sexuality, is the split in the passage between the surface of the scene and its interior turmoil. The surface calm, beneath which churn the independent forces of nature, suggests the alienation of woman within her own female body. Rachilde's ingenuity is to represent this division between surface and interior by a nearly impossible sensual contrast in which the wind is said to "sing the epithalamion in the middle of the great silence of death." A chanted wedding hymn, noise is equated with sexuality while silence remains associated with death; the difficult simultaneity transforms the silent surface of the printed page into the silent surface of the earth or, by extension, into the silent surface of the female body beneath which nature boils.

The result is a frenetic synaesthesia in the rest of the passage that oscillates constantly from the perceptible to the surmised, from the calm to the turbulent, from the cold indifference of death to the procreative demands of female sexuality. The best example of this synaesthetic frenzy equates hearing with sight: the newborn roses scream out their deliverance, in "cries one surmised without *seeing*" (emphasis added). What is not seen is open to question: it could be the roses, but it is more likely their cries. Finally, the roses that toll the tocsin reunite the two strains of displacement in the story: the displacement of the female body onto nature, and the displacement of sensual processes within the description of nature once it has been feminized. This climactic moment is brought about by the blossoming of the one-hundredth rose in a long chain of roses. At this point the hidden noise of the sexual body rises to the audible surface of the text: Rachilde means for the reader to hear the tocsin ringing. However, that noise is itself immediately displaced onto yet another combination of senses. The sentence that follows veers off into sight and smell and frames the entire description by the imagery it repeats from the opening phrase: "To the fire of the amorous sky was added the furnace of their passionate odors."

The ringing of the tocsin by the twined and interlacing roses announces the ultimate symptom of the neurotic repulsion-attraction complex of feminine sexuality at work in the dénouement of *Monsieur Vénus:* the conviction that sex and death are one. A commonplace in Decadent fiction, the connection between sex and death is particularly evident in much of Rachilde's work. Raoule de Vénérande, as we have seen, cannot fully indulge her ambiguous desire for Jacques until he is dead; in *Madame Adonis,* the restless libertin/libertine Marcelle Desambres (disguised as her brother Marcel) provokes her own murder at the hands of her male lover Louis, who is also the husband of her female lover, Louise. The mirror images of this novel announce a willful confusion of male and female desire, the better to repudiate sexual intercourse in a single murderous act, itself highly sexualized: Louis plunges a dagger into Marcelle/Marcel's breast. The point, once again, is not that one or the other of the poles of heterosexuality be eliminated. Rachilde's concern is instead that the unsayable body enter, however tenuously, into representation through the negation of its potential and shifting opposites.

A negative expression of desire, the sex-death complex is the entire premise of "The *Mortis.*" The grotesquely "natural" couplings that celebrate sexuality as the perverse vitality poured out by the plague, the promiscuous flowers, the marriage of noise and silence, and the jarringly synaesthetic mode of Rachilde's descriptions are all part of this complex. The roses carry the brunt of the association, first by their vocabularly—their *boutons* (nipples for nourishment) are also *boubons* (buboes, or pustules of poison)—and second by their definitive role in the plot. It is exactly this confusion between nourishment and poison that finishes off the Count: having gorged himself on rose petals, he dies.

Sebastiani's extended death scene at the end of the story is characterized by elaborate metonymy and displaced sexuality. The figure of the male introduces a discordant, if fleeting, note of innocence into the plague-ridden and female-dominated nature of the story: yielding to the oppressive heat of the afternoon and falsely reassured by the absence of any other living being in the city, the Count undoes the elaborate armor he had donned for protection and appears "naked like the divine bambino sprung from the loins of the Virgin Mary" (66). This sudden reference to virgin birth makes it abundantly clear that Sebastiani does not fit into the monstrously procreative world that surrounds him; like Jacques Silvert in *Monsieur Vénus* or the youngest brother in "The Harvests of Sodom," his innocence, perceived as such by the marauding female, seals his doom. It does not help his case that Sebastiani is maladroit in handling the one eminently masculine feature remaining to him in his unprotected state—his sword. As he raises his sword to protect his face, Rachilde imagines that the roses, "new women's heads decorating the balconies of Florence, seemed to shiver with modesty and lean over curiously" (66).[20] In this way their petals, which Sebastiani gathers on the tip of his sword and consumes, can literally feed him to death.

The desperate frenzy of Sebastiani's meal of roses quickly deprives him of his innocence; by the time he has tasted the first petals, he is no longer the "divine bambino" but lithe as the *couleuvre*, or serpent, that now fully belongs to this perverse Eden (67). Under these conditions, the female body, round and nourishing, benefits from a series of displacements onto food and drink. Their metonymies determined now by color and shape, the flourishing roses are simultaneously breast and pustule, fruit and fountain in a long stretch of indirect discourse by which Sebastiani consecrates his union with the feminized nature around him:

Flowers, flowers, and still more flowers! . . . If lemons and oranges were lacking, there were yellow roses! If the pomegranates and the melons never ripened, there were purple roses, red roses, pink roses! And if Asti wine did not run in rivers, this year of misfortune, one could breathe its suave and sparkling foam in the delicate aroma of the very smallest white roses, whose buds cracked like nuts beneath one's teeth! [21] (67)

Thus the roses represent the Fatal Woman, in whose embrace is death. Yet there is one more displacement in the story. This final trick of narrative displacement in "The *Mortis*" has to do with the place of the narrator or, more accurately, with her nonplace. Most of the "The *Mortis*" is recounted in the omniscient third person. The final pages, however, which recount Sebastiani's solitary procession through the decaying city, introduce a discordantly subjective voice that solemnly pronounces of the scene, "It was very beautiful" ("C'était très beau" [65]).

The voice is clearly not Sebastiani's; he remains dissociated from the text's point of view until the moment of his sexual union with the flowers, expressed in his poisonous banquet of roses/fruits/breasts. The sudden subjective statement is repeated before the reprise of the objective description: "but along the deserted streets it was even more beautiful" (65).[22] The statement makes it impossible to situate clearly the narrative voice in the story. It has been displaced from its objective or omniscient center to an indeterminate margin of incoherence that can apparently change at will. Thus, if woman's *body* is, by displacement, everywhere in nature, woman's *voice* — that of the "hysteric of letters" who wrote the story — is everywhere and nowhere: it is in nature and in the city, inside and outside the earth, above and within the narration, ultimately ready to pass judgment on the perverse fecundity of the universalized female body, of which it also pronounces, "It was very beautiful."

In this way, Rachilde realizes more fully the process of meaning at work in "The Harvests of Sodom." Her displacements of the female body join with the displacement of the female voice to stake out in "The *Mortis*" a claim to discourse beyond that of either language or the body taken independently of each other. Refusing to reduce the body to language or language to the body, Rachilde asserts the privilege of hysteria as a source and condition of narrative. Epithalamic horror in Rachilde is thus not only a refusal of sex. It is also the series of displacements of female body and voice that keeps the linguistically indomitable body beyond the reach of the discourse of reason.

No End in Sight? Mother's Body and One Last Frog

Limitless displacement, we recall, is the foundation of metonymy in the Lacanian scheme. A group of three stories from Rachilde's *Stories* and *The Demon of the Absurd* center the experience of displacement on the loss of the maternal body. Each of these three stories — "The Hermetic Chateau" ("Le château hermétique"), "The Tooth" ("La dent"), and "The Frog Killer" ("Le tueur de grenouilles") — thus depends on the experience of the incest prohibition to initiate desire for the maternal body. In other words, the maternal body becomes desirable only when it is prohibited; indeed, it is desirable by virtue of being prohibited. For Rachilde, this condition of desire entails a shift in the nature of the displacement we have seen inflicted on the female body: if the body is banished from culture in these stories as it is in "The Harvests of Sodom" and "The *Mortis,*" its entry into nature is not an automatic compensation. Rather, it is the simultaneous relationship of the body to nature *and* culture that stimulates Rachilde's reflections on desire and posits the conditions of meaning in the stories.

Of the three stories, "The Hermetic Chateau" offers perhaps the clearest representation of the creation of desire by the incest prohibition; in this story, the maternal body, emblematic in the hermetically sealed, unapproachable castle of the title, belongs both to nature and to culture. It thus doubly alienates the desire it inspires or discourages, depending on whether it is considered from the point of view of nature — which suggests in remembrance of the primordial mother-child union that one *ought* to be able to attain it — or culture — which resolutely forbids even so much as the attempt.[23]

Visiting in Franche-Comté, the narrator of the story resolves to visit a ruined chateau he perceives at the top of one of the surrounding peaks—despite the insistence of his hosts that the chateau does not really exist, that it is merely a mirage created by the sun at certain moments of the day. He nevertheless persuades his friend Téard to accompany him on an excursion to the chateau, which they never reach. Their journey, moreover, is fraught with mishaps: their descent from the peak is one accident after another, and they arrive at the picnic site where Madame Téard, the friend's mother, awaits them with the unhappy news that all of their provisions have been lost.

Tempted by nature and yet forbidden by law, one cannot return to the original mother-child union. So the narrator's adventure is inscribed within a series of examples of other persons longing for that undefined yet acutely felt "elsewhere" (of the mother's body) of which they have only remnants of consciousness, but where they know they would be at home. The first of these persons was, the first-person narrator recounts,

> a peasant woman of the Limousin, very poor, a bit crazy, whose principal monomania consisted of an eternal need of locomotion. She dreamed of a place where she would have been *better,* where she ought to have *always* lived, and since she had no knowledge of this place that, for all she knew, existed nowhere else than in her head, she used to repeat as an ejaculation: "Ah, how unhappy they are, those people who have no home!"[24] (*Contes* 121; Rachilde's emphasis)

The second, despite her superior sanity and social status, is no less obsessed with the appeal of the enigmatic "elsewhere":

> The other, a Countess de Beaumont-Landry, was hardly crazy, but she spent days dreaming about the *house of her dreams,* and this house did not represent for her a sentimental phase of her youth: it was *really, sincerely,* a dwelling built somewhere. . . . No paintings or engravings could give her any more precise indications, but she knew that that house was *over there* and that her place, coddled society lady that she was, was laid out for her in this modest place of rest. [25] (121–22; Rachilde's emphasis)

The Epithalamic Horror

This sense of eternal displacement is praised by the narrator in terms that seem a displacement of Rachilde's own style; instead of Rachilde, one might now be reading Baudelaire, Verlaine, or Jean Lorrain, as her narrator inquires, "If there is the *sister soul,* whom one seeks through all the disapointments and crimes of love, could there not also be the *brother country,* without which one is not happy in life, one cannot obtain a peaceful end?" (122; Rachilde's emphasis). The narrator goes on to speculate that the longed-for *là-bas*—"over there," or "elsewhere"—is also the place of one's very own predestined tomb (123), encountered with great joy but on rare occasions. Far more frequently, it remains elusive: "Often, also, in ecstasy before this country, we see it suddenly back away, melt away, fade away. It flees from us, abandons us, and for a reason we shall never know, for undoubtedly, *it is too frightening,* we divine that we will not reach it, that this promised land will be eternally kept away from us" (124; Rachilde's emphasis).[26]

As we have noted, this prospect of irrecuperable exile from the mother's body, worded as banishment from the ideal house, country, or tomb, is nearly pure Lacanian metonymy, expressing the eternally receding displacement of desire. The miragelike nature of the chateau to which the narrator aspires, however (it is seen most clearly when he is farthest from it, and it disappears as he approaches), clearly posits nature and culture as complicitous in the inspiration of desire. Culture is the only condition by which nature can be perceived, or in terms of the protagonist's quest for the maternal body, desire is desire only when it is most clearly opposed to its object by the irremediable barrier of the incest prohibition.

The incest taboo first appears in the story by the comparison of the "elsewhere" with a sister soul or a brother country; the intimacy thus implied is tempting—the narrator considers it a "natural" desire—but it is obviously limited by the cultural prohibition against desiring one's sister or brother. As the narrator's personal "elsewhere," the chateau remains out of reach for exactly the same reason; the incest prohibition is that "too frightening reason" imposed by culture, which renders his attempted return to the mother's body not only impossible but both pleasing (because "natural") and horrible (because forbidden) to contemplate. Thus the experience of the chateau is a paradoxically "real chimera"; the oxymoron expresses the impossibility of return to the original

135

object of desire, experienced and lost before the advent of any language that could have preserved it as integral and unambiguous: "And here is what I want to relate *in all sincerity,*" he writes, "about one of these chimerical countries that I *in all reality* found along my route" (124; Rachilde's emphasis).[27]

The foregone impossibility of the return condemns the narrator to the wandering and constant deviations that are not only the plot of the story (the impossibility of reaching the chateau) but, once again, part and parcel of Rachilde's descriptions. The chateau is said to be one with the rock from which it looms; its imposing, unconstructed aspect contrasts sharply with the cultivated countryside before it; it opposes the picture-postcard Swiss village complete with its "unpretentious bell tower, rounded off like an aspergillum, and the vineyard, with its smattering of peasants in smocks and women in bright skirts" (125). Constructed and unconstructed, natural and yet a fact of culture, the chateau, like the mother's body, resists all attempts to penetrate it. The narrator's urgent desire to "enter the chateau that I saw and that *existed* because I *had seen it!*" (132; Rachilde's emphasis) is opposed to his desperate observation that he had before him only "the rock, still the rock, shining, sweating, without a crack, without a hole" (132). Thus the two adventurers encounter the inevitability of the eternal displacement as they turn round and round the rock-chateau, increasingly aware that "*it was always farther away than we thought*" (128; Rachilde's emphasis) and that "we kept going astray, in spite of ourselves" (130).[28]

There is a second maternal figure in the story, however: Madame Téard, the mother of the narrator's companion. If the chateau figures as the natural mother to whom one is lured *because* of the incest taboo, Madame Téard is the cultural mother strictly circumscribed by this prohibition. There is no thought of scaling *her* in the story; in fact, this "exquisite, sensible old woman" ("exquise vieille femme raisonnable") cannot even imagine the chateau-mirage. "For my part, . . . I have often tried to make out the chateau," she explains to the narrator, "and I have not been able to distinguish the least little turret!" (127).[29] Whatever "natural" mother there is about her Rachilde promptly undermines: charged with providing the picnic food for the excursion, Madame Téard has to give up her nourishing role when she allows the provisions to be stolen by a wild dog. Her role as the mother prohibited by culture is clearly the more important. Not only does she not see the chateau, but she repeats the incest prohibition in the brief story she tells of a previous failure to conquer the chateau. Attempting to dissuade the narrator (and her own son!) from their quest, she tells of

> a draftee who had talked about getting some buzzard eggs out of their nest, up there, before joining his regiment, and since he was drunk the morning he attempted the ascent, he fell head over heels from your famous chateau back down to his cottage. If he did not find the buzzard eggs, he nonetheless found the police station when reporting for duty, because the simpleton had been laid up and had missed the first roll call.[30] (127)

The point of Madame Téard's story is the punishment inflicted on the witless soldier for his silly belief that he could actually scale the maternal chateau. In the narrator's failure to do the same, repression becomes the single most important determinant of his desire. As the group is safely dining at home on the evening of the expedition, the mirage reappears to the narrator more clearly and more alluringly than ever before. "Over there . . . over there," the narrator writes, "a diabolical play of purple lights, of violet shadows, brought back the ruins of the feudal castle. I made out more clearly than ever the dungeons, the rampart walk, the crenelles; and more formidably than ever, there rose, in the blood of the dying day, the *Hermetic Chateau,* the unknown homeland to which my heart was drawn" (134–35).[31] It is only by consenting to its loss that the narrator can clearly apprehend the ultimate and unobtainable object of his desire; it is only through his acquiescence to the *here* of culture that his vision of an elsewhere, of a contradictory *over there* of an inaccessible nostalgia, is restored to him, allowing him—in fact condemning him—to continue to exist in prey to a state of desire.

In contrast to the impenetrable female surfaces of "The Hermetic Chateau," "The Tooth" opens up feminine space. But it does so in order to destroy it as an object of desire. Here the physical disintegration of the female, expressed as the sudden loss of a tooth, is experienced as sexual horror and proximity to death. Instead of the unscalable surface of the maternal body withheld by the incest taboo and thus made an object of desire, the heroine of "The Tooth" is a fissured being for whom no place exists any longer within culture.

"The Tooth" brings the internal warring forces of the female body to bear on the the previously intact surface. Losing a tooth as she bites into a pistachio, the heroine, Bichette, is both revolted and incredulous. "Eaten away, but for how long? Attacked by what?" she asks in panic. "At first that caused her no suffering," the narration continues, "and now she finds herself plunged into one of those despairs that are no less terrible for lasting only one day: from now on she has a flaw!" (*Demon* 99).[32]

The newfound flaw is replete with sexual connotations: the lost tooth leaves a hole in the mouth that the victim's tongue will incessantly probe, and the tooth itself is reminiscent of Jean Lorrain's decapitated heads: it is a "little corpse" ("petite morte") in itself (102), "crowned by a dark border at the broken end" (99). The new opening "on the side, just behind the smile" (98) turns the heroine's mouth into a sort of powerless *vagina edentula* within which there echoes the refrain, "You are no longer whole!" (103). The yawning gap, moreover, is experienced as "a door just opened onto her thoughts, and she will no longer be able to keep back certain words which will spring, against her will, out of her mouth" (99).[33]

The heroine's empty mouth is a gap that will not be filled precisely because it is so openly offered. With nothing to prohibit desire, it has nothing to provoke it either. Even God no longer desires Bichette. For years, it had been her practice to avoid sleeping with her husband on the nights before she was to take Communion, thereby preserving all of her libidinal energy for the encounter with the sacred. After losing her tooth, however, she is horrified to discover that she can barely swallow the Host:

> she feels, she *sees* that God has paused. . . . He is not used to this yet, and is caught on a corner, next to the little breach! . . . In a panic she leaves the Holy Table, wishing sacrilegiously to spit in spite of her fervor. . . . Then, with a brutal thrust of her tongue, she detaches [the Host] and it is immediately swallowed; God disappears,

is swallowed up as if he were afraid, after seeing.[34] (106; Rachilde's emphasis)

From the single gap opened in the body by the loss of the tooth, there flow simultaneously life, language, and the sexual power to fascinate. Significantly, the image of a chateau reappears in "The Tooth" to compare Bichette not to the impregnable façade of "The Hermetic Chateau" but to all that is open and openly decrepit, well past its sexual prime: "she has suddenly, poor woman, the totally absurd vision of a ruined chateau she had contemplated long ago, on her wedding trip. Yes . . . she perceives the tower, over there, a tower sporting at its summit a crenelated crown and that stands out against the storm clouds as the uneven jawline of an outsized aged woman" (101).[35]

Bichette ends up burying her fallen tooth in the ground, like the "little corpse" she has felt it to be. The dirt remaining beneath her fingernails after this operation suggests that she is somehow between nature and culture: too openly available to be defended by the incest prohibition, she is no longer desirable. Unlike the façade of the "hermetic chateau," there is no barrier of repression that would place Bichette on either side of the nature/culture opposition.

Because this barrier is, in the Lacanian scheme, the necessary precondition for language, Bichette's loss of sexuality is also a loss of her power over language. In "The Hermetic Chateau," the narrator complains that the right word, had he only known it, might have breeched the impenetrable castle, with its "mute, blind façade, the threatening façade par excellence, the hermetic façade" (130). However, Téard "assured me we would not have the last word on this damnable rock" (130).[36] In "The Tooth," Bichette's exclusion from language is made evident by a series of puns on the word *tooth* itself, which her damaged body forces her not to "get."

To understand a pun is to demonstrate one's familiarity with the symbolic functions of language. A pun on *tooth,* for example, depends on the listener's knowing that there may be more than just physical teeth involved; thus, the pun shows language functioning at yet another remove from the physical experience of the body. Bichette's sense of her body, however, exacerbated by the loss of her tooth, prevents her from recognizing this symbolic distance and obliges her to take the puns literally. So, as the gap in her dentition prevents her from laughing, "it is already so long past, that time when she could laugh unrestrainedly"—literally, "with all her teeth" ("c'est déjà tellement loin, l'heure où elle riait de toutes ses dents" [100]). A second pun by her husband is more serious, throwing her into a nervous convulsion by evoking the exact opposite of her loss. Her husband uses the French expression "garder une dent," or "to keep a tooth" (for "to hold a grudge"), to describe his running quarrel with a neighbor (104).

With Bichette, Rachilde seems to be asking whether it is possible to be just a body with no symbolic function attaching to it. Missing a tooth, Bichette's body does not figure anything; it will not be long until the rest of it follows the tooth into dust. In this way, the story is almost the exact opposite of the last one to be considered here: "The Frog Killer," in which the maternal body is imagined to be accessible only through excess of symbolic function grafted on it. Thus the latter story picks up where "The Tooth" leaves off in the meditation on the role of the pun in the differentiation of the body from language: in "The Frog Killer," the misperception of figurative language becomes a perverse solution to the prohibition of desire for the mother by crudely identifying the mother with the metaphor.

First, however, a word about the genders of *frog*. Jean Lorrain's bullfrog was most often given as the masculine noun *crapaud;* Rachilde prefers the feminine *grenouille* for the story that occupies in her collection the same privileged place of horror that "The Mask" does in Lorrain's. The biological differences between these two types of frogs is less significant than the gender difference. If Rachilde opts for the feminine, she does so evidently because her frog is destined to represent the body of the mother, figuratively raped (as a body and as a figure of speech) in "The Frog Killer" as a symbolic refusal of the incest prohibition. The destruction of the maternal body becomes here the dream of an impossible language, of a language that would venture beyond metonymy in an effort to establish consistency with the original, nurturing body. As the incest prohibition, however, installs signification by repressing the desire for the mother, the violation of the primordial cultural taboo sets language at odds with culture, creating an illusory, parodic coincidence of the body, language, and desire whose power to shock is no less compelling than that of Lorrain's blinded and bloody *crapaud.*

The Epithalamic Horror

The Toniot family—composed of Toniot *père*, his spouse, and Toniot *fils*—is depicted from the outset as extracultural if not anticultural. They are poor and isolated; they live outside the bounds of the city; Toniot *père* makes their living by trapping without a permit. As for Toniot *fils,* the protagonist of the story: "He lived like an animal, going, coming, eating, sleeping, saying nothing" (*Contes* 82).[37] In fact, the animal to which he is compared is none other than the frog, scion of the male version that so tormented Lorrain. Beating him for having surprised her illicit sexual activity, Toniot's mother curses him as the "seed of a bullfrog" ("graine de crapaud" [86]). The term, still in the masculine, is further associated with the childish penis that the adolescent Toniot protects from his mother's blows:

> Squatting on his sheet, checking for injuries on his little burning limbs that will have turned blue by morning, the boy contemplated the female with an air of suffering curiosity, protecting his little sex with his left hand, for he well suspected that if she hit him there again that would be the end of his *little bullfrog,* who would give a little squeak and be dead.[38] (88; Rachilde's emphasis)

The comparison of Toniot *fils* to the frog is the beginning of the morbid pun on which the plot of the story and the son's paradoxically anticultural discourse will be based. Before this, however, the woman, all-powerful over her son, also holds the power of language. She complains that her husband refuses to speak to her and that he has passed on to their son this eminently male legacy of mutism: "he gave her a son," the narrator explains, "and she would have preferred a daughter, that is, an ally, an accomplice, a more supple creature capable of appreciating all the vapid phrases that escape from mouths driven to exasperation by days of rain" (90). The incomprehensibility of her men makes them "wicked," the woman laments to one of her few rare visitors, "so wicked, Madame, that they flap their beaks without ever saying anything!" (91).[39]

The language barrier between mother and son gives rise to the serious misinterpretations from which the story proceeds. For Toniot *fils,* the problem is to discern figurative from literal language. Concerned that someone has been stealing onions from their garden at night, Toniot *fils* resolves to "surveiller leurs oignons," that is, to "watch over their onions." His literal use of the figurative expression for "to mind someone's business" (in French, "to watch over their onions") blinds him to the fact that *no one* is stealing these particular onions: his mother has been giving them away to her lover, a voluble salesman, in exchange for his linguistic and sexual favors. The child's most serious misapprehension, however, confuses the literal and the figurative uses of the word *frog*—this time, the feminine, maternal *grenouille*—to the point of losing all reference to the real. As Toniot *fils* attempts to track down the onion thief in the middle of the night, he discovers instead his mother in the arms of the salesman, looking very much indeed like a frog: "What he sees, oh, he'll never forget it now, because it's too funny! He sees a great white frog, yes, that's it, that marvelous flexibility of the open thighs and arms, that precise and elastic stretching of limbs so pale they appear to be silver" (94–95).[40]

Sexual and linguistic acculturation—the repression of desire that would have, in Lacan, granted him access to the symbolic exchange of language—would have permitted Toniot *fils* to recognize his mother in the figurative *grenouille* thus seen exercising in the moonlight. Instead, his desire, unbound by culture, causes him to take quite literally the figurative *frog*. As a result, his entire experience becomes suffused by the figurative, henceforth to be misunderstood as the "real": "Now, he understands why they call him a bullfrog, it's because he really is the son of a [mother] frog" (95).[41]

Toniot *père* kills the mother-frog in a fit of jealous rage and is arrested and imprisoned for his crime. In his absence, Toniot *fils* accedes to the place of the stubbornly silent hunter, beyond the bounds of the city and its civilization. More important, however, his confusion between the literal and the figurative places him squarely outside the bounds of language. Unable to distinguish the maternal body from the frog, for example, he even wonders why murder should be considered a crime: "Dang!" he reflects, "there are so many more . . . *frogs* than men, anyone can see that" (98; Rachilde's emphasis).[42]

As the title predicts, Toniot *fils* becomes a killer of frogs in his own right. Each frog killed repeats the crime of the mother's sexuality that both attracts and repels her son. This time, however, it is the son who is in control; access to the maternal body is freely granted by the frogs, but only on condition that the mother remain always and everywhere a perverted figure of speech. For it is undeniable that Toniot *fils* can attract the frog-body as much as it attracts him. Time after time, he throws out his bait, "a little scrap of red sheet as long as a woman's tongue" (102–3),[43] only to discover

> there they are falling all over themselves, the poor little monsters, just to look at the red tongue the man is sticking out at them from the tip of his goddammed string. It is the chimera's tongue of fire! They fascinated [him], these charmers, little sirens, and now in his turn, he fascinates them. The stick comes up, the string whips through space, and one hears an atrocious cry of a bird being plucked alive. The frog, overly curious, is seized by the double bait that, from afar, looks like an anchor of safety. She flails her little hind legs like the legs of a girl being raped.[44] (104)

As the rape metaphor continues, so does the sense of freedom, clearly related to sexual liberty and pleasure, enjoyed by Toniot *fils:*

> No, no longer can anyone prevent him from eating his fill, from living. He is free.
>   Kneeling before the pile of little corpses, he undresses them, takes out the double ring of their golden eyes, takes off their pretty green satin dresses, their adorable white velvet panties. All that slides off pell-mell like doll's clothes, and all that remains are the little naked thighs, very pale, shaken with nervous spasms.[45] (105)

The voyeuristic slowness of this ending description accounts in large part for the lurid chill it evokes. Horror, as we saw with Lorrain's *crapaud*, poisoning the waters from which the young boy drank, is not only a matter of the unexpected; it is a creation of deliberate pacing as well. Thus this particular strip is clearly a tease. In this sensational prelude to rape, the actions may be presented as successive, but they do not constitute a syntagm or progress through a plot line so much as they repeat each other, sounding so many carefully crafted synonyms for violation.

This could bring us back to the return of the repressed in Lorrain's *crapaud,* except for one simple thing: Rachilde's motherly *grenouille* shows us that Toniot *fils* has never known the initial repression that would have permitted culturally acceptable language, separated mother from son and the maternal body from the figurative frog. Thus Toniot *fils's* discourse of desire is most chilling for the depths of incoherence that open up beneath it, careening downward to the origins of the primary process itself. Imagining itself exactly coextensive with the maternal body, this discourse does indeed bring to an end the shifts and displacements that so plagued the protagonists of the preceding stories. But it does so at a horrible price. The mother's body must be made to subsist indefinitely as a misinterpreted figure of speech — "mother" most fully available as a metaphor taken literally.

In *Feminist Novelists of the Belle Epoque,* Jennifer Waelti-Walters observes that "energy is certainly not lacking in Rachilde's novels, and plausibility is not a concern. [Her novels] are deliberately nightmarish parodies of male and female attitudes toward sexuality and marriage" (158–59). What is implausible in "The Frog Killer" — and thus source of its power to shock — is the very language it uses; its parodic intent is directed not toward such higher "forms" of sexual expression as object choices and marriage but toward the very foundation of desire. Toniot *fils* will not give up the mother, even if — or especially if? — that refusal denies him access to culture. Can it be really so bad to continually misinterpret one's metaphors, or is such misinterpretation always in some sense a rape, a forcing of the sexual boundaries by which culture and language strive to keep desire in check?

An antisocial parody of the mother-child relationship, the discourse of Toniot *fils* can be read only as a parody of language. Denying the support of language in the experience of repression, "The Frog Killer" dreams of a paradoxically anticultural language, a language perched constantly, for want of repression, on the brink of its self-annihilation. This language is the discourse of reason turned exactly on its head — trump card, perhaps, of the "hysteric of letters" who would have sensed, given the chance, that Dora had no choice but to simply slither away.

6

Neurosis and
Nostalgia

"Decadent"
Desire?

In his 1980 Goncourt Prize–winning novel, *Le jardin d'ac-climatation* (*Cronus' Children* in Howard Girven's 1986 translation), Yves Navarre suggests the bankruptcy of psychoanalysis as meta-language in the late twentieth century. "The murder of the father," an eldest son explains to his girlfriend, "this lovely Oedipus so much in style this century, is only one more idea to shore up the family as it is, to reinforce the idea it has and always will have of itself" (281–82; my translation). Navarre's thesis is that in our time psychoanalysis has become so much a part of everyday discourse that it has lost its explanatory power, its astonishing ability to change things in the psyche just by talking about them. No longer a means of evasion from society, the family, and conventional language, psychoanalysis is demystified in Navarre; for him, it entails the weary acceptance of the status quo against the allure of the unknown, the repressed, the unconscious. For Navarre, the real revolution is silence.

Navarre's attempts to debunk psychoanalysis serve a specific purpose within a body of fiction that he intends as an explicit rejection of bourgeois society.[1] The rejection of psychoanaylsis is certainly not unique to Navarre among late twentieth-century writers and, indeed, is an important organizing principle for his work. Yet one cannot help feeling that Navarre is *too* disabused of psychoanalysis; his personal quarrel with language and society obscures the fact that much more remains to be said about the kinds of evasion permitted by psychoanalytic language, particularly in its confrontation with literature.

Neurosis and Narrative

The French Decadence and Freud's first glimmerings of psychoanalysis entered Western culture in virtual lockstep with each other. Clearly, my account of this nearly simultaneous emergence has not been rigorously historical; I have been tempted not so much by questions of mutual influence as by the temporal coincidence of two discourses — Freud's and the Decadents' — that share a common interest in neurosis and that express this interest in narrative, whether or not they set out explicitly to do so. What I see in between the writings of Freud and the Decadence is thus a fascinating symbiosis, expressed as a double-edged appeal to the imaginative and the empirical, to the literary and the scientific, to the wish to be ill and to the desire to cure. Further, their common recourse to elaborately managed rhetorical structures make both eminently rereadable in the terms proposed by Lacanian textual criticism: if the signs of neurosis can be thought of as signifiers that, by the very nature of the unconscious, must behave like the signifiers of language, the vagaries of that behavior are apt to obtain in similar ways whether one is reading Freud or Proust, Lorrain or Rachilde. My purpose here has been to propose one more level of analysis, moving from the structures of language to those of narrative: if the unconscious is indeed structured like a language, narrative — particularly if it calls itself Decadent — ought to be analyzable in its structures and technical features according to the rhetorical terms Freud and Lacan brought to bear on mental (dys)function.

My analyses of stories by Proust, Lorrain, and Rachilde have attempted to demonstrate certain precise and original ways in which narrative patterns can be constructed out of moments of trauma, experimented with and then finely honed to meet the technical demands of the short story. For Proust, in his long period of hesitation before *Remembrance of Things Past*, *Pleasures and Regrets* offers a reassuring fetish presence against the prospect of his never becoming a writer at all, thus against the threat of his premature death as a writer, which the demands of his father to choose a career unmask as the threat of castration. The book holds out this fetish presence in two ways: first by its lavish physical existence (with all the ambiguities of its financing: Proust or his father?) and second by the solutions Proust devises within it to the necessity of creating probable, "realist" plots. These solutions, moreover, turn in large part on his increasing ability throughout the work to transfer the fascination with the fetish from the level of the author to that of the characters.

Jean Lorrain's various frogs and masked figures guarantee that the ambiguities of childhood experience—ambiguities concentrated in the equivocations of the signifier—will be preserved in adult perception. When the childhood repressed returns in his work as descriptive technique, it disrupts the conventions of realist metonymy to re-create the experience of horror as fragmention of the perceptual field and as the type of emigration of the signifier across the signifying field that I have referred to as "cross-marking." Thus the reference of the figure in Lorrain is not to the "real" but to the enduring effects of trauma by which his protagonists and narrators define their subjectivity. In "The Student's Tale" and "Sea-Green Eyes," the very experience of desire is a sufficient experience of trauma to make the repressed return with a vengeance, ultimately subordinating narrative logic to the circular terms of self-containment imposed by the primary process.

One of the most prolific of the female Decadents, Rachilde sees the female body and its attractive/repulsive fecundity everywhere around her. Yet she anticipates the most unforgiving mystery of psychoanalysis—the existence of the female as an unstable opposition to the male—by declining to represent the maternal body in any other way than by its unavailability. Its displacement onto the natural world is at once a despairing view from the boundary lines of culture and a mocking challenge to the very existence of that boundary. In Rachilde, then, we encounter the strangest phenomenon of all: desire rendered hideously quiescent in "The Frog Killer" by a barely tenable equation between mother's "real" body and figurative language. That equation is all the more chilling for being devised in opposition to the act of repression by which language is taken to come into being. If Rachilde's prose makes us queasy, it does so not just because it is lurid language from the ink-stained hand of a woman of letters. Rather, it does so because she imagines doing away with repression in such a way as to pose an unsettling enigma: Does the repression of repression bring us closer to the body and to nature, or does it only drive us further and further into language and the figure?

In speaking of the use of psychoanalytic constructs as technical determinants within the short stories, I used the term *constructed*.

That is perhaps an unfortunate choice of vocabulary, since it implies an intentionality that I would in no way wish to defend. It is more than vaguely ridiculous to ask, for example, whether Proust had any idea he was using the fetish to such effect in *Pleasures and Regrets,* or whether Lorrain any more than Rachilde was engaged in deliberate repressions and returns thereof. The point, after all, is that literary criticism, not unlike psychoanalysis, takes as its task to bring to light what seems hidden beneath or between the signifiers of a discourse: the text for the critic, the patient's speech for the analyst. So if the critic is to discount intentionality in stories for which psychoanalytic analysis is deemed valid, the question of interpretive hubris can be addressed to him or her in terms similar to those that critics have used in addressing Freud: How do you know that this is how things really are here? Do we not stand accused in turn of not fully listening to Dora?

I do not think it begs the question to substitute an intentionality of reading for the dead issue of an intentionality of writing. In defending my "evolutionary" reading of Proust, through which I have allowed the sequence of the stories in *Pleasures and Regrets* to represent increasing mastery of Proust's narrative voice, I suggested that the choice to read in or out of sequence (as is the reader's prerogative in a short story collection) tells us as much about the process of reading as it does about the stories themselves. As is obvious by the page numbers of my citations, I did not discuss Lorrain's or Rachilde's stories in either published or chronological order, yet they, too, by the demands of critical exegesis, demonstrate a certain crescendo: in Lorrain, one goes from the masks to the source of their horror in the frog to the logical outcome of that horror in the subjective return of the repressed as the determinant of narrative coherence. In Rachilde, the conditions of meaning, reliant on the female body, are most fully realized—if through grotesque parody—in the untenable mother metaphor of "The Frog Killer."

Bastard fiction, then, produced by "bad" boy and girl authors and read by a critic with suspicious motives . . . or perhaps, my motives are not so suspicious after all, since the most interesting question posed by the refusal of sequential reading is that of closure. When the problem of closure is left to the reader, it seems to me that reading becomes most productively self-reflexive. At the risk of reintroducing the problem of hubris, Lacan's technique of the variable analytic hour suggests how variations on closure do not force meaning so much as force it into the open. In his discussion of language and psychoanalysis known as the *Discours de Rome*, or "The Function and Field of Speech and Language in Psychoanalysis," Lacan writes,

> it is the psychoanalyst who knows better than anyone else that the question is to understand which "part" of [the patient's] discourse carries the significative term, and this is, ideally, just how he proceeds: he takes the description of an everyday event for a fable addressed to whoever hath ears to hear, a long tirade for a direct interjection, or on the other hand a simply *lapsus* for a highly complex statement, or even the sigh of a momentary silence for the whole lyrical development it replaces.
>
> It is, therefore, a beneficent punctuation, one which confers its meaning on the subject's discourse. This is why the adjournment of a session—which according to present-day technique is simply a chronometric break and, as such, a matter of indifference to the thread of the discourse—plays the part of a metric beat which has the full value of an actual intervention by the analyst for hastening the concluding moments.[2] (*Ecrits: A Selection* 43–44)

For Lacan, this "metric" punctuation allows a real measure of contact between analyst and patient, as well as with the work of psychoanalytic interpretation itself. Similarly, creating closure as one reads heightens the sense of contact with the work of interpretation that goes on in criticism. The reflection thus engendered on the activity of meaning making is only enhanced when the critical framework, moreover, is known to be mined—when, in other words, it not so much "applied" to the literary text as interrogated by a parallel discourse that evinces similar rhetorical strategies.

If the property of the signifier is to play across the field in which it finds itself—and Lorrain, of all our authors, seemed closest to this realization—then critical reading must know itself to be provisional. Reading short story collections in disrupted sequence against such a discourse of incompleteness as psychoanalysis seems an ideal way to remind the critic that reading as the creation of meaning is also the creation of lapsus and gap from which new readings will spring. Thus I do not claim that my readings of Proust, Lorrain, or Rachilde should be accepted as "normative," though clearly I think they offer something new to our understanding of neurosis and Decadence: that is, that narrative technique, and not just Decadent language or its themes, substantiates the claims of this literature to plunge its roots deeply into neurosis.

I make this point in explicit response to a question that has nagged me throughout my study of the Decadence and psycho-analysis. The question comes from a 1974 essay on "Decadent Style," in which Gayatri Chakravorty Spivak asks whether Decadent writing is not rather too exemplary of literary processes to be set apart from other types of writing. In other words, given that all literary language displays some degree of artificiality, Spivak wonders why "Decadent" artificiality should remain a separate category.

> My reading has shown that the reference to artifice is a valid and isolatable characteristic of some literary language. I would advance another step. Such a characteristic, undermining the comfortable faith in words' reference to things, takes its place with the becoming-self-conscious of the ruptures and discontinuities of literary language. Yet another step and I face the uneasy question, Why keep the old normative label—decadent style—at all. (233)

Spivak's conclusion is that it should *not* be kept other than in the critic's "cabinet of period pieces" (233). I would of course disagree because it seems to me now that the question has been poorly posed at the outset. The measure of a "neurotic" literature is not the artificiality of its style, although certainly the Decadents cultivated this artificiality as a precious part of their post-Romantic aesthetic heritage. Such a literature is more properly measured, I would suggest, through the very kinds of confrontation it invites: between the discourses of the physician and the poet, the psychoanalytic and the literary.

Neurosis and Nostalgia

This kind of confrontation returns us fruitfully as well to the criticism of psychoanalysis by Navarre. Psychoanalysis and Decadence, read in fighting tandem, return each other to the anticonventionality of their respective roots. Freud, we now say, wrote in opposition to his patients (especially Dora), but he also wrote against the establishment; the rhetorical strategies that enabled him to do so with such effectiveness were clearly akin to those that enabled him to stand his new mode of inquiry on its feet in the first place. Similarly, the aim of the Decadents was to confront bourgeois society with the dark depths of the psyche that they could only hope would rise up to submerge the banality of mass production, the Republic, and the emerging consumer society. In this case, the most instructive, and anticonventional, of the Decadents has to also be the most self-affirmingly hysterical, Rachilde herself: her impossible but alluring coincidences between culture and the pre-Oedipal, language and the primary process, would, if realized, allow us talking exiles from Mother to dream of a way to finally have our cake and eat it, too.

In the essay that I cited earlier, "Reading the Mother Tongue: Psychoanalytic Feminist Criticism," Jane Gallop refers briefly to the attraction of the primary process for the literary critic. "Those of us who are attracted to psychoanalytic theory may be particularly susceptible to the mother's charming figure," she writes, "the dream of the mother without otherness" (136). She is speaking about what elsewhere in the essay she calls the "fascination" of the pre-Oedipal "realm of fusion and indifferentiation" that is felt, in some feminist psychoanalytic criticism, to hold the key to the critique of patriarchal (post-Oedipal) language and culture (134).

I suspect that Gallop is right about the fascination of the pre-Oedipal, though I agree with her less to enter into the political critique of patriarchy than to insist once again on the unsurprising source of my attraction to the Decadents: where else can we fantasize so freely the preexistence of the very structures from which we take our breath—language, literature, culture?

The beauty of the Decadence is that its writers took their phantasms so *literally*. Turning them into literary artifacts of rare precision and candid inventiveness, the Decadence offered them as examples of the highest art it was given to the human psyche to invent. Despite its morbid and rarefied sexuality, its loud exaltation of vice and its alleged preference for evil, the arabesques of language and image make Decadent fiction, in a deep sense, child's play. So is the intensity of their call for the end of culture. Whatever the will to subversion in Proust's use of Tolstoy or Rachilde's overly maternal Mother Earth, whatever the will to perversion in Lorrain, the texts we have examined all seem retrospectively imbued with a certain fundamental, childlike naïveté. They are ignorant of trench warfare and mustard gas, concentration camps and atomic bombs, at the threshold of the century, our own, which Lawrence Langer has called the "age of atrocity." Through its language raised to high artifice and its repudiation of the psychic censor, Decadent fiction is attractive by its easy reconciliation of the pairs of opposites whose actualization could only properly be called atrocious: the seductive barbarian who would now come to destroy a society worn out by its own evolution would take the irreducible form of a poisonous mushroom cloud.

The Decadence is child's play, but by dint of the primary process, it is child's play of the highest and most serious order. At the time of this writing, my two-and-a-half-year-old son has just discovered monsters. So his feet must always be well tucked in at night to ward off the potential arrival of elephants and tigers, and, of course, the big bad wolf. In my maternal persona I reassure him there are no animals anywhere near, but I tuck his feet in just in case; just as I will tuck my own in later, *just in case*. The lure of the Decadence, I think, is precisely this just-in-case of the primary process: what if there were no secondary revision? What if the monsters got out? It is absolutely thrilling to be scared so seriously—to explain in elaborate critical language that Mother's body, after all, is always just behind the next door.

Notes
Bibliography
Index

Notes

1. Neurosis and Narrative: Principles and Strategies

1. Gearhart bases her study on the "countertransference" by which Lacan says Freud disentangled himself from the processes of identification that Dora's transferences imposed on him. Gearhart argues against such a "transcendent" Freud who would have produced a classically rational, scientific analysis of Dora, despite the manner in which his complicity with her and the adults around her compromised his objectivity. Thus she accuses Lacan of wanting to have it both ways—to wish to demonstrate the tenuousness of Freud's narration while crediting the final product with the irrefutability of scientific discourse. "Though for Lacan," Gearhart writes, "the place designated by Freud's name is empty, it nonetheless comports all the guarantees of the formal coherence of the work that the classical subject does. It is only in the name of such a subject that Lacan can claim to synthesize the conflicts left unresolved by the case" (126). Her own position is that the dual themes of female homosexuality and transference in the case make it fundamentally unresolvable within the terms imposed on it by both Freud and Lacan. Lacan's analysis of the Dora case is "L'intervention sur le transfert," *Ecrits* 215–26.

2. See Carter's *Idea of Decadence* as well as Koenraad W. Swart's *Sense of Decadence in Nineteenth Century France* and Richard Gilman's *Decadence: The Strange Life of an Epithet*. Though inexact, the appeal of the analogy with Rome lingers. Thomas Couture's large and lurid painting *Les Romains de la décadence* (*The Romans of the Decadence*), for example, occupies a prominent place in the main hall of the Musée d'Orsay in Paris.

3. In "On the Nature of Human Thought: The Primary and the Secondary Processes as Exemplified by the Dream and Other

Psychic Productions," Robert Fliess explains why, in terms of these two processes, "it is impossible to diagnose anyone as psychotic or neurotic from his dreams." The dream state is given over in all persons to the primary process, so that labels such as "sane" and "insane," "well" and "ill" fail to apply. Fliess writes, "We all develop—when dreaming—a nocturnal psychosis and perform like psychotics; we hallucinate, we indulge in delusions, and our thought largely follows the primary process because the id prevails upon the dreaming ego to an extent to which it cannot prevail ordinarily when we are awake" (214). Fliess distinguishes seven characteristics of the primary process: symbolization, picturization, condensation, allusion, the representation of the whole through a part (*pars pro toto*), concretization, and representation through opposites. Contemporary psychoanalytic literary theory confines itself largely to speaking of condensation and displacement as the chief characteristics of the primary process. It is taken as a given that the dream is concrete and pictorial, and the processes of condensation and displacement are taken to cover the other categories of allusive or contiguous representation.

4. The formulations from "Linguistique et poétique" are as follows: "la fonction poétique projette le principe d'équivalence de l'axe de la sélection sur l'axe de la combinaison" (220), and "En poésie, où la similarité est projetée sur la contiguïté, toute métonymie est légèrement métaphorique, toute métaphore a une teinte métonymique" (238).

5. In "Lacan, Poe, and Narrative Repression," Robert Con Davis offers a reading of "The Tell-Tale Heart" that illustrates the Lacanian concept of metaphor as a continual substitution of one signifier for another, repressed signifier. Working from the example of the metaphor "Moriarty is a snake," Davis writes, "we can . . . surmise that 'snake' forms a chain of association with an array of similar nouns—lizard, reptile, etc. At the same time we can posit that a 'repressed' term, one left out of the utterance, exists in a separate chain, say, of human character descriptions. We can identify the sentence's missing term (arbitrarily) as 'untrustworthy.' Further, 'snake' and 'untrustworthy' are signifiers that could fit in many other possible chains, the total system of which would be quite literally impossible to trace. However, we can speculate that there is a substitution taking place already in the original sentence that allows

156

'snake' to stand in for (or for something similar to) 'untrustworthy,' a metaphorical sutstitution of one term for another: a word in one chain takes another's place in a different chain" (989). In Davis's view, Lacan's chief contribution to literary theory has been the concept of text as "an economy of conscious and unconscious systems in various stages of disunity—a text/system governed . . . by metaphor" (989). This view is contrary to the one expressed by Peter Brooks in "Freud's Masterplot: Questions of Narrative," which considers Lacan's insights into the metonymical nature of text as his seminal contribution. For reasons that should become clear, I will be dealing principally in this study with metonymy, or displacements in the structures of Decadent narrative, rather than with metaphor as a "textual unconscious" (Davis 984), keeping in mind, however, the interweaving of the two described in Jakobson's notion of poetic language.

6. The self-referentiality of psychoanalytic discourse is at the heart of one of the main criticisms against it. In the first place, psychoanalysis cannot be scientific because it is unprovable. Second, it has little, if any, predictive value. More seriously, its theories can be said to take precedence over the empirical: psychoanalysis can always find itself, the criticism runs, wherever it looks. This is not the place to prove or disprove the validity of psychoanalytic discourse. The reader is instead referred to Adolf Grünbaum's *Foundations of Psychoanalysis: A Philosophical Critique* and to Barbara Johnson's "Frame of Reference: Poe, Lacan, Derrida." The degree to which psychoanalytic discourse is or is not self-referential is not a problem for our discussion of Decadent fiction, since this fiction in general presupposes—in fact, cultivates—the gap between signifier and referent that would have to be filled for a discourse to count as "scientific." It is instructive in this light to recall that Decadent fiction was elaborated as a deliberate refusal of the claims to "science" advanced by the Naturalist novelists.

7. Proust died in 1922; Lorrain died of a perforated colon in 1906.

2. *Common Ground: Freud and the Decadence*

1. An interesting sidelight on Freud's use of French is offered by Steven Marcus in his essay "Freud and Dora: Story, History, Case

History." Marcus points out the way in which the foreign language functions as an agency of repression opposing Freud's claims to clarity and forthrightness. Asserting his right to plain speaking and the direct use of real sexual terms, even with young women, Freud explains, "*J'appelle un chat un chat*" and "the right attitude is: '*pour faire une omelette il faut casser des oeufs*'": in other words, "I call a cat a cat" and "to make an omelet, you have to break some eggs" (Marcus 183–210; Freud 8:48, 49).

2. One of the most useful approaches I have found to poetics of this type is that of Group μ in their *General Rhetoric*. While recognizing the difficulties of positing a "degree zero" of language and of limiting the range of variations possible on it, Group μ analyzes the concept of poetic language as "deviation" from conventional or nonpoetic language. Deviation is language calling attention to itself at a certain cost to the message; deviation, Group μ writes, "is a *local* alteration of degree zero. It presents no systematic character and is, therefore, always unexpected" (38). The intuition of degree zero is what allows deviation, and therefore rhetorical or figurative intent, to be perceived. Naturally, this relationship between convention and deviation can go on and on: "the rhetoric of deviations is of such current usage in poetry that it becomes more or less systematic. Deviation is conventionalized. In this way, conditions give rise to 'deviations of deviations,' which we sometimes find in certain tongue-in-cheek texts" (38, 39).

3. In "Intertextuality and Dante's Antithetical Hypersign," Susan Noakes uses intertextuality and antithesis in Dante as a means of showing that "the intertextual hypersign demonstrates with great clarity a basic feature of sign structure: that the sign is a sign, that is, the sign means, not in itself but only by virtue of its relation to some other sign" (101). Noakes acknowledges the importance of antithesis in demonstrating the manner in which all literary texts themselves can be thought of as hypersigns, reliant for their meaning on their relation to other texts: Dante's use of intertextuality and antithesis in *The Divine Comedy*, she writes, "would tend to teach contemporary lay readers some very important things about literary language: that it is not to be read literally; that it is polyvalent; that it may simultaneously mean two things which are opposites" (99).

4. "L'esprit humain s'est vidé d'images et comblé d'idées" (1:176).

5. "Le propre de l'extrême culture est d'effacer de plus en plus les images au profit des idées" (1:151).

6. "Prononcez . . . le mot *arbre* devant un moderne, et il logera ce signe en sa tête, dans une case étiquetée et distincte; c'est là ce qu'aujourd'hui nous appelons comprendre" (*Philosophie* 1:152); "peuplé[s . . .] de signes abstraits" (1:152); "Nous ne faisons qu'entrevoir par fragments les formes colorées; elles ne persistent pas en nous; elles s'ébauchent vaguement sur la toile intérieure, elles s'enfuient aussitôt" (1:152).

7. "Ce même mot *arbre,* entendu par des esprits encore sains et simples, leur fera voir à l'instant l'arbre tout entier, avec la masse ronde et mouvante de son feuillage lumineux, avec les angles noirs que ses branches dessinent sur le bleu du ciel, avec son tronc rugueux sillonée de grosses veines, avec ses pieds enfoncés dans le sol contre le vent et l'orage, de sorte que leur pensée, au lieu de se réduire à une notation et à un chiffre, leur fournira un spectacle animé et complet" (*Philosophie* 1:153).

8. "Quand les spectateurs les contemplent [ces formes colorées] dans une fresque ou sur une toile, ils les ont déjà vues en eux-mêmes, ils les reconnaissent; elles ne sont point pour eux des étrangères, ramenées artificiellement sur la scène par une combinaison d'archéologie, un effort de volonté, une convention d'école; elles leur sont si familières, qu'ils les importent dans leur vie privée et dans leurs cérémonies publiques" (*Philosophie* 1:153).

3. *Plotting the Fetish: Proust's* Pleasures and Regrets

1. "Je trouverais déplorable que *Les Plaisirs et les jours,* oeuvre de jeunesse, écrite au collège, avant le régiment, paraisse avant qu'*A la recherche du temps perdu* ne soit terminé" (*Correspondance générale* 4:39).

2. See for example, Maurice Bardèche, *Marcel Proust romancier;* Brian G. Rogers, *Proust's Narrative Techniques;* Muriel Dominguez, "'La fin de la Jalousie': A First Start"; or Paola Placella, *Motivi proustiani: Da* Les plaisirs et les jours *alla* Recherche.

3. "Une carrière dont j'ignore le nom qui aboutit à l'inspection des beaux-arts et qui en attendant consiste en missions pour rendre

compte des diverses expositions, représentations, etc." (*Correspondance* 1:257).

4. "Je suis toujours un peu étonné que quelqu'un ait lu les *Plaisirs et les Jours*. Mon éditeur m'a assuré que personne n'était jamais venu lui demander cet ouvrage. Il faut qu'il exagère un peu" (*Correspondance* 3:457).

In *A la recherche de Marcel Proust*, André Maurois recounts the sketch invented by Proust's friends to make fun of this inflated price of *Pleasures and Regrets*. Léon Yeatmann, playing Proust, added up the book's parts: "A preface by M. France: four francs . . . Some paintings by Madame Lemaire: four francs . . . Some music by Reynaldo Hahn: four francs . . . Some prose by me: one franc . . . A few poems by me: fifty centimes . . . Total: thirteen francs, fifty centimes; that's not inflated?" ("Une préface de Monsieur France: quatre francs . . . Des tableaux de Madame Lemaire: quatre francs . . . De la musique de Reynaldo Hahn: quatre francs . . . De la prose de moi: un franc . . . Quelques vers de moi: cinquante centimes . . . Total: treize francs cinquante; ça n'était pas exagéré?" [85]). In his edition of Proust's *Correspondance*, Philip Kolb gives the price of *Pleasures and Regrets* as fifteen francs (2:219 4).

5. "'Grâce' . . . qui nous rapproche des réalités d'au-delà de la mort" (7); "les malades se sentent plus près de leur âme" (7).

6. "Quand j'étais tout enfant, le sort d'aucun personnage de l'histoire sainte ne me semblait aussi misérable que celui de Noé, à cause du déluge qui le tint enfermé dans l'arche pendant quarante jours. Plus tard, je fus souvent malade, et pendant de longs jours je dus rester aussi dans l'"arche." Je compris alors que jamais Noé ne put si bien voir le monde que de l'arche, malgré qu'elle fût close et qu'il fît nuit sur la terre" (6). André Gide saw in the Noah's ark image a foreshadowing of the older Proust, who, ill and enclosed in his room, would concentrate all his energies on the production of the *Recherche*. See Gide's essay in the commemorative volume of the *Nouvelle revue française* issued after Proust's death, "En relisant *Les plaisirs et les jours*," as well as David McDowell, "The World from the Ark," and Gerald Kamber and Richard Macksey, "'Negative Metaphor' and Proust's Rhetoric of Absence."

7. "L'ingéniosité de Mme Lemaire ne s'est jamais adaptée aussi étroitement à un talent d'auteur."

8. "C'est au Bois que je vous retrouvais souvent le matin, m'ayant aperçu et m'attendant sous les arbres, debout, mais reposé, semblable à un de ces seigneurs qu'a peints Van Dyck, et dont vous aviez l'élégance pensive. . . . Tout d'ailleurs contribuait à accentuer cette mélancolique ressemblance, jusqu'à ce fond de feuillages à l'ombre desquels Van Dyck a souvent arrêté la promenade d'un roi; comme tant d'entre eux qui furent ses modèles, vous deviez bientôt mourir et dans vos yeux comme dans les leurs, on voyait alterner les ombres du pressentiment et la douce lumière de la résignation" (5–6).

9. "Plus grave qu'aucun de nous,vous étiez aussi plus enfant" (7).

10. "Toutes [ces pages] ne sont que la vaine écume d'une vie agitée, mais qui maintenant se calme" (7–8); "Je vous donne ce livre. Vous êtes, hélas! le seul de mes amis dont il n'ait pas à redouter les critiques" (8).

11. The discrepancies of sequence between the French and English editions of *Pleasures and Regrets* point up directly the "bastard" nature of stories in collection to which I referred earlier. In both editions, "Baldassare" is the first story, but the French presents the stories according to the original 1896 edition, that is, in the order in which I discuss them here: "The Melancholy Summer of Madame de Breyves," "A Young Girl's Confession," and "The End of Jealousy." The English translation continues from "Baldassare" with "A Young Girl's Confession," "The Melancholy Summer of Madame de Breyves," and "The End of Jealousy." This would be of minor importance were it not for my reading of the four stories *in the order of the original edition* as presenting evidence of increasing narrative mastery through an increasingly technical use of the fetish. My evolutionary reading thus represents a choice to accept a particular sequence as a valid stimulus to a particular type of reading. In that way, it makes a fundamental point about the action of reading on the literary text (which is another way of showing how the signifier can play). That is, while it most likely did not occur to Proust that his arrangement of his stories could be seen to obey certain dictates of the fetish, there is no reason why this should not be available to close reading as an underlying sequence within them. And, given what will become evident about the use of fetish throughout the stories, I

think there is a clear case for speaking of increasing narrative mastery across the sequence.

"Mastery" thus becomes a judgment based on an experience of *reading* across a particular textual sequence; it is not an evaluation of Proust's linear progression as a writer, year to year and story to story, particularly since neither language edition arranges the stories in the order of their composition. "Baldassare" first appeared in *La revue hebdomadaire* in 1895 and "Madame de Breyves" in *La revue blanche* in 1893. "A Young Girl's Confession" and "The End of Jealousy" appear to have been composed expressly for *Pleasures and Regrets.* Thus is again revealed the arbitrary nature of sequence in the short story collection. While the order I chose to follow for my analysis of "mastery" has a great deal to recommend it—Proust's original arrangement, the evidence of the fetish available within this sequence, and Proust's own later comments, as we shall see, on the relative maturity of "The End of Jealousy"—it is not the only order I could have chosen. Short story collections do not demand to be read start to finish, and different sequences clearly can and do stimulate different readings and often quite disparate conclusions.

12. From a historical point of view, Taine and Alexis are not so far off the mark. In "Degeneration and the Medical Model of Cultural Crisis in the French Belle Epoque," Robert Nye points out that by 1900 in France, a new vogue of physical exercise had become well established as a response to the country's perceived physical decadence (39–40).

13. "It occurred to me, as I thought about it, that the raw material of my experience, which would also be the raw material of my book, came to me from Swann, not merely because so much of it concerned Swann himself and Gilberte, but because it was Swann who from the days of Combray had inspired in me the wish to go to Balbec, where otherwise my parents would never have had the idea of sending me, and but for this I should never have known Alber-tine. . . . had I not gone to Balbec I should never have known the Guermantes either, since my grandmother would not have renewed her friendship with Mme de Villeparisis nor should I have made the acquaintance of Saint-Loup and M. de Charlus and thus got to know the Duchesse de Guermantes and through her her cousin, so that even my presence at this very moment in the house of the Prince de Guermantes, where out of the blue the idea for my work had just

come to me (and this meant that I owed to Swann not only the material but also the decision), came to me from Swann" (*Remembrance* 3:953–54).

14. While an equally plausible psychoanalytic reading might motivate the mother's appearance as a figuration of dread and make it impossible for her *not* to appear at the moment of the Young Girl's greatest guilt, the narrative difficulties Proust encounters through *Pleasures and Regrets* support a reading of her appearance as *narratively* unmotivated and hence problematic.

15. "Très différent des *Plaisirs et les Jours*. . . . cependant une partie ressemble (mais en tellement mieux) à la 'Fin de la jalousie'" (*Correspondance générale* 4:99).

4. *The Return of the Repressed: Lorrain's* Masked Figures and Phantoms

1. "On ne voit pas leur visage"; "mystère attirant et répulsif du masque"; "Pourquoi pas des stryges sous ces larges camails, encadrant des faces figées de velours ou de soie? Pourquoi pas du vide et du néant sous ces vastes blouses de pierrot drapées à la façon de suaires sur des angles aigus de tibias et d'humérus? . . . Le masque, c'est la face trouble et troublante de l'inconnu, c'est le sourire du mensonge, c'est l'âme même de la perversité qui sait corrompre en terrifiant" (21–22).

2. "La délicatesse de l'organisme mental est telle que l'incident le moins grave en apparence peut occasionner les plus sérieux désordres" ("La Main gantée" 310); "strophes moroses, comme anémiées de spleen" ("Le visionnaire" 298); "c'est dans la réalité que je deviens visionnaire. Ce sont les êtres en chair et en os rencontrés dans la rue, c'est le passant, c'est la passante, les anonymes mêmes de la foule coudoyés qui m'apparaissent dans des attitudes de spectres, et c'est la laideur, la banalité même de la vie moderne qui me glacent le sang et me figent de terreur" ("Le Possédé" ["The One Possessed"] 305).

In "Jean Lorrain, chroniqueur d'une fin de siècle," Jacques Dupont relates Lorrain's tendencies toward vicious caricaturization to dimly perceived urgings of the unconscious. Dupont writes, "This tendency toward caricatural exaggeration is neither fortuitous nor bereft of signification. One of the most often neglected aspects of the fin de siècle is this propensity for a grating baroque style, derisive or parodic, that serves as an inverted symmetry or deforming mirror for the tendency to spiritualize, faced with the mystified and deceptive pathos of beauty that is phantasmagoric and often empty. Ugliness and cruelty (return of the repressed?) take their places in the affirmation of art, gain for themselves a force of emphasis that creates one of the historical links between this period and our own, marked by the stigmata of modernism in its most aggressive or negative forms" (121).

3. "Vous la supprimez, vous, la Folie, cette dernière citadelle où un homme d'esprit, à terme de patience, pourrait encore se retrancher! . . . —Vous la supprimez, oui et non. Mais enfin vous l'analysez, vous expliquez, la déterminez, la localisez . . . vous la guérissez au besoin, et par quels moyens! par l'électricité et la thérapeutique. Vous avez tué le fantastique, Monsieur" (329).

4. "Toutes morphinées, cautérisées, dosées, droguées de romans psychothérapiques et d'éther, médicamentées, anémiées, androgynes, hystériques, et poitrinaires" (332); "damnables cadavres échappés du cimetière et vomis par la tombe à travers les vivants, fleurs de charnier jaillies pour séduire, envoûter et perdre les jeunes hommes" (331).

5. "Toutes ces grimaces flottantes dans les ténèbres, ricanements équivoques de pierres qui regardent, d'arbres qui veulent saisir, agrandissements subits d'objets inanimés, qui s'animent dans l'ombre et que l'ombre déforme et dont l'ombre menace, qui les a vus enfant, les retrouvera sûrement dans les masques; les masques, cette épouvante errante de nos rues et de nos musées, qu'ils soient le grossier cartonnage au rabais des marchands de jouets, ou le chef-d'oeuvre de cire éclos sous les doigts modeleurs; car le masque, c'est le rire du mystère, c'est le visage du mensonge fait avec la déformation du vrai, c'est la laideur voulue de la réalité exagérée pour cacher l'inconnu" (42–43).

6. "Oh! les grands arbres bruissants des fonds de parcs d'automne humides et solitaires, les interminables corridors des vieux logis de province à demi abandonnés, les greniers hauts comme des cathédrales, . . . les chambres inhabitées des maisons de campagnes des grands-parents aujourd'hui morts, la chambre qu'on n'ouvrait jamais parce qu'il s'y était passé quelque chose (une aïeule y avait été

séquestrée), mais la vérité est qu'on y tenait la réserve des fruits et des confitures. . . . Oh! tous ces châteaux d'épouvante effrités aujourd'hui dans nos âmes sceptiques, mais qui tenaient jadis une si formidable place dans notre enfance effarée et inquiète, de quelle atmosphère frissonnante et glacée ils s'emplissaient pour nous à la tombée de la nuit, surtout au retour de l'automne, dans ces mois brumeux et pourris d'incessantes ondées, de torrentielles pluies" (41–42).

7. "Oh! la tristesse de ces chambres d'hôtel, les soirs d'été pluvieux" (45).

8. "Entre les hauts lambris du salon dit des Dames, violemment éclairé, un seul couple valsait; deux femmes, une énorme dondon que nous voyions de dos, avec, entre ses bras, une belle créature somptueusement vêtue d'une robe de brocart, la chair des bras et des seins nus, très blancs, jaillie, comme une fleur, hors d'un étrange corsage . . . , corsage de princesse de foire ou de reine de féerie, car l'immense traîne de la robe rose s'enroulait par deux fois autour de la dondon. . . . La belle fille, un grand éventail de satin bleu déployé sur son visage, valsait éperdument, entraînait la grosse femme à la taille carrée; et la valseuse rose avait les plus beaux yeux du monde, des cheveux noirs luisants et souples, tordus sur la nuque en gros câble, des pieds menus et des mains fines élégamment gantées, tandis que sa partenaire, gainée dans une espèce de sac de soie grise, exhibait des chevilles de charretier et un cou à gros bourrelets, ignoblement rouge et grenu sous les poils jaunes d'une perruque de clown. . . . Dans un coin, assise à la turque, les jambes croisées parmi les coussins d'un fauteuil, une naine en japonaise égratignait une guitare" (46–47).

9. "Une barbe de sapeur, une très belle barbe brune encadrait ce visage, ondoyait en deux pointes soyeuses entre les seins: la dame était barbue comme un roi de légende. La valseuse éperdue était une femme à barbe, sa partenaire un affreux gros homme glabre, maquillé et fardé et déguisé en femme" (47).

10. "Tout cela nous apparut expliqué, évident, dans l'éclair de la porte ouverte et aussitôt refermée; mais nous avions eu un moment de stupeur, la sensation d'une chute dans un gouffre, dans de l'absurde, de l'impossible" (47).

11. "[Ses jambes] étaient moulées dans un maillot de soie noire qu[i] l'enserrait tout entier, car son burnous s'était un peu ouvert;

mais, chose bizarre, tandis que sa jambe droite était haut gantée d'un bas de femme, un bas de soie vert glauque, serré au-dessus du genou d'une jarretière de moire, l'autre pied avait une chaussette d'homme, une chaussette de soirée à semis de fleurettes, si bien qu'il était double ce masque, et joignait au charme terrifiant de sa face de goule le trouble équivoque d'un sexe incertain" (25).

12. "Quitter Paris pour échapper à une obsession de ressemblance animale se dégageant pour lui de tout visage humain" ("La main gantée" 310).

13. "La vie moderne, luxueuse et dure, a fait à ces hommes comme à ces femmes des âmes de bandits ou de garde-chiourme; l'envie, la haine et le désespoir d'être pauvre font aux uns des têtes aplaties et revêches, des faces aiguisées et retor[s]es de musaraignes et de vipères; l'avarice et l'égoïsme donnent aux autres des groins de vieux porcs avec des machoires de requins" ("Le possedé" 307).

14. "Les aventures les plus extraordinaires peuvent se ruer maintenant sur M. et Mme la conseillère: l'autruche a ouvert la porte du surnaturel" (44).

Lorrain calls the Hoffmann story "Le Docteur Cinabre" ("Doctor Cinabre"). To my knowledge, there is no story of this name in the Hoffmann bibliography. Lorrain is most likely referring to the long Hoffmann *märchen,* or fairy tale, *Little Zaches, Surnamed Zinnober* (*Klein Zaches genannt Zinnober*), published in 1819, abridged and translated into French as "Petit Zacharie" in 1832, and then translated in full in 1836. It appears under the title "Petit Zacharie, surnommé Cinabre" in an 1840 edition of Hoffman's stories. (In *La fortune d'Hoffmann en France,* Elizabeth Teichmann traces the various translations and editions of the stories in France, along with their critical reception.) The ostrich appears in *Little Zaches* to introduce the hero Balthasar and his friend Fabian into the quarters of the mage Doctor Prosper Alpanus, who is to reveal to them the enchantment to which the mean and misshapen Zinnober owes his ill-gotten worldly gains. Lorrain may have gotten the erroneous story line by confusion with Hoffman's personage the Councillor Krespel, hero of the story by the same name, known in France as "Le Conseiller Krespel."

Lorrain's errors may be based on misreadings, poor memory, or limited hearsay knowledge of Hoffman's works. Their potential source, however, is far less significant than their actual presence, which reveals a reshuffling of external material consistent with the working of the primary process. Hoffmann's ostrich, greeting ordinary people at the opening of a simple door, is in fact more striking a presence in Lorrain's version than in the original, where he is just one of the many wonders encountered by Balthasar and Fabian during their visit to the wizard. Among these wonders are a couple of frogs in the garden; as the groundskeeper and his wife, the two frogs escort the visitors to the gate. As we shall soon see the importance of the frog as a creature of trauma for Lorrain, it is easy to speculate on their presence in *Little Zaches* as the stimulus for the willful/unwillful, primary process "confusions" in Lorrain's reading.

15. "Des visages humains plus effroyables encore" (43); "la raison peut perdre pied, et la réalité de la vie même se continue alors dans du cauchemar" (43).

16. "Eh bien, à l'autruche près, j'ai vécu, cet été, le conte du *Docteur Cinabre*" (44).

17. "Vous finiriez par voir des têtes de renards sur les épaules de vos amis . . . à moins que vous ne preniez ma servante pour une autruche, la gigantesque et fallacieuse autruche qui vient ouvrir la porte aux visiteurs et fait à la famille Mock épouvantée de si belles révérences dans le *Docteur Cinabre* [*Little Zaches*]" (374).

18. "La grenouille est mon animal favori: J'en ai dix-sept dans mon cabinet de travail; d'abord un orchestre de dix rainettes vertes en faïence, tout à fait exquises, deux de bronze, une en verre filé, venue de Londres, un tableau de Mme Desbordes où il y en a trois, plus un grès de Carriès. Il y en a dix-sept en tout et je ne compte pas les portraits de femmes" (qtd. in Jullian 167–68).

19. "Dans vos *Sensations et Souvenirs,* vous avez raconté une petite mésaventure d'écolier, pas bien méchante en elle-même, mais dont l'affreuse impression n'a pas laissé que de me troubler. Vous savez? l'histoire du crapaud, la soudaine apparition dans une source, où vous veniez de boire, d'un flasque et monstrueux batracien! Circonstance aggravante, l'ignoble bête avait les yeux crevés, et l'eau, que vous veniez de puiser, en prit dans votre bouche un effroyable goût de sang. . . . cette rencontre faite il y a plus de vingt-cinq ans, vous ne pouvez encore en évoquer la minute sans sentir votre coeur chavirer sous vos côtes, et remonter à vos lèvres une indicible nausée de dégoût" (233).

20. Semiotic studies of realist literature have demonstrated the extent to which literary description depends on the allusive effects of metonymy to create its impression of a coherent and recognizable "real" world. In "Trollope's Metonymies," for instance, Michael Riffaterre has shown how metonymic details prompt the reader to fill in the unstated physical and moral characteristics of the characters in a novel; thus metonymy collaborates in the realist illusion. Even as they denounce metonymy's totalizing effects, such postmodern critics as Mathieu Bénézet recognize the suggestive power of this figure. Claude Ollier's refusal to describe faces in his novels is for Bénézet a rejection not only of realism but of the narrative authority on which the realist pretense is based; in such works, writes Bénézet enthusiastically, "doing away with the face seems to indicate that *the hero no longer possesses the power of the narrative . . .* [he is no longer the] site from which semes are organized and distributed" (154).

21. This phenomenon of reader identification is for Bénézet a basic element of the reader's interaction with the text. Elsewhere in *Le roman de la langue,* he writes, "Should we rout the reader? Forbid him any phenomenon of identification whatever? That would be to not recognize that you need only present one feature, one vowel, one 'sparkle of a shoulder' (Valéry) to make the specular process work, to inspire 'projection' on the part of the reader" (29).

22. "La terreur, c'est surtout de l'imprévu" (41); "Eh bien, moi aussi j'ai un crapaud dans ma vie, et ce crapaud est une histoire de masques: et, puisque vous les aimez et semblez en faire collection, la voilà, mon aventure de bal masqué" (233).

23. In *The Delights of Terror: An Aesthetics of the Tale of Terror,* Terry Heller muses about aesthetic closure in the fantastic, the horrible, and the terrifying. On the one hand, reading all stories, even scary ones, is an exercise in completion. Heller writes, "As we read we engage in a process of creating provisional unities; we hypothesize wholes, practicing for the final concretization of the work" (3). On the other hand, terror and the horrible threaten the reader's projection toward the whole by tempting him or her not to finish reading: "If the individual reader encounters an image that is an especially powerful evocation of a personal terror, then, in the absence of extraordinary buffers in the work, the reading must end. The anxiety aroused by the image takes precedence over aesthetic

experience" (57). Another way of saying this is that Lorrain's description requires the aesthetic experience to be identical to the anxiety aroused by the series of images. There are no "buffers" to protect the reader's progress in this passage. Rather, each successive image buffets the reader between anxiety and pleasure. This is what makes the description read as fragmented.

24. "En février dernier, comme je descendais vers six heures je ne sais quel escalier de rédaction, je bousculais étourdiment un chapeau haut de forme enfoui dans le collet relevé d'une longue pelisse fourrée" (254).

25. My translation of *l'égrégore,* which is not standard French, is based on this evocative description provided by none other than the electrician Forbster in the story: the *égrégore* "is the imperceptible and deleterious influence of a being made of shadows, of a dead man or woman taking up residence beside you in the form of a living being, insinuating himself into your life and your habits, creeping into your heart, your preferences, and taking odious root there, breathing into you with his damned mouth a fatal passion, some madness, the madness of an artist or a dilettante, and step by step, under his hallucinatory and fascinating obsession, laying you out one pleasant evening in some cold grave" ("c'est l'insensible et délétère influence d'un être de ténèbres, d'un mort ou d'une morte s'installant auprès de vous sous l'aspect d'un vivant, s'insinuant dans votre vie et vos habitudes, s'immisçant dans votre coeur, dans vos admirations et y prenant une odieuse racine, vous soufflant de sa bouche damnée une passion fatale, une folie quelconque, folie d'artiste ou d'amateur, et d'étapes en étapes, sous son hallucinante et fascinante obsession, vous couchant un beau soir dans le froid d'une fosse" [339–40]).

26. "Un masque de verre, un masque hermétique sans yeux et sans bouche, . . . rempli jusqu'aux bords d'éther, de liquide poison" (286).

27. "Elle me poursuivait comme une obsession. . . . Modelée en pleine cire, elle était d'une délicatesse de tons et de détails infinie et dans la pénombre de l'atelier, où je venais d'entrer sur les pas de Gormas, cette tête disait non, immobile sur son socle, presque surnaturelle par l'intensité de la bouche orgueilleuse et des yeux de lapis. . . .

"Les mains croisées derrière le dos, Gormas attachait comme moi sur la cire peinte deux yeux devenus lointains de rêve et d'admiration.

"—Oui, cela réconcilie avec la vie, reprenait-il en poursuivant sa pensée, et cela console presque de l'ennui d'y marcher. On peut y rencontrer de semblables créatures, et encore les rencontre-t-on? Non, car vous croiseriez Rayon-d'Aube dans la rue (c'est ainsi que nous l'appelons), que vous ne la reconnaîtriez pas. La meilleure preuve en est que vous l'avez déjà cent fois vue et qu'elle ne vous a pas frappé" (210–11).

28. "Si la théorie des avatars est vraie, c'est dans quelque couloir tendu de tapisseries des châteaux de Blois ou d'Amboise que Ringel avait dû rencontrer jadis cette insidieuse et souriante créature" (213); "entre Mme Catherine et René le Florentin, dans une société adonnée tout entière à la science des philtres et des envoûtements" (215).

29. "Un petit Italien [que] j'ai rencontré . . . dans la rue, un soir de décembre, grelottant, hâve et mendiant presque" (216); "Oui, il est bien mort, le petit Antonio Monforti et à Beaujon, n'est-ce pas, Gormas?" (217).

30. "Que le primitif, qu'il admirait si sincèrement, était un simple surmoulage du Louvre décapité pour la circonstance . . . , que la décollation de ce buste était de mon invention et que c'était moi qui en avais donné l'ordre et la commande au mouleur avec aggravation de grumelots de sang . . . que le barbare coloriage de ce plâtre, le vert glauque des aveugles prunelles, le rose fané des lèvres, les touches d'or des cheveux jusqu'à la pourpre humide des caillots étaient mon oeuvre de peintre ou plutôt l'emploi maladroit d'une journée de paresse" (274).

31. "Toutes les perversités et toutes les audaces" (274); "Je n'ai rien à vous dire de plus . . . que mutiler un chef-d'oeuvre est un véritable meurtre et que c'est là un jeu quelquefois dangereux" (275).

32. "J'étais bien bon d'accorder attention aux billevesées qui lui avaient passé par la tête [à de Romer] à propos du moulage entrevu chez moi; à ce compte les ateliers de sculpteurs seraient peuplés de visionnaires et l'Ecole des beaux-arts une succursale de chez Charcot, tandis que tous les sculpteurs de ma connaissance se trouvaient être au contraire de joyeux vivants râblés et barbus aux idées et aux teints clairs, plus préoccupés de sensations que de songes" (276).

33. "D'un grain de peau si uni et si pâle qu'on eût dit un précieux objet d'art" (277); "avec une plaie rouge entre les deux

épaules et du sang en filets [qui] coulait du cou béant" (279); "sur le tapis sombre les deux pieds [du corps] se tordaient, convulsés dans une angoisse atroce; à ce moment la tête darda sur moi son regard d'outre-tombe et je roulai brisé sur le tapis" (279).

34. "Sans avoir repris connaissance, stupide et muette" (134); "N'est-ce pas une belle vengeance de masque?" (134).

35. "Souplesse presque féline" (417); "tout angoissait comme une énigme dans ce mystérieux de Burdhe" (417); "était un être à la fois répulsif et attirant" (417).

36. "Les intailles romaines ont je ne sais quelle ardeur intense. Il y avait là dans le chaton d'une bague une tête adolescente couronnée de lauriers, quelque jeune César, à l'expression exténuée et jouis-sante, à la fois désirante et lasse, dont je vais rêver pendant bien des nuits" (424); "sous les paupières à peine soulevées luit et sommeille une eau si verte, l'eau morne et corrompue d'une âme inassouvie, la dolente émeraude d'une effrayante luxure!" (425).

37. "L'air est lourd, empesté d'alcool, d'odeurs de crasse et de haillons, des bras nus agitent des piques et avec un grand cri je vois soudain monter dans le ciel de plomb une tête coupée, une tête exsangue aux yeux éteints et fixes, que des hommes ivres se passent de mains en mains, soufflètent et baisent sur les lèvres. L'un d'eux porte, enroulé autour de son bras nu, comme un paquet de lanières sanglantes, tout un noeud de viscères; il ricane, les lèvres ornées d'une équivoque moustache blonde pareille aux poils frisé d'un sexe . . . et ce sont autour de la moustache postiche des propos ignobles, des gros rires outrageants; et la tête oscille au-dessus de la foule, brandie au bout d'une pique" (432).

38. "A la place où la chair est plus douce et plus blanche, . . . comme une morsure ou la succion d'un baiser long et lent" (421).

39. "Des rampements de spectre et des frôlements d'âme! Eh bien! cette nuit de fièvre et d'épouvante, moi, qui ne suis ni superstitieux ni nerveux, je l'ai vécue dans des circonstances si étranges qu'il faut, ma foi, que je vous la raconte" (266).

40. "La terreur, c'est surtout de l'imprévu, avez-vous dit dans un de vos contes" (183); "une histoire de plus à ajouter à votre série de masques, car c'est une véritable histoire de masques que cette aventure d'hôtel garni, où il y eut, au moment critique, une si terrible, une si inattendue substitution de personne" (184); "Avouez que c'est une belle histoire de masque" (190).

41. "Qu'un poète de la jeune école, effaré du verdâtre de son teint et de ses costumes, a pu écrire ce distique: La grenouille le voit et l'appelle sa soeur / Et le haricot en reverdit de peur" (208–9).

42. "Je n'étais alors qu'un pauvre étudiant en droit, peu préoccupé de l'extériorité des choses et il fallait, pour que cette femme eût attiré mon attention, qu'elle tranchât en effet violemment sur la grise uniformité des autres pensionnaires de l'hôtel" (35).

43. "Il m'était arrivé plus d'une fois de la coudoyer dans l'escalier de l'hôtel; . . . et chaque fois ça avait été de ma part des frôlements et des hardiesses de main traînant sur la rampe et tâchant d'y rencontrer la sienne, car cet énigmatique sourire ombré et ces yeux prometteurs me lancinaient; mais j'en avais été chaque fois pour mes frais. Je n'étais pas son type, il fallait le croire" (37).

44. "Oh! errer, toute une nuit, libre sous le masque, coudoyer, frôler, avec la certitude de n'être jamais reconnue, toutes les luxures, tous les vices qu'on soupçonne et tous ceux qu'on ne soupçonne pas" (38); "Et puis vraiment, tu es trop innocente, ma petite Suzanne" (39); "Moi, vois-tu, je me passe toutes mes fantaisies. . . . Ce n'est pas bien malin pourtant, le truc de l'hôtel meublé où l'on a une chambre au mois sous un faux nom; ainsi moi qui te parle" (39).

45. "L'hôtelière faisait un effort et, prenant son trousseau de clés à sa ceinture, *enjambait* le cercueil, et, *les jambes écartées, à cheval au-dessus du mort,* ouvrait l'armoire et passait à sa client impassible tout un amoncellement de satins, de velours et de dentelle" (40).

46. "Ses yeux, mais ils sont bleus, d'un bleu-vert un peu pâle. La mer, quand elle est grosse et moutonne, a cette teinte de bleu, un bleu un peu verdâtre. Baudry, votre grand peintre, avait cette teinte de bleu quand il peignait les vagues, ces vagues où il met, ruisselants d'écume, des corps de femmes si savoureusement blancs" (347).

47. "Serge, tenté par la température, avait voulu absolument se baigner, [elle racontait] qu'il lui avait confié les rames, s'était dévêtu, avait quelque temps nagé derrière la barque, joyeux et folâtrant sous le clair de lune, puis qu'à sa grande terreur [de Nelly], il s'était soudain enfoncé dans les flots et n'avait plus reparu" (348).

48. "Mais je vois très bien Nelly, assise à l'avant de la barque et ramant doucement et poussant le bateau, tandis que nage à lentes et souples brassées mon regretté ami Serge; la lune les baigne tous deux comme d'une gaze de lumière, argentant le torse de Serge hors

de l'eau et le corsage blanc de Nelly dans sa barque; ils sont très beaux tous deux, ils vont ainsi une heure se regardant dans les yeux, se souriant l'un à l'autre; puis Serge se fatigue, peu à peu il s'essouffle, il voudrait remonter, il dit à Nelly: 'Arrête,' Nelly ne l'entend pas, la lèvre souriante, le regard dans le sien, elle rame doucement et le bateau fuit toujours; Serge, d'abord, croit qu'elle plaisante. . . . Quelle belle nuit pour mourir! Serge a compris, il bat la vague, il râle, de l'eau déjà plein la bouche, mais les yeux fixés sur les yeux de Nelly; devant lui la barque oscille. Elle sourit toujours appuyant sur la rame, et l'eau mugit dans les oreilles de Serge agonisant, qui se cramponne en vain à l'écume des vagues et coule dans l'ombre verte et lunaire des flots" (348–49).

49. " J'ai toujours retrouvé depuis [le regard de Serge] dans les yeux de Nelly" (349).

50. "Vous calomniez Nelly, et puis, il ne faut pas faire mentir les légendes" (349).

5. *The Epithalamic Horror: Displacement in Rachilde*

1. "Un fichu métier, le plus fichu métier possible" (viii); "est immoral, en ce sens qu'il gâte un bon ménage sur vingt, produit des enfants adultères sous le spécieux prétexte d'un trop plein cérébral, porte aux vices contre nature—toujours pour la même raison . . . trouble l'harmonie du foyer, tâche les doigts et embête ferme les directeurs de journaux" (viii).

2. "Je suis donc chien de lettres, à mon grand regret hystérique de lettres, et si on pense que je ne mérite ni cet excès d'honneur ni cette indignité . . . je suis androgyne de lettres" (xi).

3. "Il faut en moyenne un an pour écrire un bon roman, six mois pour en faire un passable, trois mois pour en faire un mauvais . . . ceux qui les écrivent en un mois et demi, comme mes pareilles, rentrent dans la catégorie des hystériques. . . . Pendant ces différentes lunes de miel de *l'autoresse,* avec son roman, elle ne cause plus, elle prend un air de poule constipée, ne se peigne plus, horrible détail, ne digère plus, a des cauchemars ou bien égratigne son amoureux" (ix).

4. "Les racontars malpropres sont expulsés de l'ombre, [et] la femme vindicative s'en sert toujours pour apprendre à Paul que

Caroline le trompe, ce dont Jacques . . . est obligé de répondre dans un duel meurtrier" (viii).

5. "J'ai écrit des histoires. — Elles sont peu morales. En cela elles ressemblent à la vie. C'est même le seul contact quelles [*sic*] aient avec la vie, me paraît-il" (xi); "toutes les critiques du monde n'empêchent pas un auteur d'être lu du moment que cet auteur plaît au public" (xii).

6. "Règle générale: on a tort d'être une femme de lettres. Il y a toujours mieux à faire. Pour les unes, la prostitution hygienique de la société. Pour les autres, le mari." (vi)

7. "I did not succeed in mastering the transference in good time," Freud wrote in his postcript to the Dora case. "Owing to the readiness with which Dora put one part of the pathogenic material at my disposal during the treatment, I neglected the precaution of looking out for the first signs of transference. . . . In this way the transference took me unawares, and, because of the unknown quantity in me which reminded Dora of Herr K., she took her revenge on me as she wanted to take her revenge on him, and deserted me as she believed herself to have been deceived and deserted by him" (7:118–19).

8. "Tu vois, si j'écrivais à la *Monatschrift* pour donner ma version à moi (ça serait justifié d'un point de vue *scientifique,* qu'on m'écoute aussi), d'abord ils ne la publieraient pas et puis ils y trouveraient sûrement la confirmation que je suis hystérique. C'est peut-être vrai que je suis hystérique; ce qui ne me plaît pas c'est surtout qu'on dirait que ce n'est pas à moi d'en juger! c'est possible que je souffre de la 'petite hystérie.' Et après? Vois, l'hystérie jusqu'ici ne servait à rien. Il fallait bien la faire servir. C'est fait: maintenant elle est recherchée, chez les professeurs. Crois-tu que ça arrange les choses?" (16–17).

9. This is my translation of Beauvoir's résumé of the case (*Deuxième sexe* 2:233). While generally faithful to the original, Parshley's translation leaves out much of de Beauvoir's insistence on the details of dysfunction that recall others we have seen thus far: spying on one's parents in "The End of Jealousy," for example, and the physical self-mutilation that recalls Rachilde's sarcastic reasons for why women should not be writers. For the sake of comparison, here are both passages, Parshley's followed by the original: "She suffered from vomiting, took morphine every night, flew into rages,

refused to bathe, stayed in her room. She was engaged, said she loved her fiancé and had given herself to him, but later admitted she had felt no pleasure and recalled his kisses with disgust. She adored her mother but felt herself not loved enough; she could not bear the thought of marrying and leaving home, fell sick, offended her fiancé, and declared she wished to give up all thought of marriage and remain at home, always, like a child. Her mother insisted, but a week before the wedding day she committed suicide" (433–34).

"Au moment où Stekel fait sa connaissance, elle souffre de vomissements, prend de la morphine tous les soirs, refuse de se laver, mange au lit, reste enfermée dans sa chambre. Elle est fiancée et affirme aimer ardemment son fiancé. Elle avoue à Stekel qu'elle s'est donnée à lui. . . . Plus tard, elle dit qu'elle n'en a eu aucun plaisir: qu'elle a même gardé de ses baisers un souvenir répugnant et c'est là la source de ses vomissements. On découvre en fait qu'elle s'est donnée pour punir sa mère dont elle ne se sentait pas assez aimée: enfant, elle épiait ses parents la nuit parce qu'elle avait peur qu'ils ne lui donnent un frère ou une soeur; elle adorait sa mère. 'Et maintenant elle devait se marier, quitter la maison paternelle, abandonner la chambre à coucher de ses parents? c'était impossible.' Elle se fait grossir, gratte et abîme ses mains, s'abrutit, devient malade, essaie d'offenser son fiancé de toute manière. Le médecin la guérit mais elle supplie sa mère de renoncer à cette idée de mariage: 'Elle voulait rester à la maison, toujours, pour rester l'enfant.' Sa mère insistait pour qu'elle se marie. Une semaine avant le jour du mariage on la trouva dans son lit, morte: elle s'était tuée d'une balle de revolver."

It is not the least interesting of the English omissions that the doctor who erroneously declares her cured (but of what?) in the French does not appear at all in the English. The return from the English to the French—in which the cure is mentioned only because it is illusory—seems once more to emphasize de Beauvoir's fascination with all that does not go right with women.

10. "Oeuvre que je ne renie pas et que je préfère à mes autres oeuvres, parce que les mères préfèrent toujours les fils bossus aux fils droits" (xviii).

11. "Nulle odeur ne lui était plus odieuse que celle des pommes" (23); "Mlle de Vénérande s'imagina qu'elle mangerait peut-être bien une de ces pommes sans trop de révolte" (28).

12. "Ces imaginations [de Rachilde] sentent la mort" (19).

13. "Elle se fit petite, toute petite, rampa, humblement serpentine, se glissa dans la cuve où fermentait le moût, et, ramenant sur elle des monceaux de grappes écrasées, elle demeura inerte, augmentant le sang du raisin de tout le vin exquis de ses veines. Comme elle agonisait encore, ils descendirent dans l'auge et la foulèrent aux pieds, tandis que jaillissaient, des prodigieuses graines noires à reflets d'yeux roulants, un regard de suprême malédiction" (80).

14. "Tous entourèrent la femme. C'était une de ces rodeuses d'amour que les sages de Sodome venaient de chasser de leur ville. Dans une juste et formidable colère, des hommes de Dieu s'étaient réunis pour se débarrasser de ces démentes, qu'une fringale de passions mauvaises hantait du crépuscule à l'aurore. Se condamnant virilement à une chasteté de plusieurs années pour ne pas donner le meilleur de leurs forces, durant le temps des récoltes, à ces gouffres de voluptés qu'étaient les filles de Sodome, ne gardant que les mères en gésine et les vieilles, ils avaient répudié jusqu'à leurs épouses, jusqu'à leurs soeurs" (77).

15. "A cette aurore, la terre fumait comme une cuve emplie d'un moût infernal, et la vigne, située au centre de l'immense plaine, rutilait sous un soleil levant déjà féroce, un soleil pourpre à chevelure de braise qui faisait fermenter d'avance les grappes énormes, dont les grains, d'une grosseur surnaturelle, prenaient des reflets d'yeux roulants, tout noirs jaillis de leurs orbites. . . . Pareille à la bête trop féconde, qu'aucun lien ne doit entraver aux heures douloureuses des parturitions multiples, elle [la vigne] se roulait sur le sol avec d'effrayantes convulsions, lançant des jets furieux de guirlandes, bras implorants qui se tendaient vers le soleil, semblant à la fois souffrir et délirer d'une joie coupable mais paradisiaque, tandis que ses moelles surchauffées débordaient d'elle en l'inondant d'une rosée de larmes épaisses. Elle mettait bas n'importe où ces prodigieux fruits d'un brun lustré, velouté, mystérieuse éclosion du mortel bitume, le rappelant par leur nuance charbonneuse, leur nuance de sucre satanique distillé à travers des violences de volcan" (69–70).

16. Though based on the word *mort* for death or a dead man, *mortis* has no ready English translation. It is not standard French and is most closely related to the Latin genitive *mortis*, "of death." I take the *mortis* in the story to be a reference to the hero, Count Sebastiani Ceccaldo-Rossi, and could venture the not wholly satisfactory paraphrase of the title that he is "the one marked for death."

17. "Aucune femme ne traversait la ville, et à remuer les tas de corps en putréfaction sur les places publiques on n'aurait pas exhumé le moindre lambeau de jupe. Les femmes avaient disparu, ne laissant aucun souvenir de leur grâce. Peut-être avaient-elle fui dès le début du fléau? Peut-être étaient-elles mortes les premières—de peur—avant la maladie?" (59).

18. "Folles de leurs corps, escaladant les grilles de fer, débordant des urnes de bronze, retombant des balcons dorés, [elles] rompaient leurs dernières attaches patriciennes pour s'unir aux [fleurs] vagabondes en de monstrueuses noces" (53); "toutes brûlantes des parfums défendus, que pimentait le fumier humain" (53).

19. "Dans l'amoureux incendie d'un ciel de juin, par les marches encore blanches des escaliers croulants vers l'Arno devenu presque noir, [les fleurs] les plus sauvages, guerrières déjà très habituées aux obstacles, montèrent à l'assaut de la ville. . . . le vent de la révolte enlaça des branches à des branches, tressa des guirlandes, suspendit des couronnes, éleva des arcs de triomphe, chanta l'épithalame au milieu du grand silence de la mort.

"Les roses, bouches de braise, flammes de chair, léchant l'incorruptibilité des marbres, éclaboussèrent jusqu'aux faîtes les longues colonnes pures de taches rouges comme du vin, pourpres comme du sang, et qui, la nuit, formaient des signes ronds, s'extravasant en brun, marquant d'ombres violettes la peau des monuments pâles, pareilles à des traces de doigts profondément enfoncés. Les roses, sur tous les tons, du safran aux couleurs de la lie, de l'écarlate furieuse aux nuances des tendres membres des nouveau-nés, hurlèrent leur délivrance. C'étaient des gueules ouvertes inlassablement, poussant des clameurs qu'on devinait sans les voir. Elles secouaient, au-dessus du charnier, leur gros boutons tout fiévreux d'éclore, bubons crevant de sève, prêts à éclater en giclements de pus, et l'horrible menace s'achevait dans des torrents de senteurs enivrantes, violentes, exaspérées comme des cris. . . .

"Une espèce raccrocheuse [de roses] s'étant introduite dans un clocher, ayant lancé, par une ogive, la forêt de ses épines féroces s'agrippa le long d'une corde, la fit onduler sous le poids de ses jeunes têtes, et lorsque la centième s'épanouit, pleine de rosée, calice lourd de larmes, la corde se tendit, vibra . . . l'on perçut un son de cloche: les roses sonnaient le tocsin! A l'incendie du ciel amoureux s'ajoutait la fournaise de leurs odeurs passionnées" (53–55).

20. "Nu comme le divin bambino qui vient d'issir du flanc de la vierge Marie" (66); "nouvelles têtes de femme ornant les balcons de Florence, semblèrent frémir de pudeur et se pencher curieusement" (66).

21. "Des fleurs, des fleurs, encore des fleurs! . . . Si les citrons et les oranges manquaient, il y avait les roses jaunes! Si les grenades, les melons, les pastèques n'arrivaient pas à mûrir, il y avait les roses pourpres, les roses rouges, les roses roses! Et si le vin d'Asti ne coulait point à flots, cette année de malheur, on humait sa mousse pétillante et suave dans l'arome délicat des très petites roses blanches, dont les boutons craquaient, sous la dent, comme de simples noisettes!" (67).

22. "Mais le long des rues désertes c'était encore plus beau" (65).

23. In "Reading the Mother Tongue: Psychoanalytic Feminist Criticism," Jane Gallop refers to the difficulty of situating the mother within patriarchy. For all the homage paid to the mother in psychoanalytic theories of early infancy, she points out, the mother is never present as subject; she is, rather, an object for the infant who identifies with her, as well as for the father who will necessarily disrupt the mother-child dyad at the moment of the Oedipal passage. Gallop writes, "The mother tongue, the language we learn at our mother's breast, *is* patriarchal language. That is where we learned the language which feminism has taught us to see as full of masculinist bias. In trying to move beyond the father, the mother looks like an alternative, but if we are trying to move beyond patriarchy, the mother is not outside. . . . Although the father may be absent from the pre-Oedipal, patriarchy constitutes the very structure of the mother-child dyad. The early mother may appear to be outside patriarchy, but that very idea of the mother (and the woman) as outside of culture, society, and politics is an essential ideological component of patriarchy" (133).

Rachilde's displacements of the mother from culture to nature and back again make an even more fundamental point. There is a strong intuition in Rachilde, particularly in "The Hermetic Chateau," that in order to recognize nature, one is first obliged to recognize culture. As with Saussure's description of linguistic value or Lacan's insistence on the barrier of repression, recognition is primarily a matter of recognizing difference. Because it de-natures the maternal body by forbidding access to it (and installing, again in Lacanian terms, the reign of metonymy), culture bestows a quirky kind of blessing on a literary project like Rachilde's, which proceeds as an exploitation of the possibilities for the creation of meaning by displacement. Rachilde's originality, however—perhaps even her feminism in spite of herself—is that she turns that cultural blessing against itself. That is, insofar as she accepts the Oedipal prohibition as the foundation of culture, Rachilde can be said to write *within* culture. However, she writes more persuasively *against* culture no less by her continual reminders of what is lost by the incest prohibition—union with the mother—than by her taunting perceptions of what is gained: restless desire, irresolvable nostalgia, and the inability of language to coincide with the object of desire. We shall see this writing against culture most clearly, I think, in "The Frog Killer."

24. "Une paysanne du Limousin, fort pauvre, un peu folle, dont la principale monomanie consistait en un éternel besoin de locomotion. Elle rêvait d'un endroit où elle aurait été *mieux,* où elle aurait dû vivre *toujours,* et comme elle ne connaissait pas cet endroit, que, du reste, elle ignorait même s'il existait autre part que sous son crâne, elle répétait jaculatoirement: 'Ah! ils sont bien malheureux, ceux qui n'ont pas de pays!'" (*Contes* 121).

25. "L'autre, une comtesse de Beaumont-Landry, avait toute sa raison, mais elle songeait des journées entières à la *maison de ses rêves,* et cette maison ne représentait pas, pour elle, une phrase sentimentale de son jeune temps: c'était *réellement, sincèrement,* une demeure bâtie quelque part. . . . Ni tableaux, ni gravures, ne lui donnaient d'indications plus précises, mais elle savait que cette maison était *là-bas,* et que sa place, à elle, une choyée mondaine, était marquée dans ce modeste endroit de repos" (121–22).

26. "S'il y a l'*âme soeur,* que l'on cherche à travers toutes les déceptions et tous les crimes d'amour, n'y aurait-il pas aussi le *pays frère,* sans lequel on ne vit pas heureux, on ne peut obtenir une fin paisible?" (122); "tombe à soi" (123); "Souvent, aussi, extasiés devant ce pays, nous le voyons tout à coup reculer, se fondre, s'évanouir. Il nous fuit, nous abandonne, et pour une raison qui ne nous sera jamais donnée, car, sans doute, *elle est trop effrayante,* nous devinons que nous ne l'atteindrons pas, que cette terre promise nous sera éternellement dérobée" (124).

27. "Et voici ce que je veux raconter *bien sincèrement,* au sujet d'un de ces pays de chimère que j'ai *bien réellement* trouvé sur ma route" (124).

28. "Clocher naïf, arrondi en goupillon, et le vignoble, où s'éparpillaient des paysans en blouse et des femmes en jupes claires" (125); "entrer dans le château que j'avais vu, et qui *existait* puisque je *l'avais vu!*" (132); "La roche, toujours la roche, luisante, suintante, sans une fissure, sans un trou" (132); "*c'était toujours plus loin qu'on ne le pensait*" (128); "on déviait, malgré soi" (130).

29. "Moi, . . . j'ai souvent essayé de me figurer le château, et je n'ai pas pu découvrir la moindre tourelle!" (127).

30. "Un conscrit qui avait parié de dénicher des oeufs de buse, là-haut, avant d'aller au régiment, et, comme il était gris le matin où il tenta son ascension, il a dégringolé de votre fameux château jusqu'à sa chaumière. S'il n'a pas trouvé des oeufs de buse, il a toujours trouvé de la salle de police en arrivant chez son capitaine, car il a fallu le soigner et il a manqué le premier appel, le nigaud" (127).

31. "Là-bas . . . là-bas, un jeu diabolique de lumières pourpres, d'ombres violettes, faisait réapparaître les ruines du castel féodal. Je distinguais plus nettement que jamais les donjons, le chemin de ronde, les créneaux; et, plus formidablement que jamais, se dressait, dans le sang du jour agonisant, le *Château hermétique,* la patrie inconnue qui attirait mon coeur" (134–35). Often translated as "homeland," *patrie* is by etymology "fatherland," but it also carries the connotation, particularly apt in this context, of "motherland."

32. "Minée, mais depuis combien de temps? Attaquée par quoi? Cela ne lui a causé d'abord aucune souffrance, et maintenant elle se trouve plongée dans un de ces désespoirs qui, pour ne durer qu'un jour, n'en sont que plus terribles: elle a désormais une tare!" (*Démon* 99).

33. "Couronnée d'un liséré sombre à l'endroit de la cassure" (99); "sur le côté, un peu en arrière du sourire" (98); "Tu n'es plus entière!" (103); "une porte [qui] vient de s'ouvrir sur ses pensées, et elle ne saura plus garder certains mots qui jailliront, sans qu'elle le veuille, de sa bouche" (99).

34. "Elle devine, elle *voit* que Dieu s'arrête. . . . Il n'a pas encore l'habitude de ça, et se laisse retenir par un coin, du côté de la petite brèche! . . . Elle quitte affolée la Sainte Table, ayant l'envie sacrilège de cracher en dépit de sa ferveur. . . . Alors, elle le détache d'un coup

brutal de la langue, et la déglutition s'opère subitement; Dieu disparaît, s'engouffre comme s'il avait eu peur, après avoir constaté" (106).

35. "Elle a brusquement, la pauvre femme, la vision très absurde d'un château en ruines contemplé, autrefois, durant son voyage de noces. Oui . . . elle aperçoit la tour, là-bas, une tour qui porte à son sommet une couronne crénelée et qui met, dans des nués d'orage, comme la mâchoire inégale d'une colossale vieille" (101).

36. "Façade muette, aveugle, la menaçante façade par excellence, la façade hermétique" (130); "m'avoua qu'on ne savait pas le fin mot de cette satanée roche" (130).

37. "Il vit en état d'animal, allant, venant, mangeant, dormant, sans rien dire" (*Contes* 82).

38. "Accroupi sur son drap, tâtant ses petits membres cuisants qui seraient bleuis au matin, le garçon contemplait la femelle d'un regard de curiosité souffrante, protégeant son petit sexe de sa main gauche, car il se doutait bien que si elle frappait encore par là ce serait fini du *petit crapaud,* qui ferait couac et serait mort" (88).

39. "Il lui avait fait un garçon, et elle eût préféré une fille, c'est-à dire une alliée, une complice, une créature plus souple, capable d'apprécier toutes les phrases vaines qui s'élancent des bouches exaspérées par les journées de pluie" (90); "si méchants, Madame, qu'ils claquent du bec, sans jamais rien dire!" (91).

40. "Ce qu'il voit, il ne l'oubliera plus, parce que c'est trop drôle! Il voit une grande grenouille blanche, oui, c'est bien cela, cette flexibilité merveilleuse des cuisses et des bras ouverts, cet étirement élastique et précis de membres si pâles qu'ils en paraissent argentés!" (94–95).

41. "Maintenant, il comprend pourquoi on le traite de *crapaud,* c'est qu'il est réellement le fils d'une grenouille" (95).

42. "Dame! il y a beaucoup plus de . . . *grenouilles* que d'hommes, ça se devine" (98).

43. "Un petit morceau de drap rouge de la longueur d'une langue de femme" (102–3). The French word *appas* means both "bait" and "sexual attraction."

44. "Les voilà qui se pressent les uns sur les autres, les pauvres petits monstres, pour contempler la langue rouge que leur tire l'homme du bout de son fil maudit. C'est la langue de feu de la chimère! Elles ont fasciné, charmeuses petites sirènes, et, à son tour,

il les fascine. La gaule se relève, le fil fouette l'espace, et on perçoit un atroce cri d'oiseau plumé vif. La grenouille, trop curieuse, est saisie par le double hameçon qui, de loin, a l'air d'une ancre de salut. Elle agite ses petites pattes de derrière comme des jambes de fille qu'on viole" (104).

45. "Non, plus personne ne peut l'empêcher de manger à sa faim, de vivre. Il est libre. A genoux devant le tas des petits cadavres, il les déshabille, leur ôte la double boucle de leurs yeux d'or, leur enlève leur jolie robe de satin vert, leurs mignonnes culottes de velours blanc. Tout cela glisse pêle-mêle comme des vêtements de poupée, et il ne reste plus que les cuissettes nues, très pâles, agitées de frissons nerveux" (105).

6. Neurosis and Nostalgia: "Decadent" Desire?

1. A more extended treatment of Navarre and the "post-psycho-analytic" novel may be found in my "After the *Nouveau Roman:* Some New Names in French Fiction."

2. This essay has also been translated, with notes and commentary, by Anthony Wilden as *The Language of the Self: The Function of Language in Psychoanalysis* and subsequently as *Speech and Language in Psychoanalysis.*

For a discussion of the various "punctuations" that condition alternate readings of the preface Huysmans wrote for the 1903 reedition of *Against the Grain,* see my "Amazing Grace: *A rebours* Twenty Years After."

Bibliography

Primary Works

Beauvoir, Simone de. *Le deuxième sexe.* 2 vols. 1949. Paris: Gallimard, 1976.

———. *The Second Sex.* Trans. and ed. H. M. Parshley. New York: Knopf, 1971.

Freud, Sigmund. *The Complete Standard Edition of the Psychological Works of Sigmund Freud.* Trans. and ed. James Strachey. 24 vols. London: Hogarth Press and the Institute of Psycho-Analysis, 1953–74.

Hoffmann, E. T. A. *Three Märchen of E. T. A. Hoffmann: Little Zaches Surnamed Zinnober; Princess Brambilla; Master Flea.* Trans. C. E. Passage. Columbia: U of South Carolina P, 1971.

———. *A rebours.* 1884. Vol. 9 of *Oeuvres complètes de J.-K. Huysmans.* Paris: Editions G. Crès, 1928.

Huysmans, Joris-Karl. *Against the Grain.* Trans. J. Howard. New York: Lieber and Lewis, 1922.

Lorrain, Jean. *Masques et fantômes.* Ed. Francis Lacassin. Collection Modern Style. Paris: Union Générale d'Editions 10/18, 1974.

———. *Monsieur de Phocas, Astarté.* Paris: Albin Michel, 1929.

———. *Le jardin d'acclimatation.* Paris: Flammarion, 1980.

Navarre, Yves. *Cronus' Children.* Trans. Howard Girven. New York: Riverrun, 1986.

Proust, Marcel. *Correspondance de Marcel Proust.* Ed. Philip Kolb. 13 vols. Paris: Plon, 1970–85.

———. *Correspondance générale de Marcel Proust.* Ed. R. Proust and P. Brach. 6 vols. Paris: Plon, 1935.

———. *Jean Santeuil, précédé par* Les plaisirs et les jours. Ed. P. Clarac and Y. Sandre. Paris: Gallimard, Bibliothèque de la Pléiade, 1971.

Bibliography

————. *Les plaisirs et les jours*. Paris: Calmann-Lévy, 1896.

————. *Pleasures and Regrets*. Trans. L. Varese. New York: Ecco, 1949.

————. *A la recherche du temps perdu*. Ed. P. Clarac and A. Ferré. 3 vols. Paris: Gallimard, Bibliothèque de la Pléiade, 1954.

————. *Remembrance of Things Past*. Trans. C. K. Scott Moncrieff, T. Kilmartin, and A. Mayor. 3 vols. New York: Random, 1981.

————. *Selected Letters 1880–1903*. Trans. R. Manheim. Ed. P. Kolb. Garden City, NY: Doubleday, 1983.

Rachilde. *Contes et nouvelles, suivis du théâtre*. Paris: Mercure de France, 1900.

————. *Le démon de l'absurde*. Paris: Mercure de France, 1894.

————. *Madame Adonis*. Paris: Monnier, 1888.

————. *Monsieur Vénus*. Paris: F. Brossier, 1889; Paris: Flammarion, 1977.

Secondary Works

The secondary works have been grouped into specific subject areas; authors may therefore appear in more than one area.

DECADENCE

Amprimoz, Alexandre. "Note sur l'histoire des Hydropathes." *Romance Notes* 21 (1981): 305–308.

Aspects du Décadentisme européen. *Revue des sciences humaines* 153 (1974).

Autour du Symbolisme. *Revue des sciences humaines* 77 (1955).

Baju, Anatole. *L'école décadente*. Paris: Vanier, 1887.

Balakian, Anna, ed. *The Symbolist Movement in the Literature of European Languages*. Budapest: Akadémiai Kiadó, 1982.

Bancquart, Marie-Claire. *Images littéraires du Paris fin de siècle*. Paris: Labyrinthe, 1979.

————. "Introduction: Decadence." *Romantisme* 13.42 (1983): 3–8.

Beauclair, Henri, and Gabriel Vicaire. *Les Déliquescences, poèmes décadents d'Adoré Floupette*. Paris: Lion Vanné, 1885.

Besnard-Coursodon, Micheline. "*A rebours:* Le corps parlé." *Revue des sciences humaines* 170–71 (1978): 52–58.

Bibliography

Billy, André de. *L'époque 1900: 1885–1905.* Paris: Tallandier, 1951.

Bourget, Paul. *Essais de psychologie contemporaine.* Paris: Lemerre, 1885.

Carter, A. E. *The Idea of Decadence in French Literature 1830–1900.* Toronto: U of Toronto P, 1958.

Colin, René-Pierre. "Les Décadents: Nuanceurs ou barbares de l'idée." *Romantisme* 13.42 (1983): 47–53.

El Gammal, Jean. "Décadence, politique et littérature à la fin du XIXe siècle." *Romantisme* 13.42 (1983): 23–33.

Garber, Frederick. "The Structure of Romantic Decadence." *Nineteenth-Century French Studies* 1 (1973): 84–104.

Gilman, Richard. *Decadence: The Strange Life of an Epithet.* New York: Farrar, 1979.

Gourmont, Rémy de. *Le livre des masques.* Paris: Mercure de France, 1923.

Guiral, Pierre, "Les écrivains français et la notion de décadence de 1870 à 1914." *Romantisme* 13.42 (1983): 9–21.

Hamlyn, D. W. *Schopenhauer.* The Arguments of the Philosophers. London and Boston: Routledge and Kegan Paul, 1980.

Hansen, Eric C. *Disaffection and Decadence: A Crisis in French Intellectual Thought 1848-1898.* Washington, DC: UP of America, 1982.

Hughes, H. Stuart. *Consciousness and Society: The Reorganization of European Social Thought 1890–1930.* New York: Vintage-Random, 1977.

Huret, Jules. *Enquête sur l'évolution littéraire.* Paris: Charpentier, 1901.

Jackson, A. B. *La revue blanche.* Paris: Minard, 1960.

Jankélévitch, V. "La Décadence." *Revue de métaphysique et de morale* 55 (1950): 337–69.

Jullian, Philippe. *Robert de Montesquiou.* Paris: Perrin, 1966.

Kahn, Gustave. *Symbolistes et Décadents.* Paris: Léon Vanier, 1902.

Kaminsky, Alice R. "The Literary Concept of Decadence." *Nineteenth-Century French Studies* 4 (1976): 371–84.

Kingcaid, Renée A. "Amazing Grace: *A rebours* Twenty Years After." *L'esprit créateur* 27.3 (1987): 68–78.

Lehmann. A. G. *The Symbolist Aesthetic in France 1885–1895.* Oxford: Basil Blackwell, 1968.

Lethève, Jacques. *Impressionnistes et Symbolistes devant la presse.* Paris: Armand Colin, 1959.

Bibliography

————. "Un mot témoin de l'époque fin de siècle: Esthète." *Revue d'histoire littéraire de la France* 64 (1964): 436–46.

————. "Le thème de la décadence dans les lettres françaises à la fin du XIXe siècle." *Revue d'histoire littéraire de la France* 63 (1963): 46–61.

Livi, F. *J.-K. Huysmans:* A rebours *et l'esprit décadent.* Paris: Nizet, 1972.

Mazel, Henri. *Aux beaux temps du Symbolisme, 1890–1895.* Paris: Mercure de France, 1943.

Michaud, Guy. *Message poétique du Symbolisme.* 3 vols. Paris: Nizet, 1947.

Michel, Alain. "Tradition antique et philosophies de la décadence dans la littérature française autour de 1880." *Romantisme* 13.42 (1983): 55–76.

Milner, John. *Symbolists and Decadents.* London: Studio Vista, 1971.

Mitchell, Robert L. "The Déliquescence of Décadence: Floupette's Eclectic Target." *Nineteenth-Century French Studies* 9 (1981): 247–56.

Nordmann, Jean-Thomas. "Taine et la décadence." *Romantisme* 13.42 (1983): 35–46.

Nye, Robert A. "Degeneration and the Medical Model of Cultural Crisis in the French Belle Epoque." *Political Symbolism in Modern Europe: Essays in Honor of George L. Mosse.* Ed. Seymour Drescher and David Warren Sabean. New Brunswick, NJ: Transaction, 1982. 19–41.

Palacio, Jean de. "La féminité dévorante: Sur quelques images de la manducation dans la littérature décadente." *Revue des sciences humaines* 44 (1977): 601–18.

————. "Messaline décadente, ou la figure du sang." *Romantisme* 11.31 (1981): 209–28.

————. "Motif privilégié au jardin des supplices: Le mythe de la décollation et le décadentisme." *Revue des sciences humaines* 39 (1974): 39–61.

Peyre, Henri. *Qu'est-ce que le symbolisme?* Paris: Presses Universitaires de France, 1974.

Pierrot, Jean. *L'imaginaire décadent 1880–1900.* Paris: Presses Universitaires de France, 1977.

Praz, Mario. *The Romantic Agony.* Trans. A. Davidson. London: Oxford UP, 1933.

Bibliography

Raynaud, Ernest. *En marge de la mêlée symboliste*. Paris: Mercure de France, 1936.

———. *La mêlée symboliste*. Paris: Renaissance du livre, 1918–22.

Reed, John R. *Decadent Style*. Athens: Ohio UP, 1985.

Ribot, Théodule. *La philosophie de Schopenhauer*. Paris: Librairie Germer Baillère, 1874.

Richard, Noël. *A l'aube du symbolisme*. Paris: Nizet, 1961.

———. *Le mouvement décadent*. Paris: Nizet, 1968.

Ridge, George Ross. *The Hero in French Decadent Literature*. Athens: U of Georgia P, 1961.

Riffaterre, Michael. "Decadent Features in Maeterlinck's Poetry." *Language and Style* 7 (1974): 3–19.

Roosbroeck, G. L. *The Legend of the Decadents*. New York: Columbia UP, 1927.

Shattuck, Roger. *The Banquet Years*. Garden City, NY: Doubleday, 1958.

Sontag, Susan. *Illness as Metaphor*. New York: Farrar, 1977.

Spivak, Gayatri Chakravorty. "Decadent Style." *Language and Style* 7 (1974): 227–34.

Swart, Koenraad W. *The Sense of Decadence in Nineteenth Century France*. The Hague: Martinus Nijhoff, 1964.

Symons, Arthur. *The Symbolist Movement in Literature*. London: Heineman, 1899. New York: Dutton, 1919.

Taine, Hippolyte. *Philosophie de l'art*. 2 vols. Paris: Hachette, 1901.

———. *Voyage en Italie*. 2 vols. Paris: Hachette, 1884.

Teichmann, Elizabeth. *La fortune d'Hoffmann en France*. Geneva: Droz; Paris: Minard, 1961.

West, Thomas G. "Schopenhauer, Huysmans and French Naturalism." *Journal of European Studies* 1 (1971): 313–24.

Williams, Roger L. *The Horror of Life*. Chicago: U of Chicago P, 1980.

Dora

Bernstein, Isidor. "Integrative Summary: On the Re-viewings of the Dora Case." Kanser and Glenn 83–91.

Chodorow, Nancy. *The Reproduction of Mothering*. Berkeley and Los Angeles: U of California P, 1978.

Cixous, Hélène. *Portrait of Dora*. Trans. Sarah Burd. *Diacritics* 13.1 (1983): 2–32.

Bibliography

Cixous, Hélène, and Catherine Clément. *La jeune née.* Paris: Union Générale d'Editions 10/18, 1975.

Collins, Jerre, J. Ray Greene, Mary Lydon, Mark Sachner, and Eleanor Honig Skoller. "Questioning the Unconscious: The Dora Archive." *Diacritics* 13.1 (1983): 37–42.

Decker, Hannah S. "The Choice of a Name: 'Dora' and Freud's Relationship to Breuer." *Journal of the American Psychoanalytic Association* 30.1 (1982): 113–36.

Deutsch, Felix. "A Footnote to Freud's 'Fragment of the [*sic*] Analysis of a Case of Hysteria." *Psychoanalytic Quarterly* 16 (1957): 159–67.

Gallop, Jane. *The Daughter's Seduction: Feminism and Psychoanalysis.* Ithaca: Cornell UP, 1982. 132–50.

Geahchan, Dominique J. "Haine et identification négative dans l'hystérie." *Revue française de psychanalyse* 37 (1973): 337–57.

Gearhart, Suzanne. "The Scene of Psychoanalysis: The Unanswered Questions of Dora." *Diacritics* 9.1 (1979): 114–26.

Glenn, Jules. "Freud's Adolescent Patients: Katharina, Dora and the 'Homosexual Woman.'" Kanser and Glenn 23–47.

Hertz, Neil. "Dora's Secrets, Freud's Techniques." *Diacritics* 13.1 (1983): 65–76.

Kanser, Mark. "Dora's Imagery: The Flight from a Burning House." Kanser and Glenn 72–82.

Kanser, Mark, and Jules Glenn, eds. *Freud and his Patients.* New York: Jason Aronson, 1980.

Langs, Robert J. "The Misalliance Dimension in the Case of Dora." Kanser and Glenn 58–71.

Lewin, Karl K. "Dora Revisited." *Psychoanalytical Review* 60 (1974): 519–32.

Lubtchansky, Jacqueline. "Le point de vue économique dans l'hystérie à partir de la notion de traumatisme dans l'œuvre de Freud." *Revue française de psychanalyse* 37 (1973): 373–405.

McCaffrey, Phillip. *Freud and Dora: The Artful Dream.* New Brunswick, NJ: Rutgers UP, 1984.

Maddi, Salvatore R. "The Victimization of Dora." *Psychology Today* Sept. 1974: 91–100.

Major, René. "L'hystérie: Rêve et révolution." *Revue française de psychanalyse* 37 (1973): 303–12.

Mannoni, Octave. *Fictions freudiennes.* Paris: Seuil, 1978.

Bibliography

Marcus, Steven. "Freud and Dora: Story, History, Case History." *Freud: A Collection of Critical Essays.* Ed. P. Meisel. Englewood Cliffs, NJ: Prentice-Hall, 1981. 183–210.

Mitchell, Juliet. *Psychoanalysis and Feminism.* London: Allen Lane, 1974.

Moscovitz, Jean-Jacques. "D'un signe qui lui serait fait, ou aspects de l'homo-sexualité dans 'Dora.'" *Revue française de psychanalyse* 37 (1973): 359–72.

Ramas, Maria. "Freud's Dora, Dora's Hysteria: The Negation of a Woman's Rebellion." *Feminist Studies* 6 (1980): 472–510.

Rieff, Philip. "Introduction." *Dora: An Analysis of a Case of Hysteria.* By Sigmund Freud. New York: Collier, 1963. 7–20.

Rogow, Arnold A. "A Further Footnote to Freud's 'Fragment of an Analysis of a Case of Hysteria.'" *Journal of the American Psychoanalytic Association* 26 (1978): 330–56.

Scharfman, Melvin A. "Further Reflections on Dora." Kanser and Glenn 48–57.

Shimmel, Ilana. "Rêve et transfert dans 'Dora.'" *Revue française de psychanalyse* 37 (1973): 313–21.

Suleiman, Susan Rubin. "Nadja, Dora, Lol V. Stein: Women, Madness and Narrative." *Discourse in Psychoanalysis and Literature.* Ed. Shlomith Rimmon-Kenan. London and New York: Methuen, 1987. 124–51.

LORRAIN

Berg, Christian. "Le Dîner de têtes." *Art nouveau: Littérature et beaux-arts à la fin du 19e.* Editions de l'Université de Bruxelles 3 (1981): 9–24.

Dupont, Jacques. "Jean Lorrain, chroniqueur d'une fin de siècle." *Aspekte des Literature des Fin de siècle in der Romania.* Ed. Albert Gier and Angelika Corbineau-Hoffmann. Tübingen: Niemeyer, 1983. 116–23.

Guyaux, André. "Jean Lorrain et les illuminations: La citation clandestine." *Travaux de linguistique et de littérature* 24.2 (1986): 93–107.

Jullian, Philippe. *Jean Lorrain ou le Satiricon 1900.* Paris: Fayard, 1974.

Lacassin, Francis. "Préface: Jean Lorrain ou le bal des fantômes." *Masques et fantômes.* By Jean Lorrain. Paris: Union Générale d'Editions 10/18, 1974. 7–17.

Bibliography

McLendon, Will L. "The Grotesque in Jean Lorrain's New Byzantium: *Le vice errant.*" *Pre-Text/Text/Context: Essays on Nineteenth-Century French Literature.* Ed. Robert L. Mitchell. Columbus: Ohio State UP, 1980. 25–35.

──────. "Jean Lorrain: Impresario de l'art nouveau." *Orbis Litterarum* 39 (1984): 54–64.

──────. "Travel as Hunger Urge in the Works of Jean Lorrain." *South Central Review* 2.1 (1985): 13–24.

Mourier-Casile, Pascaline. *De la chimère à la merveille.* Lausanne: L'Age d'Homme, 1986.

Schuerewegen, Franc. "Histoires de pieds: Gautier, Lorrain et le fantastique." *Nineteenth-Century French Studies* 13 (1985): 200–210.

Tunner, Erika. "Lore Lay—Loreley: Romantique ou décadente?" *Romantisme* 13.42 (1983): 167–75.

Ziegler, Robert E. "The Spectacles of Self: Decadent Aesthetics in Jean Lorrain." *Nineteenth-Century French Studies* 14 (1986): 312–23.

PROUST

Bailey, Ninette. "Couleur picturale et couleur poétique dans *Les plaisirs et les jours.*" *Bulletin de l'Association des Amis de Marcel Proust et de Combray* 16 (1966): 411–22.

Bardèche, Maurice. *Marcel Proust romancier.* 2 vols. Paris: Les Sept Couleurs, 1971.

Bataille, Georges. "Proust et la mère profanée." *Critique* 1 (1946): 601–11.

Berthier, Philippe. "Barbey d'Aurevilly et Proust." *Revue des lettres modernes* 260–63 (1971): 23–60.

Billy, Robert de. *Marcel Proust: Lettres et conversations.* Paris: Editions des Portiques, 1930.

Blum, Léon. Rev. of *Les plaisirs et les jours. La revue blanche* 1 July 1896: 46.

Bonnet, Henri. "Proust en 1896." *Europe* 48 (1970): 120–29.

──────. "Proust et Darlu." *Bulletin de l'Association des Amis de Marcel Proust et de Combray* 14 (1964): 217–21.

Brée, Germaine. "Une étude du style de Proust dans les *Plaisirs et les jours.*" *French Review* 15 (1942): 401–9.

Carassus, Emilien. *Le snobisme et les lettres françaises de Paul Bourget à Marcel Proust.* Paris: Armand Colin, 1966.

Bibliography

Clogenson, Y. E. "Proust et Huysmans." *Revue de Paris* 70.9 (1963): 50–62. Rpt. in Fabre-Luce de Gruson 15–34.

Cohn, Robert G. "Proust and Mallarmé." *French Studies* 24 (1970): 262–75.

Dominguez, Muriel. "'La fin de la jalousie': A First Start." Joiner 23–31.

Doubrovsky, Serge. *La place de la madeleine: Ecriture et fantasme chez Proust.* Paris: Mercure de France, 1974.

Du Maire, L. "Marcel Prousts Novellen *Les plaisirs et les jours* als Vorlaufer seines Romans." Thesis. U of Hamburg, 1954.

Ellison, David R. *The Reading of Proust.* Baltimore: Johns Hopkins UP, 1984.

Fabre-Luce de Gruson, Françoise, ed. *Entretiens sur Marcel Proust.* Paris and The Hague: Mouton, 1966.

Ferré, André. *Les années de collège de Marcel Proust.* Paris: Gallimard, 1959.

Florival, Ghislaine. *Le désir chez Proust.* Louvain and Paris: Nauwelaerts, 1971.

Fretet, Jean. *L'aliénation poétique: Rimbaud, Mallarmé, Proust.* Paris: Janin, 1946.

Galand, René. "Proust et Baudelaire." *PMLA* 65 (1950): 1011–34.

Gauthier, Patrick. "Proust et Gustave Moreau." *Europe* 48 (1970): 237–41.

Gicquel, Bernard. "La composition des *Plaisirs et les jours.*" *Bulletin de l'Association des Amis de Marcel Proust et de Combray* 10 (1960): 249–61.

Gide, André. "En relisant *Les plaisirs et les jours.*" *Nouvelle revue française* 20 (1923): 123–26.

Gourmont, Jean de. "Comment débuta Marcel Proust." *Mercure de France* 185 (1926): 701–3.

Gregh, Fernand. "Livres illustrés." *Revue de Paris* 15 Dec. 1896: n. pag.

———. Rev. of *Les plaisirs et les jours. Revue de Paris* 15 July 1896: n. pag.

Gunn, Daniel. *Psychoanalysis and Fiction: An Exploration of Literary and Psychoanalytic Borders.* Cambridge: Cambridge UP, 1988.

Henry, Anne. "*Les plaisirs et les jours*: Chronologie et métempsychose." *Etudes proustiennes.* Vol. 1. Les Cahiers Marcel Proust n. s. 6. Paris: Gallimard, 1963. 69–93.

Bibliography

Hodson, W. L. "Proust's Methods of Character Presentation in *Les plaisirs et les jours* and *Jean Santeuil.*" *Modern Language Review* 57 (1962): 41–46.

Houston, J. P. "Proust, Gourmont, and the Symbolist Heritage." *Modern French Criticism from Proust and Valéry to Structuralism.* Ed. J. K. Simon. Chicago: U of Chicago P, 1971. 41–60.

Jackson, Elizabeth R. *L'évolution de la mémoire involontaire dans l'œuvre de Proust.* Paris: Nizet, 1966.

Johnson, J. Theodore, Jr. "Proust et Gustave Moreau." *Bulletin de l'Association des Amis de Marcel Proust et de Combray* 28 (1979): 614–39.

———. "Proust's Early 'Portraits de peintres.'" *Comparative Literature Studies* 4 (1967): 397–408.

Joiner, L. D., ed. *The Art of the Proustian Novel Reconsidered.* Winthrop Studies on Major Modern Authors. Rock Hill, SC: Winthrop College, 1979.

Josipovici, Gabriel D. "Proust: A Voice in Search of Itself." *Critical Quarterly* 13 (1971): 105–23.

Juin, Hubert. "Proust, fin de siècle." *Ecrivains de l'avant-siècle.* Paris: Seghers, 1972. 231–43.

Kamber, Gerald, and Richard Macksey. "'Negative Metaphor' and Proust's Rhetoric of Absence." *Modern Language Notes* 85 (1970): 858–83.

Kasell, Walter. "Writing and the Return to Innocence: Proust's 'La confession d'une jeune fille.'" Joiner 33–42.

Kingcaid, Renée A. "Running with the 'In' Crowd: Proust *Pasticheur.*" *Selecta: Journal of the Pacific Northwest Council on Foreign Languages* 4 (1983): 10–16.

Kolb, Philip. "Les Phares de Proust." Fabre-Luce de Gruson 105–28.

Languth, William. "The World and Life of the Dreams." *Yale French Studies* 34 (1965): 117–30.

Lorrain, Jean. "Pall-Mall Semaine." Rev. of *Les plaisirs et les jours. Le journal* 15 July 1896: n. pag.

———. "Pall-Mall Semaine." Rev. of *Les plaisirs et les jours. Le journal* 3 Feb. 1897: n. pag.

McDowell, David. "The World from the Ark." *Hudson Review* 2 (1949): 151–60.

Massis, Henri. *Le drame de Marcel Proust.* Paris: Seuil, 1937.

Bibliography

Maurois, André. *A la recherche de Marcel Proust, avec de nombreux inédits.* Paris: Hachette, 1949.

Maurras, Charles. "Un poète, deux pamphlétaires, un sociologue, et un moraliste." Rev. of *Les plaisirs et les jours. Revue encyclopédique* 22 Aug. 1896: 584.

Milly, Jean. *Les pastiches de Proust.* Paris: Armand Colin, 1970.

Monnin-Hornung, Juliette. *Proust et la peinture.* Geneva: Droz, 1951.

O'Brien, Justin. "The Wisdom of the Young Proust." *Romanic Review* 45 (1954): 121–34. Rpt. in *Contemporary French Literature.* Ed. L. S. Roudiez. New Brunswick, NJ: Rutgers UP, 1971. 60–84.

Paganini, Maria. "Intertextuality and the Strategy of Desire: Proust's 'Mélancolique villégiature de Mme de Breyves.'" Trans. J. Beizer. *Yale French Studies* 57 (1979): 136–63.

Perret, Paul. "A travers champs." Rev. of *Les plaisirs et les jours. La liberté* 26 June 1896: n. pag.

Peytard, Jean. "Un Prénom en quête de personnage: Honoré dans *Les plaisirs et les jours. Cahiers de lexicologie* 51.2 (1987): 215–28.

_____. "Sur les variantes des noms de personnages dans 'La Mort de Baldassare Silvande, Vicomte de Sylvanie': Marcel Proust, *Les plaisirs et les jours." Hommages à Jacques Petit.* Ed. Michel Malicet. Paris: Belles Lettres, 1985. 801–12.

Picon, Gaetan. "Proust et la naissance d'une voix." *Critique* 188 (1963): 3–20.

Placella, Paola. *Motivi proustiani: Da* Les plaisirs et les jours *alla Recherche. Naples: Giannini, 1976.*

Price, Larkin B. *"Materials for a Critical Edition of Marcel Proust's Les plaisirs et les jours." DA* 26 (1965): 3348–49. Wisconsin.

Rambaud, Henri. "Le premier livre de Marcel Proust." *La revue universelle* 19 (1924): 232–37.

Robert, Louis de. *Comment débuta Marcel Proust.* Paris: Gallimard, 1969.

Rogers, Brian G. *Proust's Narrative Techniques.* Geneva: Droz, 1965.

Sarkany, Stéphane. "Pragmatique et réception de *Les plaisirs et les jours." Proust et le texte producteur.* Ed. John Erickson and Irene Pages. Guelph, Ontario: University of Guelph, 1980. 115–22.

Soucy, Robert. "Bad Readers in the World of Proust." *French Review* 44 (1971): 677–86.

Bibliography

Splitter, Randolph. *Proust's* Recherche: *A Psychoanalytic Interpretation*. London and Boston: Routledge and Kegan Paul, 1981.

Strauss, Bernard. *The Maladies of Marcel Proust: Doctors and Disease in His Life and Work*. New York and London: Holmes and Meier, 1980.

Wilson, Edmund. "Marcel Proust." *Axel's Castle: A Study of the Imaginative Literature of 1870–1930*. New York: Scribner's, 1931. 132–90.

Wright, Ralph. "A Sensitive Petronius." *Nineteenth Century and After* 93 (1923): 378–99. Rpt. in *Marcel Proust: An English Tribute*. Ed. C. K. Scott Moncrieff. London: Chatto and Windus, 1923. 31–52.

PSYCHOANALYSIS, SEMIOTICS, AND LITERARY THEORY

Barthes, Roland. *Elements of Semiology*. Trans. A. Lavers and C. Smith. London: Jonathan Cape, 1967.

Beaujour, Michel. "Some Paradoxes of Description." *Yale French Studies* 61 (1981): 27–59.

Bénézet, Mathieu. *Le roman de la langue: Des romans 1960–1975*. Paris: Union Générale d'Editions 10/18, 1977.

Benveniste, Emile. *Problèmes de linguistique générale*. Paris: Gallimard, 1966.

Bonaparte, Marie. "Poe and the Function of Literature." Phillips, *Art and Psychoanalysis* 54–87.

Bonnefis, Philippe. "The Melancholic Describer." Trans. Jeremy Raw. *Yale French Studies* 61 (1981): 145–75.

Bowie, Malcolm. *Freud, Proust and Lacan: Theory as Fiction*. Cambridge: Cambridge UP, 1987.

Brooks, Peter. "Freud's Masterplot: Questions of Narrative." Felman, *Literature and Psychoanalysis* 280–300.

———. "The Idea of a Psychoanalytic Literary Criticism." *Critical Inquiry* 13 (1986): 334–48. Rpt. in Rimmon-Kenan 1–18.

Bryson, Norman. *Tradition and Desire: From David to Delacroix*. Cambridge: Cambridge UP, 1984.

Burke, Kenneth. "Freud—and the Analysis of Poetry." Meisel 73–94.

Clark, Ronald W. *Freud: The Man and the Cause*. New York: Random, 1980.

Clarke, D. S., Jr.. *Principles of Semiotic*. London and New York: Routledge and Kegan Paul, 1987.

Bibliography

Clément, Catherine. *The Lives and Legends of Jacques Lacan.* Trans. A. Goldhammer. New York: Columbia UP, 1983.

Danto, Arthur C. "Freudian Explanations and the Language of the Unconscious." Smith 325–53.

Davis, Robert Con. "Lacan, Poe, and Narrative Repression." Davis, *Lacan and Narration* 983–1005.

——, ed. *Lacan and Narration : The Psychoanalytic Difference in Narrative Theory.* Baltimore: Johns Hopkins UP, 1983.

Derrida, Jacques. "Freud and the Scene of Writing." Trans. A. Bass. Meisel, *Freud* 145–82.

Dix, Carol. *The New Mother Syndrome: Coping with Postpartum Stress and Depression.* Garden City, NY: Doubleday, 1985.

Evans, Mary. *Simone de Beauvoir: A Feminist Mandarin.* London: Tavistock, 1985.

Felman, Shoshana. "Beyond Oedipus: The Specimen Story of Psychoanalysis." Davis, *Lacan and Narration* 1021–53.

——. *La folie et la chose littéraire.* Paris: Seuil, 1978.

——. "On Reading Poetry: Reflections on the Limits and Possibilities of Psychoanaytic Approaches." *The Literary Freud: Mechanisms of Defense and the Poetic Will.* Ed. J. H. Smith. New Haven: Yale UP, 1980. 119–48.

——. "To Open the Question." Felman, *Literature and Psychoanalysis* 5–10.

——. "Turning the Screw of Interpretation." Felman, *Literature and Psychoanalysis* 94–207.

——, ed. *Literature and Psychoanalysis: The Question of Reading: Otherwise.* Baltimore: Johns Hopkins UP, 1982.

Flieger, Jerry Aline. "The Purloined Punchline: Joke as Textual Paradigm." Davis, *Lacan and Narration* 941–67.

——. "Trial and Error: The Case of the Textual Unconscious." *Diacritics* 11.1 (1982): 56–67.

Fliess, Robert. "On the Nature of Human Thought: The Primary and the Secondary Process as Exemplified by the Dream and Other Psychic Productions." *Readings in Psychoanalytic Psychology.* Ed. Morton Levitt. New York: Appleton-Century-Crofts, 1959. 213–20.

Gallop, Jane. *Reading Lacan.* Ithaca: Cornell UP, 1985.

——. "Reading the Mother Tongue: Psychoanalytic Feminist Criticism." *The Trial(s) of Psychoanalysis.* Ed. Françoise Meltzer.

Bibliography

Chicago: U of Chicago P, 1987. 125–40.

Genette, Gérard. *Figures II*. Paris: Seuil, 1969.

———. *Figures III*. Paris: Seuil, 1972.

Girard, René. *Deceit, Desire, and the Novel: Self and Other in Literary Structure*. Trans. Y. Freccero. Baltimore: Johns Hopkins UP, 1976.

Group µ [J. Dubois et al.]. *A General Rhetoric*. Trans. P. B. Burrell and E. M. Slotkin. Baltimore: Johns Hopkins UP, 1981.

Grünbaum, Adolf. *The Foundations of Psychoanalysis: A Philosophical Critique*. Berkeley and Los Angeles: U of California P, 1984.

Hamon, Philippe. "Rhetorical Status of the Descriptive." Trans. Patricia Baudoin. *Yale French Studies* 61 (1981): 1–26.

Hartman, Geoffrey H., ed. *Psychoanalysis and the Question of the Text*. Baltimore: Johns Hopkins UP, 1978.

Heller, Terry. *The Delights of Terror: An Aesthetics of the Tale of Terror*. Urbana and Chicago: U of Illinois P, 1987.

Hertz, Neil. "Freud and the Sandman." *Textual Strategies: Perspectives in Post-Structrualist Criticism*. Ed. J. V. Harari. Ithaca: Cornell UP, 1979. 296–321.

Holland, Norman N. *The Dynamics of Literary Response*. New York: Oxford UP, 1968.

Jakobson, Roman. "Linguistique et poétique." *Essais de linguistique générale*. Vol. 1. Paris: Minuit, 1963. 209–48.

Johnson, Barbara. "The Frame of Reference: Poe, Lacan, Derrida." Felman, *Literature and Psychoanalysis* 457–505.

Josipovici, Gabriel. *Writing and the Body*. Princeton: Princeton UP, 1982.

Kermode, Frank. *The Sense of an Ending: Studies in the Theory of Fiction*. London: Oxford UP, 1975.

Kingcaid, Renée. "After the Nouveau Roman: Some New Names in French Fiction." *Review of Contemporary Fiction* 8.2 (1988): 300–312.

Kofman, Sarah. *The Enigma of Woman: Woman in Freud's Writings*. Trans. Catherine Porter. Ithaca: Cornell UP, 1985.

Kristeva, Julia. *Desire in Language: A Semiotic Approach to Literature and Art*. Trans. L. S. Roudiez. New York: Columbia UP, 1980.

———. "The Pain of Sorrow in the Modern World: The Works of Marguerite Duras." *PMLA* 102 (1987): 138–52.

Lacan, Jacques. *Ecrits*. Paris: Seuil, 1966.

Bibliography

_____. *Ecrits: A Selection*. Trans. Alan Sheridan. New York: Norton, 1977.

_____. "Seminar on 'The Purloined Letter.'" Trans. Jeffrey Mehlman. *Yale French Studies* 48 (1972): 38–72.

_____. *Speech and Language in Psychoanalysis*. Trans. Anthony Wilden. Baltimore: Johns Hopkins UP, 1981. Rpt. of *The Language of the Self: The Function of Language in Psychoanalysis*. By Jacques Lacan. Trans. Anthony Wilden. New York: Dell, 1968.

Langer, Lawrence. *The Age of Atrocity: Death in Modern Literature*. Boston: Beacon, 1978.

Laplanche, Jacques, and Serge Leclaire. "The Unconscious: A Psychoanalytic Study." Trans. P. Coleman. *Yale French Studies* 48 (1972): 118–78.

Laplanche, Jacques, and J.-B. Pontalis. *The Language of Psycho-Analysis*. Trans. D. Nicolson-Smith. New York: Norton, 1973.

Leavy, Stanley A. "The Significance of Jacques Lacan." Smith 271–92.

LeGuern, Michel. *Sémantique de la métaphore et de la métonymie*. Paris: Larousse, 1973.

Lemaire, Anika. *Jacques Lacan*. Trans. D. Macey. London and Boston: Routledge and Kegan Paul, 1977.

Lesser, Simon O. *Fiction and the Unconscious*. New York: Vintage-Random, 1962.

Lévi-Strauss, Claude. *Anthropologie structurale*. Paris: Plon, 1958.

_____. *The Elementary Structures of Kinship*. Trans. J. H. Bell et al. Boston: Beacon, 1969.

Lodge, David. *The Modes of Modern Writing: Metaphor, Metonymy, and the Typology of Modern Literature*. Ithaca: Cornell UP, 1977.

Loewald, Hans W. "Primary Process, Secondary Process, and Language." Smith 235–70.

Lubbock, Percy. *The Craft of Fiction*. New York: Viking, 1957.

Mahony, Patrick J. *Freud as a Writer*. New Haven: Yale UP, 1987.

Mannoni, Octave. *Clefs pour l'imaginaire ou l'autre scène*. Paris: Seuil, 1969.

Mehlman, Jeffrey. "The Floating Signifier: From Lévi-Strauss to Lacan." *Yale French Studies* 48 (1972): 10–37.

_____. *A Structural Study of Autobiography: Proust, Leiris, Sartre, Lévi-Strauss*. Ithaca: Cornell UP, 1974.

Bibliography

Meisel, Perry. "Introduction: Freud as Literature." Meisel, *Freud* 1–35.

———, ed. *Freud: A Collection of Critical Essays.* Englewood Cliffs, NJ: Prentice-Hall, 1981.

Miel, Jan. "Jacques Lacan and the Structure of the Unconscious." *Yale French Studies* 36–37 (1966): 104–11. Rpt. in *Structuralism*. Ed. J. Ehrmann. Garden City, NY: Anchor-Doubleday, 1970. 94–101.

Mykyta, Larysa. "Lacan, Literature and the Look: Woman in the Eye of Psychoanalysis." *SubStance* 39 (1982): 49–57.

Newsom, Robert. *A Likely Story: Probability and Play in Fiction.* New Brunswick, NJ: Rutgers UP, 1988.

Noakes, Susan. "Intertextuality and Dante's Antithetical Hypersign." *Semiotics 1984*. Ed. John Deely. Lanham, MD: UP of America, 1985. 95–103.

Paley, Marlene G. "A Feminist's Look at Freud's Feminist Psychology." *American Journal of Psychoanalysis* 39 (1979): 179–83.

Phillips, William. "Introduction: Art and Neurosis." Phillips *Art and Psychoanalysis* xiii–xxiv.

———, ed. *Art and Psychoanalysis.* Cleveland and New York: Meridian-World, 1957.

Ragland-Sullivan, Ellie. *Jacques Lacan and the Philosophy of Psychoanalysis.* Urbana and Chicago: U of Illinois P, 1986.

Rieff, Philip. *Freud: The Mind of the Moralist.* Chicago: U of Chicago P, 1979.

Riffaterre, Michael. "Descriptive Imagery." *Yale French Studies* 61 (1981): 107–25.

———. *Semiotics of Poetry.* Bloomington: Indiana UP, 1978.

———. "Trollope's Metonymies." *Nineteenth-Century Fiction* 37 (1982): 272–92.

Rimmon-Kenan, Shlomith, ed. *Discourse in Psychoanalysis and Literature.* London and New York: Methuen, 1987.

Rogers, Robert. *Metaphor: A Psychoanalytic View.* Berkeley and Los Angeles: U of California P, 1978.

Saussure, Ferdinand de. *Cours de linguistique générale.* Paris: Payot, 1974.

Schafer, Roy. "Narration in Psychoanalytic Dialogue." *On Narrative.* Ed. W. J. T. Mitchell. Chicago: U of Chicago P, 1981. 25–49.

Schofer, Peter, and Donald Rice. "Metaphor, Metonymy and Synec-doche Revis(it)ed." *Semiotica* 21 (1977): 121–49.

Scholes, Robert. *Semiotics and Interpretation*. New Haven: Yale UP, 1982.

Sharpe, Ella Freeman. "Psycho-Physical Problems Revealed in Language: An Examination of Metaphor." *Collected Papers on Psycho-Analysis*. Ed. M. Brierley. London: Hogarth, 1950. 155–58.

Silverman, Kaja. *The Subject of Semiotics*. Oxford and New York: Oxford UP, 1983.

Skura, Meredith Anne. *The Literary Use of the Psychoanalytic Process*. New Haven: Yale UP, 1981.

Smith, J. H., ed. *Psychoanalysis and Language*. New Haven and London: Yale UP, 1978.

Spivak, Gayatri Chakravorty. "The Letter as Cutting Edge." Felman, *Literature and Psychoanalysis* 208–26.

Stierle, Karlheinz. "The Reading of Fictional Texts." *The Reader in the Text: Essays on Audience and Interpretation*. Ed. Susan Suleiman and Inge Crosman. Princeton: Princeton UP, 1980. 83–105.

Todorov, Tzvetan. *The Fantastic: A Structural Approach to a Literary Genre*. Trans. R. Howard. Ithaca: Cornell UP, 1977.

Wilden, Anthony. "Freud, Signorelli, and Lacan: The Repression of the Signifier." *American Imago* 23 (1966): 332–66.

Wright, Elizabeth. *Psychoanalytic Criticism: Theory in Practice*. London and New York: Methuen, 1984.

RACHILDE

Besnard-Coursodon, Micheline. "*Monsieur Vénus, Madame Adonis:* Sexe et discours." *Littérature* 54 (1984): 121–27.

Dauphiné, Claude. *Rachilde: Femme de lettres 1900*. Perigueux: Fanlac, 1985.

———. "Sade, Rachilde, et Freud: Lecture de *La Marquise de Sade.*" *Bulletin de l'Association des Professeurs de Lettres* 17 (1981): 55–59.

Hawthorne, Melanie C. "*Monsieur Vénus:* A Critique of Gender Roles." *Nineteenth-Century French Studies* 16 (1987–88): 162–79.

Waelti-Walters, Jennifer. *Feminist Novelists of the Belle Epoque*. Bloomington: Indiana UP, 1990.

Bibliography

Ziegler, Robert E. "The Suicide of 'La Comédienne' in Rachilde's *La jongleuse.*" *Continental, Latin-American and Francophone Women Writers*. Ed. Enice Myers and Ginette Adamson. Lanham, MD: UP of America, 1987. 55–61.

Index

Anchoring points, 33. *See also* Punctuation; Upholstery buttons

Art, Decadent concept of, 6, 14, 15, 38, 97, 105, 150, 151, 157n.6; in Lorrain, 80, 82, 96–98, 99, 100, 163–64n.2, 168–69n.23; and neurosis, 6; and return of the repressed, 79–80

Aubert, Edgar, 40–41

Authority, narrative, 16, 37, 100, 168n.20

Bardèche, Maurice, 37, 53, 159n.2

Barrès, Maurice, 123

Baudelaire, Charles, 5, 135

Beauclair, Henri, 5

Beauvoir, Simone de, 111, 116–22; critique of Freud and psychoanalysis in, 116–17, 120; interest in sexual dysfunction, 116–19, 174–75n.9; and reproduction, female, 118–19. Works: *Second Sex, The,* 116–22; discrepancies between French and English editions of, 174–75n.9; *Very Easy Death, A,* 121

Behavior, bad, 80; in case of Elisabeth von R., 78; and Decadents, 6, 148; in Dora case, 80; in Freud's grandson,

77–78, 79; in Lorrain, 80; in Proust, 60–61, 62, 63–64, 69; in war neurotics, 78, 79

Bénézet, Mathieu, 91, 168nn. 20, 21

Billy, Robert de, 37, 40–41

Body, 23, 25, 30, 31, 66, 68, 69–71, 72, 74, 95, 97, 100, 111, 112–16, 123, 130, 137, 138–40, 147

—female: in Beauvoir, Simone de, 116–22; and displacement in Rachilde, 17, 122–33; in Dora case, 115–16; and hysteria, 113–22; in Rachilde, 14, 17, 112, 122, 123, 124, 132–33, 139–40, 144, 147, 148

—maternal, 10, 68, 72, 122, 133, 134, 135, 136, 138, 140, 142, 147, 152, 178–79n.23

Breuer, Josef, 19

Brooks, Peter, 156–57n.5

Bryson, Norman, 32

Carter, A. E., 5, 155n.2

Case study, 105, 110; in Beauvoir, Simone de, 117–18; and relation to short story, 15, 23

Castration, 9, 10, 40, 72, 73, 74, 101, 121, 146; anxiety, 38, 39; and cinema, 71–72; and rela-

Index

tion to fetish object, 38–40,
146
Censor, psychic, 8, 11, 20, 152
Chain, signifying, 10–11
Charcot, Doctor Jean Martin, 18–
23, 98. Work: *Leçons du mardi
de la Salpêtrière (1887–88)*, 21
Clément, Catherine, 32
Closure, narrative, 168n.23; in
Lorrain, 99–100, 107; in short
story collections, 15, 148–50
Condensation, 8–9, 10, 11, 21, 89,
155–56n.3
Condition seconde, 19–21, 112
Constancy principle, 76
Countertransference, 155n.1
Couture, Thomas, 155n.2
Cross-marking, 85–87, 88, 100,
101, 147
Culture, 17, 32, 117, 120, 138,
140, 141, 142, 144, 146, 147,
151, 152; and Decadence, 30–
31; opposed to nature in
Rachilde, 133, 135, 136, 137,
139, 178–79n.23

D'Annunzio, Gabriele, 14
Daudet, Lucien, 15
Dauphiné, Claude, 15, 112
Davis, Robert Con, 9, 156–57n.5
Death: in Lorrain, 95, 96–97, 101,
102, 103, 106, 109–10; in
Proust, 38, 40–52, 66, 74, 146;
in Rachilde, 124–25, 126, 127,
128, 129, 130–32, 137, 143
—instincts, 78; and return of the
repressed, 79–80
Decadence, French, 21–22, 30–31,
45, 150–52; historical
relationship to psychoanalysis,

8, 19, 146; literary definitions
of, 5, 6; models of, 6–7, 29,
155n.2; semiotic approach to,
8, 13, 29, 33–34
Deformation (descriptive
technique in Lorrain), 81–82,
83, 84–86, 87, 163–64n.2
*Déliquescences, poèmes décadents
d'Adoré Floupette, Les*, 5
Description (narrative technique),
14; in Lorrain, 86, 87, 90, 92–
94, 95, 147, 168–69n.23; in
Rachilde, 122–33, 136, 143
Des Esseintes, Jean des Floressas
(protagonist of *Against the
Grain*), 5, 6, 19, 104
*Diagnostic and Statistical Manual of
Mental Disorders*, 119
Displacement, 8–9, 10, 11, 21, 89,
93, 94, 104, 107, 111, 133,
135–36, 144, 147, 155–56n.3,
156–57n.5, 178–79n.23; as
descriptive technique in
Rachilde, 122–33
Dix, Carol, 119
"Docteur Cinabre, Le." *See*
Hoffman, *Little Zaches,
Surnamed Zinnober*
Dora (Bauer, Ida), 1–4, 17, 24,
111, 114–16, 117, 121, 144, 148,
151, 155n.1
Dora case. *See* Freud, Sigmund,
"Fragment of an Analysis of a
Case of Hysteria"
Dreams, 2, 8–9, 11, 24, 57, 59,
76, 77, 78, 81, 98, 101, 104,
114, 120, 151, 155–56n.3
Duncan, Isadora, 117

El Gammal, Jean, 7

202

Index

Evans, Mary, 120, 121

Fantastic, 16, 75–76, 82, 88, 89, 98, 102, 168n.23
Fetish, 35; and castration, 38–40; definition of, 38–39; in Lorrain, 101; in Proust, 16, 43, 44, 45, 47, 48, 51, 52, 55, 56–57, 66, 68, 69, 72, 73, 74, 146–47, 148
Fetishism, 14; feminist critique of, 39–40; as narrative strategy in Proust, 14, 38, 40, 43, 51–52, 55–56, 74, 161–62n.11
Field, perceptual, 16, 92, 94, 95, 97, 100, 103, 147
Flaubert, Gustave, 16
Fliess, Robert, 155–56n.3
Fort-da game, 77, 104–5
France, Anatole, 35, 160n.4
Franco-Prussian War (1870), 7
Frau K. (Dora case), 2, 3, 4, 115, 116
Freud, Sigmund, 1–4, 8–9, 11, 13, 17, 18–29, 38–40, 48, 76–80, 81, 99, 104, 105, 113–16, 117, 118, 119, 120, 121, 123, 146, 148, 151, 155n.1, 157–58n.1. Works: *Beyond the Pleasure Principle*, 76–80; "Case of Elizabeth von R., The," 25–29; Charcot obituary, 19–20, 21; "Fetishism," 38–40; "Fragment of an Analysis of a Case of Hysteria," 1–4, 8–9, 17, 22, 24, 114–16, 123, 155n.1, 157–58n.1; *Interpretation of Dreams, The*, 8–9, 21, 24, 114, 120; *Leçons du mardi de la Salpêtrière (1887–88)* (translation of

Charcot), 21; *On the History of the Psycho-Analytic Movement*, 22; "Preliminary Communication" *(Studies on Hysteria)*, 19; *Report to the Faculty of Medicine*, 18–19; *Studies on Hysteria*, 1, 19, 23, 24, 29, 76, 78, 115; *Totem and Taboo*, 48
Frog: as image in Lorrain, 87, 88, 90–91, 92–94, 99, 103, 104, 140, 143, 144, 147, 148, 166–67n.14; as image in Rachilde, 13, 133, 140, 141, 142–44; as signifier in Lorrain, 94
Fuocu, Il (The Flame, D'Annunzio) 28

Gallimard, Gaston, 36
Gallop, Jane, 151, 178–79n.23
Gautier, Théophile, 5
Gearhart, Suzanne, 4, 155n.1
Gicquel, Bernard, 44–45
Gide, André, 16, 160n.16. Work: *Journal*, 16
Glenn, Jules, M.D., 2
Goncourt, Jules, and Edmond de, 5
Grandjean, Charles, 36
Group μ, 158n.2
Grünbaum, Adolf, 157n.6

Hahn, Reynaldo, 35, 160n.4
Hallucination: in Lorrain, 75, 81, 97, 101, 103; in Proust, 16, 52, 53, 54, 58–59, 62, 64–65, 66, 71
Head, decapitated: as image in Lorrain, 95–99, 100–103, 138; as image in Rachilde, 138
Head metonymy. *See* Metonymies, head

Index

Health, Willie, 40, 41, 42–43; dedication of *Pleasures and Regrets* to, 40–43

Heller, Terry, 168–69n.23

Henry, Anne, 51, 74

Heredity: as factor in degeneration, 21–22; as factor in hysteria, 19, 21–22

Herr K. (Dora case), 2, 4, 115, 174n.7

Hertz, Neil, 22–23

Heterosexuality, 130; and fetishism, 39

Hoffman, E. T. A., 76, 88, 89, 90, 104; French translations of, 164, 166–67n.14. Works: "Councillor Krespel," 166–67n.14; *Little Zaches, Surnamed Zinnober*; 89–90, 166–67n.14

Homosexuality, 90, 155n.1; and fetishism, 39; in Rachilde, 126

Huysmans, Joris-Karl, 5, 7, 34, 104. Work: *Against the Grain*, 6, 14, 19, 34, 104

Hypersign, 24, 158n.3

Hypertrophy: and Decadence, 5, 29–31, 34; in Lorrain, 92; and signification, 29–34

Hysteria, 18–23, 24; and body, 113–22; in case of Elizabeth von R., 25–29; and Dora case, 24, 116; etiology of (Charcot), 19, 22; etiology of (Freud), 21–23; in Lorrain, 82, 99, 110; in Proust, 45, 47; in Rachilde, 111, 112–13, 121–22, 133, 151; sexual factors in, 17, 21–22, 115; textual approach to, 24–29

Illness, 11, 118, 119, 146, 155–56n.3; in Freud, 23, 25, 26, 28; in Proust, 41, 42, 43–44, 45, 51, 60, 160n.6

Illusion, realist, 16, 66, 91–94, 95, 146, 168n.20

Incest prohibition, 133, 134, 135–37, 138, 140, 178–79n.23

Interpretation, 1, 3, 4, 17, 71, 114; in literary criticism, 148, 149; in psychoanalysis, 24, 29, 114, 148, 149; resistance of hysterical symptom to, 20–21, 23, 24

Jakobson, Roman, 9–10, 11, 14, 156–57n.5

Jaloux, Edmond, 37

Johnson, Barbara, 157n.6

Josipovici, Gabriel, 113

Joyce, James, 14

Jullian, Philippe, 16, 90

Kaminsky, Alice R., 6

Kasell, Walter, 61

Kofman, Sarah, 39–40

Lacan, Jacques, 4, 8, 9–13, 32–33, 93, 133, 135, 139, 146, 148–49, 155n.1, 156–57n.5, 178–79n.23. Works: *Ecrits: A Selection*, 10, 32, 33, 149; *Function and Field of Speech and Language in Psychoanalysis, The*, 149, 182n.2; "L'intervention sur le transfert," 155n.1; "Seminar on 'The Purloined Letter,'" 89

Langer, Lawrence, 152

Langs, Robert J., M.D., 3

Language, 9, 61, 64, 68–70, 86,

Index

92, 136, 141–42, 145–46, 147,
149, 151, 152, 157n.6, 157–
58n.1, 178–79n.23; and body,
66, 113–16, 120–22, 123, 132–
33, 139–40, 141–42, 144; and
Decadence, 5, 8, 13, 34; and
hysteria, 115, 119–22; and
neurotic symptom, 13; and
psychoanalysis, 13; and
unconscious, 10, 11, 13
—figurative or poetic, 4, 9–10, 11–
13, 14, 23–24, 44, 45–47, 92,
140, 141–42, 143, 144, 147,
156–57n.5, 158n.2. *See also*
Metaphor; Metonymy; Trope
La Salpêtrière, 18, 19
Léautaud, Paul, 112
Lemaire, Madeleine, 35, 37, 41,
42, 160n.4
Lorrain, Jean, 5, 6, 13, 14, 15, 16,
34, 75, 80, 81, 82, 83, 88, 89,
90, 91, 93–94, 100, 103, 104,
135, 138, 140, 141, 143, 144,
146, 147, 148, 149, 150, 152,
157n.7, 163–64n.2, 166n.14,
168–69n.23. Works: "Bad
Lodgings," 94–95; *Crime of the
Rich, The*, 75; criticism of
Pleasures and Regrets, 15, 35,
42; *Drinkers of Souls*, 75;
Feelings and Memories, 75, 90–
91, 92, 99; "Gloved Hand,
The," 81, 87; "Green Bean,"
104; "Janine," 103–4; "January
Night," 90; "Life-Sucker, The,"
95; "Magic Lantern," 82; "Man
Possessed by the Devil, A,"
100–103; "Man with the Wax
Heads, The," 95–100, 101;
"Mask, The," 90–94, 95, 99,
102, 103, 140; "Masked Figure,
The," 13; *Masked Figures and
Phantoms*, 16, 75, 76, 80, 82,
90, 94, 99, 100, 103, 105, 110;
"Masks from London and
Elsewhere," 95; "Mask's
Revenge, The," 99; *Monsieur de
Phocas*, 14; "One of Them, or
the Soul of the Mask," 80, 86–
87, 90, 100; "One Possessed,
The," 87; *Paints and Poisons*,
75; *Possessed of the Devil*, 75;
"Posthumous Complaint," 97–
100, 102; "Sea-Green Eyes," 16,
105, 108–10; *Stories of Masked
Figures*, 75; *Stories of Simple
Souls*, 75; "Student's Tale, The,"
16, 105–7; "Three Masked
Figures," 83–84, 85–85, 88–
90, 92, 100; "Unknown Crime,
An," 95; "Unquiet Night, An,"
103; "Visionary, The," 81;
Wandering Vice, The, 75

Maeterlinck, Maurice, 5
Mallarmé, Stéphane, 5
Mannoni, Octave, 116
Marcus, Stephen, 3, 157–58n.1
Massis, Henri, 59
Maurois, André, 160n.4
Maurras, Charles, 35
Meaning, 2, 11, 13, 29, 31, 117,
122, 124, 126, 132, 133, 148,
149–50, 178–79n.23;
insistence of, 8, 10; provisional
nature of, 33; suspension of, 17,
126. *See also* Signification
Mendès, Catulle, 113
Mercure de France, 15

Index

Metaphor, 9, 33, 104, 107, 110, 156–57n.5; definition of (Lacan), 11–12; in poetic language (Jakobson), 9–10; in Proust, 41, 45, 46–47, 49; in Rachilde, 17, 125, 140, 143, 144, 148

Metonymies, head (descriptive feature in Lorrain), 94–103, 108

Metonymy, 9, 34, 91–92, 109, 156–57n.5; definition of (Lacan), 11–13; in Lorrain, 16, 91, 92–94, 95, 97, 100, 101, 147; in poetic language (Jakobson), 9–10; in Proust, 46, 48, 56; in Rachilde, 122, 123, 124–25, 126, 127, 131, 135, 140, 178–79n.23; and realist illusion, 91–94, 95, 147, 168n.20

Montesquiou, Robert de, 104

Mother, 77, 92, 104, 151, 178–79n. 23; as concept within patriarchy, 178–79n.23; and desire (Lacan), 10, 12; in Proust, 60, 61–62, 63, 64, 65, 68, 72, 163n.14; in Rachilde, 125, 133, 134, 136, 137, 140, 141–42, 144, 147

Narrative: neurosis as structuring principle of, 16, 29, 80, 146–48; treatment of hysteria through ("talking cure"), 23, 25–29, 113–15

Navarre, Yves, 145, 151, 182n.1. Work: *Cronus' Children (Le jardin d'acclimatation)*, 145

Neurosis, 13–14, 20–22, 48, 76–77, 113, 114, 117, 119, 130, 146, 155–56n.3; and Decadence, 4–6, 8, 23, 33–34, 150; and figurative language, 4; in Lorrain, 76, 80, 81, 82, 87, 92, 100, 104, 105–10; and narrative structure, 16, 29, 80; in Proust, 43–44, 45–46, 48, 52–53, 56–57, 59, 62, 66

Noakes, Susan, 158n.3

Nye, Robert A., 5, 162n.12

Oedipal crisis, 10, 11, 12–13, 145, 178–79n.23

Ollier, Claude, 168n.20

Ostrich: in Hoffman, 88, 89, 166–67n.14; in Lacan, 89, 93; in Lorrain, 87, 88–90, 166–67n.14

Paganini, Maria, 53

Parshley, H. M., 174–75n.9

Patriarchy, 120, 151

Penis envy: and relation to fetishism, 39–40; as rhetorical strategy in Freud, 40

Perret, Paul, 35

Pleasure principle: and death instincts, 78–80; and return of the repressed, 76–80

Plot, 9, 14; in Dora case, 115, 123; in Lorrain, 14, 108; in Proust, 16, 52, 56–59, 61, 64, 66, 146; in Rachilde, 123, 124, 126, 131, 136, 141, 143

Poe, Edgar Allan, 9, 76, 104, 156n.5. Works: "Purloined Letter, The," 89; "Tell-Tale Heart, The," 156–57n.5

Point of view, 14, 16, 23; in Proust, 44–45, 47, 48, 56, 57–

59; in Rachilde, 132, 133

Pre-Oedipal, 11, 12, 151, 178–79n.23

Primal scene, 71, 174–75n.9

Primary process, 9, 10, 12, 81, 114, 121, 151, 155–56n.3; and Decadence, 152; in Lorrain, 16, 81, 86, 88, 89, 147, 166–67n.14; in Proust, 44–45, 47, 48, 69; in Rachilde, 144, 151

Proust, Dr. Adrien (father of Marcel), 36, 37, 38, 51, 74, 146

Proust, Jeanne, née Weil (mother of Marcel), 60

Proust, Marcel, 6, 13, 14, 15, 16, 34, 35–38, 43, 45, 48, 51, 52, 59, 60, 67, 74, 104, 146, 148, 150, 152, 157n.7, 160nn. 4, 6; 161–62n.11. Works: "Death of Baldassare Silvande, The," 13, 42, 43–52, 56, 57, 66, 72, 161–62n.11; "End of Jealousy, The," 44, 52, 65–74, 161–62n.11, 174n.9; "Fragments from Italian Comedy," 44; "Melancholy Summer of Madame de Breyves," 44, 52–59, 64, 65, 66, 72, 161–62n.11; *Pleasures and Regrets*, 15, 16, 35–38, 40–43, 45, 52, 53, 59, 61, 65, 74, 146–47, 148, 160n.4, 161–62n.11; discrepancies between French and English editions of, 161–62n.11; "Portraits of Painters and Musicians," 35, 42, 44, 45; *Remembrance of Things Past*, 36, 42, 43, 45, 53, 57, 60, 63, 72, 146, 160n.6; *Remembrance of Things Past*: *Swann's Way*, 56,

74; *Remembrance of Things Past: Time Regained*, 45, 62; "Violante; or Worldly Vanities," 44; "Young Girl's Confession, A," 44, 52, 59–65, 66, 72, 73, 161–62n.11

Psychoanalysis: critique of, 116–17, 120, 145, 151, 157n.6; historical relationship to French Decadence, 8, 19, 146; in Lacanian rereading of Freud, 8, 9, 10–13; and narrative structure, 3–4, 146, 147; origins of, 22–23; in relation to literary criticism, 13, 146, 148–50

Punctuation, 33, 149, 182n.2. *See also* Anchoring points; Upholstery buttons

Rachilde (Marguerite Vallette), 6, 13, 14, 15, 17, 34, 111–13, 121–22, 123, 131, 132–33, 134, 135, 136, 139, 140, 144, 146, 147, 148, 150, 151, 152, 174n.9, 178–79n.23; as "androgyne of letters," 111; and career as women of letters, 111; as "hysteric of letters," 111, 132, 144; nervous breakdown of, 112–13; opinion of her own work, 113, 122; and writing compared to *condition seconde*, 112; and writing compared to prostitution, 113. Works: *Demon of the Absurd, The*, 124, 133, 138; "Frog Killer, The," 13, 17, 133, 140–44, 147, 148, 178–79n.23; "Harvests of Sodom, The," 122, 124–26,

131, 133; "Hermetic Chateau, The," 13, 133–37, 139, 144, 178–79n.23; *Madame Adonis*, 130; preface to, 111, 112, 113; *Monsieur Vénus*, 15, 111, 122–24, 130, 131; "*Mortis*, The," 122, 127–33; *Stories*, 17, 127, 133, 134, 141, 144; "Tooth, The," 133, 137–40

Realism. *See* Illusion, realist

Reed, John R., 6, 14–5

Renaissance, Italian, 7, 30, 31, 32

Repetition: as structuring principle in Lorrain, 80, 103–4; of traumatic event in Freud, 76–78, 79; of traumatic event in Proust, 64–65. *See also* Repressed, return of the

Representation, literary, 130; and fetishism in Proust, 40, 43, 47, 48–52, 55–56; and return of the repressed, 80

Repressed, return of the, 144, 148; and death instincts, 79–80; in Lorrain, 14, 76, 80, 82, 83–84, 86, 87, 88, 89–90, 91, 92–93, 102, 147, 163–64n.2; and masochism, 77; and narrative structure, 76, 103–11; and pleasure principle, 76–80; and sublimation in art, 80; and symbolization, 77; and war neuroses, 76–77

Repression, 1, 8, 9, 11–13, 20, 22–23, 31, 68, 77, 81, 97, 101, 103, 108, 114, 120, 121, 137, 139, 140, 142, 144, 145, 147, 148, 156–57n.5, 157–58n.1; barrier of (Lacan), 11–12, 139, 178–79n.23; and formation of

unconscious (Lacan), 10, 12–13. *See also* Repressed, return of the

Reproduction, female: in Beauvoir, Simone de, 118–19; in Rachilde, 122, 125–26, 127–28, 131, 147

Richard, Noël, 5

Riffaterre, Michael, 168n.20

Rogers, Brian G., 72, 159n.2

Rollinat, Maurice, 103

Romans of the Decadence, The, 155n.2

Rome, Imperial, and Decadence, 7, 35, 155n.2

Saussure, Ferdinand de, 9, 178–79n.23

Secondary process (secondary revision), 9, 10, 81, 114, 121, 152, 155–56n.3

Sexuality, equivocal, 6; in Lorrain, 75, 85–86, 87, 100; in Rachilde, 122–24, 130. *See also* Cross-marking; Signifier, equivocal

—female: in Beauvoir, Simone de, 116–19; in Freud, 40; in Rachilde, 122, 125–26, 127–30, 139, 141, 142

Short story, 15, 147; in collection, 14–15; and neurosis, 15, 105; and relation to case study (Freud), 15, 23; and sequence in reading, 148, 149–50, 161–62n.11

Sign, 24, 29, 30, 32, 33, 80, 158n.3

Signification, 8, 31, 83–84, 89, 94, 96, 105, 140; in Decadence,

Index

4, 8, 13–14; in psychoanalysis, 11, 12, 22, 23–29, 32, 33; in Taine, 30–32. *See also* Meaning
Signified, 34, 87, 88, 95, 108; opposed to signifier, 1, 8, 10, 11–13, 33, 47
Signifier, 34, 68, 69, 70, 72, 92, 94, 95, 100, 102, 103, 108, 146, 148, 149, 156–57n.5; in Decadence, 8, 13, 33–34, 157n.6; equivocal, or unrestricted (Lorrain), 76, 80, 81, 82–83, 84, 86–87, 88, 89, 95, 100, 102, 147; opposed to signified, 1, 8, 10, 11–13, 33, 47; in psychoanalysis, 22, 23–24, 25, 29; treasury of (Lacan), 32
Silverman, Kaja, 71, 81
Spivak, Gayatri Chakravorty, 150
Stekel, Wilhelm, 118
Style, Decadent, 14, 15, 34, 150
Suleiman, Susan Rubin, 3
Suture, 71–72
Symbolic (Lacan), 12, 71, 142
Symbolism, 6
Symptom, hysterical or neurotic, 19–20, 22, 26, 27, 28, 29, 48; as signifier, 23–24, 29, 68

Taine, Hippolyte, 6, 29–34, 46, 162n.12. Works: *Journey to Italy*, 30; *Philosophy of Art*, 30
Talking cure. *See* Narrative, treatment of hysteria through
Thought, omnipotence of, 48–51, 52
Todorov, Tzvetan, 75
Tolstoy, Leo, 51–52, 56, 74, 152. Works: "Death of Ivan Ilyich, The," 51, 74; *War and Peace*, 51, 74

Transference, 2, 3, 80, 114, 115, 155n.1
Trauma: childhood, in Lorrain, 16, 81, 82–84, 87, 88, 89, 90–91, 94, 95, 102, 104, 110, 147, 166–67n.14; childhood, and relation to adult neurosis, 21, 81, 82, 83–84, 87, 147; and hallucination, 52, 59, 64–65, 66, 67–68; neurotic, 16, 76, 99, 146
Tree: in Lacan, 32–33; in Taine, 30–32
Trope, 4. *See also* Language, figurative or poetic; Metaphor; Metonymy

Ulysses (Joyce), 14
Unconscious, 8, 9, 114, 145, 163–64n.2; formation of, 10, 11–13; structured as a language, 11, 13, 146
Upholstery buttons, 33. *See also* Anchoring points; Punctuation

Vagina dentata, 101
Vagina edentula, 138
Vallette, Alfred, 15
Vallette, Marguerite. *See* Rachilde
Value, linguistic, 9, 31, 178–79n.23
Varese, Louise, 55
Verdichtung, 11. *See also* Condensation
Verlaine, Paul, 135
Verschiebung, 11. *See also* Displacement
Vicaire, Gabriel, 5

Waelti-Walters, Jennifer, 144
Wright, Elizabeth, 80

Zola, Emile, 5

Renée A. Kingcaid earned her Ph.D. in romance languages and literatures from Ohio State University in 1982, where she was awarded both a Graduate Associate Teaching Award and a Presidential Dissertation Fellowship. She has taught at Montana State University in Bozeman and is currently an associate professor of French at Saint Mary's College, Notre Dame, Indiana. She has published on nineteenth- and twentieth-century French literature in such journals as *L'Esprit Créateur, French Forum,* and *The Review of Contemporary Fiction,* for which she also reviews recent French fiction. A long-time fan of the Decadence, she is presently engaged in a semiotic study of mysticism in the novels of Joris-Karl Huysmans.